Early praise for *Rails, Angular, Postgres, and Bootstrap, Second Edition*

Rails, Angular, Postgres, and Bootstrap, Second Edition is an informative and engaging tool for Rails developers to level up their skills. Dave uses real-world product examples to explain concepts, making it feel natural to apply your newfound database and front-end expertise to your everyday work.

➤ **Cameron Jacoby**
Software engineer, Stitch Fix

This book is a great introduction to modern full-stack development. You'll learn how to create rich front-end experiences and performant databases, all the while working with the joy that is Rails.

➤ **Matthew White**
Author of *Deliver Audacious Web Apps with Ember*

I found this to be an excellent book. It is well written, correct, and up to date; covers exciting OSS technologies; and has a clear sense of its audience and its needs. I intend to recommend this book to my Rails team—it will expand our competencies even further.

➤ **Tibor Simic**
Developer, Ingemark

I recommend *Rails, Angular, Postgres, and Bootstrap, Second Edition* without question. It is a great book for any developer who needs a straightforward and rich experience with the full-stack web development philosophy. It is also a great choice for any developer who wants to pair his or her Rails knowledge with bleeding-edge tools and progressively ascend to full-stack.

➤ **Peter Perlepes**
Software engineer, Adaplo

Rails, Angular, Postgres, and Bootstrap, Second Edition

Powerful, Effective, Efficient, Full-Stack Web Development

David Bryant Copeland

The Pragmatic Bookshelf

Raleigh, North Carolina

Many of the designations used by manufacturers and sellers to distinguish their products are claimed as trademarks. Where those designations appear in this book, and The Pragmatic Programmers, LLC was aware of a trademark claim, the designations have been printed in initial capital letters or in all capitals. The Pragmatic Starter Kit, The Pragmatic Programmer, Pragmatic Programming, Pragmatic Bookshelf, PragProg and the linking *g* device are trademarks of The Pragmatic Programmers, LLC.

Every precaution was taken in the preparation of this book. However, the publisher assumes no responsibility for errors or omissions, or for damages that may result from the use of information (including program listings) contained herein.

Our Pragmatic books, screencasts, and audio books can help you and your team create better software and have more fun. Visit us at *https://pragprog.com*.

The team that produced this book includes:

Publisher: Andy Hunt
VP of Operations: Janet Furlow
Executive Editor: Susannah Davidson Pfalzer
Development Editor: Katharine Dvorak
Indexing: Potomac Indexing, LLC
Copy Editor: Liz Welch
Layout: Gilson Graphics

For sales, volume licensing, and support, please contact *support@pragprog.com*.

For international rights, please contact *rights@pragprog.com*.

Printed in the United States of America.
ISBN-13: 978-1-68050-220-6
Printed on acid-free paper.
Book version: P1.0—June 2017

Contents

Acknowledgments

I'd like to first thank my wife Amy, who gave me the encouragement and space to spend time every morning writing this book (twice).

I'd also like to thank my first edition editor, Fahmida Rashid, as well as the editor of this edition, Katharine Dvorak, who helped me navigate the ever-changing JavaScript ecosystem so we could give you an updated book that actually went to print.

I'd further like to thank the many people who reviewed this new edition: Luis Miguel Cabezas Granado, Fabrizio Cucci, Cameron Jacoby, Nigel Lowry, David McClain, Nick McGinness, Peter Perlepes, Sven Riedel, Tibor Simic, and Matthew White.

Finally, I'd like to thank the contributors to the software you're learning about in this book. To the people who have given their free time to make Ruby, Rails, Postgres, Angular, Bootstrap, PhantomJS, Testdouble, Poltergeist, Devise, Capybara, RSpec, Database Cleaner, Yarn, and all the other open source software that are far too numerous to list here, thank you. Without your work, most developers would have a hard time doing their jobs.

Introduction

Think about what part of an application you're most comfortable working with. If you're a Rails developer, there's a good chance you prefer the back end, the Ruby code that powers the business logic of your application. What if you felt equally comfortable working with the database, such as tweaking queries and using advanced features of your database system? What if you were *also* comfortable working with the JavaScript and CSS necessary to make dynamic, usable, attractive user interfaces?

If you had that level of comfort at every level of the application stack, you would possess great power as a developer to quickly produce high-quality software. Your ability to solve problems would not be restricted by the tools available via a single framework, nor would you be at the mercy of hard-to-find specialists to help you with what are, in reality, simple engineering tasks.

The Rails framework encourages developers not to peer too closely into the database. Rails steers you away from JavaScript frameworks in favor of its *sprinkling* approach, where content is all rendered server-side. This book is going to open your eyes to all the things you can accomplish with your database, and set you on a path that includes JavaScript frameworks. With Rails acting as the foundation of what you do, you'll learn how to embrace all other parts of the application stack.

The Application Stack

Many web applications—especially those built with Ruby on Rails—use a layered architecture that is often referred to as a *stack*, since most diagrams (like the ones used in this book) depict the layers as stacked blocks.

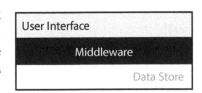

Rails represents the middle of the stack and is called *middleware*. This is where the core logic of your application lives. The bottom of the stack—the data store—is where the valuable data saved and manipulated by your application lives. This is often a relational database management system (RDBMS). The top of the stack is the user interface. In a web application, this is HTML, CSS, and JavaScript served to a browser.

Each part of the stack plays a crucial role in making software valuable. The data store is the canonical location of the organization's most important asset—its data. Even if the organization loses all of its source code, as long as it retains its data, it can still survive. Losing all of the data, however, would be catastrophic.

The top of the stack is also important, as it's the way the users view and enter data. To the users, the user interface *is* the database. The difference between a great user interface and a poor one can mean the difference between happy users and irritated users, accurate data and unreliable data, a successful product and a dismal failure.

What's left is the part of the stack where most developers feel most comfortable: the middleware. Poorly constructed middleware is hard to change, meaning the cost of change is high, and thus the ability of the organization to respond to changes is more difficult.

Each part of the stack plays an important role in making a piece of software successful. As a Rails developer, you have amassed many techniques for making the middleware as high quality as you can. Rails (and Ruby) makes it easy to write clean, maintainable code.

Digging deeper into the other two parts of the stack will have a great benefit for you as a developer. You'll have more tools in your toolbox, making you more effective. You'll also have a much easier time working with specialists, when you *do* have access to them, since you'll have a good grasp of both the database and the front end. That's what you learn in this book. When you're done, you'll have a holistic view of application development, and you'll have a new and powerful set of tools to augment your knowledge of Rails. With this holistic view, you can build seemingly complex features easily, sometimes even trivially.

You'll learn *PostgreSQL*, *Angular*, and *Bootstrap*, but you can apply many of the lessons here to other data stores, JavaScript libraries, and CSS frameworks. In addition to seeing just how powerful these specific tools can be, you're going to be emboldened to think about writing software beyond what is provided by Rails.

PostgreSQL, Angular, and Bootstrap: The Missing Parts of Our Stack

If all you've done with your database is create tables, insert data, and query it, you're going to be excited when you see what else you can do. Similarly, if all you've done with your web views is sprinkle some jQuery calls to your server-rendered HTML, you'll be amazed at what you can do with very little code when you have a full-fledged JavaScript framework. Lastly, if you've been hand-rolling your own CSS, a framework like Bootstrap will make your life so much simpler, and your views will look and feel so much better.

In this book, we focus on PostgreSQL (or simply *Postgres*) as our data store —the bottom of the stack—and Angular (or just *Angular*) with Bootstrap as our front end—the top of the stack. Each of these technologies is widely used and very powerful. You're likely to encounter them in the real world, and they each underscore the sorts of features you can use to deliver great software outside of what you get with Rails.

With these chosen technologies, our application stack looks like this:

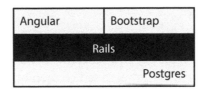

In each chapter, I highlight the parts of the stack you'll be focusing on and call out the various aspects of these technologies you'll be learning. Not every chapter focuses on all parts of the stack, so at the start of each chapter, you'll see a roadmap like this of what you'll be learning:

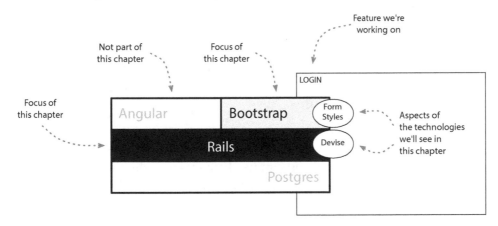

Let's get a taste of what each has to offer, starting with PostgreSQL.

PostgreSQL

PostgreSQL[1] is an open source SQL database released in 1997. It supports many advanced features not found in other popular open source databases such as MySQL[2] or commercial databases such as Microsoft SQL Server.[3] Here are some of the features you'll learn about (and I'll show you how to use them with Rails):

Check constraints

You can create highly complex constraints on your table columns beyond what you get with not null. For example, you can require that a user's email address be on a certain domain, that the state in a U.S. address be written exactly as two uppercase characters, or even that the state in the address must already be on a list of allowed state codes.

While you can do this with Rails, doing it in the database layer means that no bug in your code, no existing script, no developer at a console, and no future program can put bad data into your database. This sort of data integrity just isn't possible with Rails alone.

Advanced indexing

In many database systems, you can only index the values in the columns of the database. In Postgres, you can index the *transformed* values. For example, you can index the lowercased version of someone's name so that a case-insensitive search is just as fast as an exact-match search.

Materialized views

A database view is a logical table based on a SELECT statement. In Postgres a *materialized view* is a view whose contents are stored in an actual table— accessing a materialized view won't run the query again like it would in a normal view.

Advanced data types

Postgres has support for enumerated types, arrays, and dictionaries (called HSTOREs). In most database systems, you have to use separate tables to model these data structures.

Free-form JSON...that's indexed

Postgres supports a JSON data type, allowing you to store arbitrary data in a column. This means you can use Postgres as a document data store, or for storing data that doesn't conform to a strong schema (something

---

1.   https://www.postgresql.org
2.   https://www.mysql.com
3.   http://www.microsoft.com/en-us/server-cloud/products/sql-server

you'd otherwise have to use a different type of database for). And, by using the JSONB data type, you ensure that the JSON fields can be indexed, just like a structured table's fields.

Although you can serialize hashes to JSON in Rails using the TEXT data type, you can't query them, and you certainly can't index them. JSONB fields can interoperate with many systems other than Rails, and they provide great performance.

Angular

Angular[4] is a JavaScript framework created and maintained by Google. Angular allows you to model your user interface as *components*, which combine a model, template, and code all into one self-contained class. This means your view is not a static bit of HTML, but a full-blown application. By adopting the mind-set that your front end is a dynamic, connected interface comprised of components, and not a set of static pages, you open up many new possibilities.

Angular provides powerful tools for organizing your code and lets you structure your markup to create intention-revealing, testable, manageable front-end code. It doesn't matter how small or large the task—as your UI gets more complex, Angular scales much better than something more basic like jQuery.

As an example, consider showing and hiding a section of the DOM using jQuery. You might do something like this:

```
jquery_example.html
<section>
  <p>You currently owe: $123.45</p>
  <button class="reveal-button">Show Details</button>
  <ul style="display: none" class="details">
    <li>Base fee: $120.00</li>
    <li>Taxes: $3.45</li>
  </ul>
</section>
<script>
  $(".reveal-button").click(function($event) {
    $(".details").toggle();
  });
</script>
```

It's not much code, but if you've ever done anything moderately complex, your markup and JavaScript becomes a soup of magic strings, classes starting with js-, and oddball data- elements.

---

4.   https://angular.io

An Angular version of this might look like the following:

```
var DetailsComponent = Component({
  template: '\
    <section> \
      <p>You currently owe: $123.45</p> \
      <button on-click="toggleDetails()">Show/Hide Details</button> \
      <ul *ngIf="showDetails"> \
        <li>Base fee: $120.00</li> \
        <li>Taxes: $3.45</li> \
      </ul> \
    </section> \
    '
}).Class({
  constructor: function() {
    this.showDetails = false;
  },
  toggleDetails: function() {
    this.showDetails = !this.showDetails;
  }
});
```

It may seem oddly shaped, but it should reveal its intent much more clearly than the jQuery version, despite the extra bits of code. Without knowing Angular at all, you can piece together that when the button is clicked, it calls the toggleDetails button, and if showDetails is true, we'll show the detailed information inside the ul. This all maps closely to the user's actions and intent. There's nothing in this code about locating DOM elements or handling browser events. And, when you need to do fancier or more complex interactions in your front end, writing code this way is still easy to manage.

Unlike Postgres—where there are very few comparable open source alternatives that match its features and power—there are many JavaScript frameworks comparable to Angular. Many of them are quite capable of handling the features covered in this book. We're using Angular for a few reasons. First, it's quite popular, which means you can find far more resources online for learning it, including deep dives beyond what is covered here. Second, it allows you to compose your front end similarly to how you compose your back end in Rails, but it's flexible enough to allow you to deviate later if you need to.

If you've never done much with JavaScript on the front end, or if you're just used to jQuery, you'll be pleasantly surprised at what Angular gives you:

Clean separation of code and views

> Angular models your front end as an application with its own routes, controllers, and views. This makes organizing your JavaScript easy and tames a lot of complexity.

Unit testing from the start

Testing JavaScript—especially when it uses jQuery—has always been a challenge. Angular was designed from the start to make unit testing your JavaScript simple and convenient.

Clean, declarative views

Angular views are just HTML. Angular adds special attributes called directives that allow you to cleanly connect your data and functions to the markup. You won't have inline code or scripts, and a clear separation exists between view and code.

Huge ecosystem

Because of its popularity, there's a large ecosystem of components and modules. Many common problems have a solution in Angular's ecosystem.

It's hard to fully appreciate the power of a JavaScript framework like Angular without using it, but we'll get there. We'll turn a run-of-the-mill search feature into a dynamic, asynchronous live search, with very little code.

Bootstrap

Bootstrap[5] is a *CSS framework* created by Twitter for use in their internal applications. A CSS framework is a set of CSS classes you apply to markup to get a particular look and feel. Bootstrap also includes *design components*, which are classes that, when used on particular HTML elements in particular ways, produce a distinct visual artifact, like a form, a panel, or an alert message.

The advantage of a CSS framework like Bootstrap is that you can create full-featured user interfaces without writing any CSS. Why be stuck with an ugly and hard-to-use form like this?

Amount (in dollars)
$
Amount
.00
Transfer cash

By just adding a few classes to some elements, you can have something polished and professional like this instead:

$ Amount .00 Transfer cash

---

5.   http://getbootstrap.com

Bootstrap includes a lot of CSS for a lot of different occasions:

Typography

Just including Bootstrap in your application and using semantic HTML results in pleasing content with good general typography.

Grid

Bootstrap's grid makes it easy to lay out complex, multicolumn components. It can't be overstated how important and powerful this is.

Form styles

Styling good-looking forms can be difficult, but Bootstrap provides many CSS classes that make it easy. Bootstrap-styled forms have great spacing and visual appeal, and feel cohesive and inviting to users.

Components

Bootstrap also includes myriad *components*, which, as mentioned earlier, are CSS classes that, when applied to particular markup, generate a visual component like a styled box or alert message. These components can be great inspiration for solving simple design problems.

It's important to note that Bootstrap is not a replacement for a designer, nor are all UIs created with Bootstrap inherently usable. There are times when a specialist in visual design, interaction design, or front-end implementation is crucial to the success of a project.

But for many apps, you don't need these specialists (they are very hard to find when you do). Bootstrap lets you produce a professional, appealing user interface without them. Bootstrap also lets you realize visual designs that might seem difficult to do with CSS.

Even if you have a designer or front-end specialist, the skills you'll learn by using Bootstrap will still apply—your front-end developer isn't going to write every line of markup and CSS. They are going to hand you a framework like Bootstrap that enables you to do many of the things we'll do in this book.

Now that you've gotten a taste of what we'll be covering, let's talk about how you're going to learn it.

How to Read This Book

If you've already looked at the table of contents, you'll see that this book isn't divided into three parts—one for Postgres, one for Angular, and one for Bootstrap. That's not how a full-stack developer approaches development. A full-stack developer is given a problem to solve and is expected to bring all forces to bear in solving it.

For example, if you're implementing a search, and it's slow, you'll probably consider both creating an index in the database as well as performing the search with Ajax calls to create a more dynamic and snappy UI. You should use features at every level of the stack to get the job done, as shown in the following diagram.

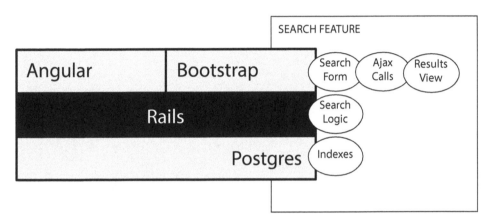

This holistic approach is how you're going to learn these technologies, and you'll have the most success reading the book in order. We'll build a Rails application together, adding features one at a time. These features will demonstrate various aspects of the technologies you're using.

Shine, the Application We'll Build

Throughout the chapters in this book we'll create and add features to a Rails application. We're creating this application for the customer service agents at the hypothetical company where we work. Our company has a public website that its customers use, but we want a separate application for the customer service agents. You've probably seen or heard about internal-facing apps like this. Perhaps you've even worked on one (most software *is* internally facing).

The application will be called *Shine* (since it allows our great customer service to *shine through* to our customers). The features that we'll build for this application involve searching for, viewing, and manipulating customer data.

For example, we'll allow the user to search for customers in a manner similar to what is shown in the figures on page xx. Users will also be allowed to click through and view or edit a customer's data.

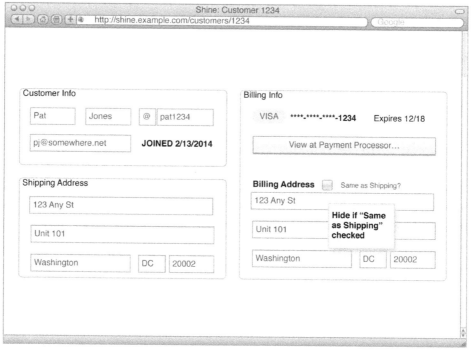

These features may seem simple on the surface, but there's hidden complexity that you'll be able to tame with Postgres, Angular, and Bootstrap. In each chapter, you'll make a bit of progress on Shine, and you'll learn features of Postgres, Angular, Bootstrap, and Rails in the process.

How We'll Build Shine

To keep things simple, each chapter focuses on a single technology, and you complete features over several chapters. We'll do as much setup as we can in Chapter 1, *Set Up the Environment*, on page 1. Because our goal is to bring together several technologies that weren't designed as a single package, we'll have to do a bit more configuration up front, but once that configuration is done, we'll be ready to add features and get the most out of everything.

The first feature we build is a registration and login system, which allows us to style the user interface with Bootstrap as well as secure the underlying database with Postgres. We'll style the login in Chapter 2, *Create a Great-Looking Login with Bootstrap and Devise*, on page 15, and tighten up the security by learning about *check constraints* in Chapter 3, *Secure the User Database*, on page 29.

We then move on to a customer search feature, which is a fertile ground for learning about full-stack development. In Chapter 4, *Perform Fast Queries with*, on page 37, we implement a basic fuzzy search, and you learn how to examine Postgres's *query plan* to understand why our search is slow. We then use Postgres's advanced indexing features to make it fast. In Chapter 5, *Create Clean Search Results*, on page 55, you learn how to use some of Bootstrap's built-in components and helper classes to create nontabular search results that look great.

Chapter 6, *Build a Dynamic UI with Angular*, on page 65, is an introduction to Angular, which we use to make our customer search much more dynamic. This chapter explores how to set up and manage Angular code, as well as how to read user input and do Ajax calls to our Rails application.

With a fully implemented customer search, we pause in Chapter 7, *Test This Fancy New Code*, on page 91 to discuss how to write tests for everything you've learned. Testing has always been a big part of Rails, so whenever we veer off Rails's golden path, it's important to make sure we have a great testing experience.

Chapter 8, *Create a Single-Page App*, on page 127 is our first step in building a more complex feature that shows customer details. We turn our customer search into a client-side, single-page application that allows the user to navigate from search results to customer details without reloading the page. This gives you an opportunity to learn about Angular's router and navigation features.

In Chapter 9, *Design Great UIs with*, on page 155, you learn about a powerful web design tool called *the grid* and how Bootstrap implements it. We use it to create a dense UI that's clean, clear, and usable. In Chapter 10, *Cache Complex Queries*, on page 169, we implement the back end of our customer details view by turning a query of highly complex joins into a simple auto-updated cache using Postgres's *materialized views*.

In Chapter 11, *Asynchronously Load Data*, on page 193, you learn how Angular's asynchronous nature allows us to keep our front end simple, even when we need data from several sources. We finish off our customer detail page feature, as well as our in-depth look at these technologies, by exploring how to effectively use forms with Angular in Chapter 12, *Wrangle Forms and*, on page 221.

All of this is just a small part of what you can do with Bootstrap, Angular, and Postgres, so in Chapter 13, *Dig Deeper*, on page 249, we'll survey some of the other features we don't have space to get to.

To help you keep track of where we are, each chapter starts with a diagram (like the one shown on page xiii) that shows which parts of the stack we are focusing on, what feature we're building, and what aspects of each technology you are learning in that chapter.

When it's all said and done, you'll have the confidence needed to solve problems by using every tool available in the application stack. You'll be just as comfortable creating an animated progress bar as you will be setting up views and triggers in the database. Moreover, you'll see how you can use these sorts of features from the comfort of Rails.

Example Code

The running examples in the book are extracted from fully tested source code that should work as shown, but you should download the sample code from the book's website at https://pragprog.com/titles/dcbang2/source_code. Each step of our journey through this topic has a different subdirectory, each containing an entire Rails application. While the book shows you only the changes you need to make, the downloadable code records a snapshot of the fully working application as of that point in the book.

Command-Line Execution

We'll be running a lot of commands in this book. Rails development is heavily command line driven, and this book shows the commands you need to execute as we go. It's important to understand how to interpret the way we're using them in the book. Each time you see a command-line *session*, the text will first show how you call the command line, followed by the expected output.

In the following example, we invoke the command line bundle exec rails generate devise:install. This is the command you'd type into your terminal and press Return. The lines *following* the command line display expected or example output.

```
$ bundle exec rails generate devise:install
    create  config/initializers/devise.rb
    create  config/locales/devise.en.yml
```

Sometimes I need to show a command-line invocation that won't fit on one line. In this case, I use backslashes to show the continuation of the command (which is how you'd actually run a multiline command in a shell like bash). The last line *won't* have a backslash. For example, here we're typing everything from rails to shine.

```
$ rails new --skip-turbolinks \
            --skip-spring \
            --skip-test-unit \
            -d postgresql \
            shine
    create
    create  README.rdoc
    create  Rakefile
    create  config.ru
    create  .gitignore
    create  Gemfile
```

The sample output won't always match exactly what you see, but it should be close. It's included so you have a way to sanity-check what you're doing as you follow along.

A second form of command-line session is when we interact with Postgres. I'll indicate this by executing rails dbconsole first and then showing SQL commands inside the Postgres command-line interpreter. In the following listing I'm executing rails dbconsole; then I'm executing select count(*) from users; inside Postgres (note how the prompt changes slightly). After that you see the expected or sample results of the command.

```
$ rails dbconsole
shine_development=> select count(*) from users;
+--------+
| count |
+--------+
|    100 |
+-------+
```

What You Need to Know

This book covers a lot of advanced topics in web development. However, my hope is that you can get a lot out of it regardless of your skill level. Nevertheless, the code and concepts are written assuming some basic exposure to the topics at hand:

Ruby and Rails

Much of the Rails content in the book is in configuration, specifically to get Rails to work with Angular, Bootstrap, and the ecosystem in which they live. If you've created a simple Rails app, and you know what controllers, models, views, migrations, and tests are, you should have no problem understanding the Rails code. If you're new to Rails, check out *Agile Web Development with Rails 5.1 [RC17]*.

SQL

I also assume you know some SQL. If you know the basics of how to select, update, and insert data, along with how to do a join, you know everything you need to understand the Postgres parts of this book. For those of you new to SQL, there are many online courses that can teach you the basics.

JavaScript

You don't need to be a JavaScript expert, but you should know the basics of how JavaScript works as a language. *JavaScript, the Good Parts [Cro08]* is a quick read and should give you these basics if you need them. You don't have to know *any* Angular. I'll cover what you need and assume you've never seen any Angular code.

CSS

There's (almost) no actual CSS code in this book. You just need to know what CSS is and what it does. All the styling you'll do will be using Bootstrap, and I don't assume any prior knowledge.

I wrote the book with the following versions of the tools and libraries:

- Ruby 2.4.1
- Rails 5.1.1
- Bootstrap 3.3.7
- Angular 4.1.3

- Postgres 9.6
- Webpack 2.6.1
- Node 7.10.0
- Devise 4.3.0
- Karma 1.7.0

For everything else you need, I'll show you how to set up and install as we get to it. We'll be using a lot of third-party libraries and tools—integrating them together is what this book is about. Pay particular attention to the versions of libraries in Gemfile and package.json that are included in the example code download. While I've tried to make the code future compatible, there's always a chance that a point release of a library breaks something.

Online Forum and Errata

While reading through the book, you may have questions about the material, or you might find typos or mistakes. For the latter, you can add issues to the errata for the book at https://pragprog.com/titles/dcbang2/errata. Think of it as a bug-reporting system for the book.

For the former—questions about the material—you should visit the online forum on the book webpage at https://pragprog.com/titles/dcbang2. There, you'll be able to interact with other readers and me to get the most out of the material.

I hope you're ready to start your journey in full-stack application development! Let's kick it off by creating our new Rails application and doing all the up-front setup for our development environment.

## CHAPTER 1

Set Up the Environment

Before you get into learning Postgres, Angular, and Bootstrap, there's a bit of setup to do first. Setup is never fun, and it's often difficult to figure out by just looking at documentation, especially when the tools aren't designed together. This isn't to say that Postgres, Angular, and Bootstrap aren't great tools that *can* work with Rails, but given what you're accustomed to with Rails, setting up these tools may be more work than you're used to.

Setup can also be distracting when trying to learn something new, despite being crucially important, since you have to be able to actually use the new tools you're learning. This is what you'll do in this chapter. By the end, you'll have a shell of the Rails application you'll be working on throughout the rest of the book. You'll have Postgres installed and set up, and you'll have configured Webpack to serve up Bootstrap, as well as the JavaScript you'll write in later chapters.

You'll do this in three steps. First, you'll install Ruby, Rails, and Postgres, which should be straightforward. Next, you'll create the Rails application you'll be building throughout the rest of the book using some particular options that aren't the default. Finally, you'll set up Yarn and Webpack—two tools you might not be familiar with. Yarn is a tool you'll use to manage JavaScript libraries (akin to Ruby gems), and Webpack is a replacement asset pipeline. Webpack is highly complex and feature rich, but for our purposes, it's the perfect tool to manage our JavaScript and CSS, because it overcomes some shortcomings in the Rails asset pipeline, which we won't be using (I'll explain why soon).

Installing Ruby, Rails, and Postgres

Most of what we'll do in building our example Rails application, Shine, are commands you can execute or code you'll enter, but getting Ruby, Rails, and

Postgres installed on your system is much more system-specific. Fortunately, the authors of these technologies have made the installation process as pain-free as possible. First, start with Ruby and Rails.

Ruby and Rails

If you don't have Ruby installed, follow the instructions on Ruby's website.[1] I recommend using an installer or manager, but as long as you have Ruby 2.3.1 or later installed and the ability to install gems you'll be good to go.

With Ruby installed, you'll need to install Rails. This is usually as simple as

```
$ gem install rails
```

Be sure to get the latest version of Rails, which is 5.0.0.1 as of this writing.

Next, you'll need access to a Postgres database.

Postgres

Postgres is free and open source, and you can install it locally by looking at the instructions for your operating system on their website.[2] Be sure you get at least version 9.5—some of the features I'll discuss were introduced in that version. When we create our Rails application in the next section, we'll create a user to access the database.

An alternative is to use a free, hosted version of Postgres, such as Heroku Postgres.[3] You can sign up on their website, and they'll give you the credentials to access the hosted database from your computer. (You'll learn where to use them in the next section when we configure Rails to access Postgres.)

With Ruby, Rails, and Postgres installed, let's create the Rails application and get a basic view working.

Creating the Rails Application

We really don't need much more than the basic Rails application we'll generate with rails new, but because we know we're using Postgres, and later in the book we'll be using Angular, there are a few options you should set now.

First, we want to tell Rails to use Postgres as our database (it uses SQLite by default). We also don't want to use TurboLinks,[4] because it's going to clash

---

1.   https://www.ruby-lang.org/en/downloads
2.   http://www.postgresql.org/download
3.   https://www.heroku.com/postgres
4.   https://github.com/rails/turbolinks

with the JavaScript you'll be writing later on when you start to use Angular. We're skipping Spring[5] as well, mostly because it isn't 100% reliable, and it could cause your experience with these examples to not mimic the one in the book. Finally, we're skipping Test::Unit as our testing framework, because we're going to be using RSpec.[6] As you see in Chapter 7, *Test This Fancy New Code*, on page 91, we have good reasons to use RSpec, so bear with me for now.

Now that you've installed Rails, we can use the rails command-line app to create Shine:

```
$ rails new shine \
          --skip-turbolinks \
          --skip-spring     \
          --skip-test       \
          -d postgresql
```

If you get an error installing the pg gem, it could be that your Postgres install is in a nonstandard place. You may need to run gem install pg --with-pg-config=«path to your pg_config». (To locate *that* highly depends on how you installed Postgres. You want to find the executable named pg_config and this usually lives inside the bin directory of wherever you installed Postgres.)

The rails new command creates the new application as you'd expect. Because almost all of our work will be in this Rails app, let's go ahead and change the current directory to the shine directory that contains the new Rails application:

```
$ cd shine
```

Before you run the Rails application, you'll need to set up your database. If you've installed Postgres locally, you'll need to create a user (if you're using Postgres-as-a-service, you should have a user created already and should skip this step). Our user will be named shine and have the password shine. You can create it using the command-line app installed with Postgres called createuser.

```
$ createuser --createdb --login -P shine
```

You'll be prompted for a password, so enter shine twice, as requested. --createdb tells Postgres that our user should be able to create databases (needed in a later step). The --login switch will allow our user to log in to the database and -P means we want to set our new user's password right now (which is why you were prompted for a password). See *If the createuser Command Isn't Found on Your System,* on page 4 if your system doesn't have createuser available.

---

5. https://github.com/rails/spring
6. http://rspec.info

Next, modify config/database.yml so the app can connect to the database:

```
default: &default
  adapter: postgresql
  encoding: unicode
➤ host: localhost
➤ username: shine
➤ password: shine
  pool: <%= ENV.fetch("RAILS_MAX_THREADS") { 5 } %>

development:
  <<: *default
  database: shine_development

test:
  <<: *default
  database: shine_test
```

If you're using Postgres-as-a-service, use the credentials you were given instead of what's shown here. Typically, you'll get a URL, so manually break it up into the pieces needed in config/database.yml. The URL is usually of the form postgres://some_user:their_password@some_host.com:PORT/database_name.

If the createuser Command Isn't Found on Your System

In some Linux installations, the createuser command isn't available. While you should consult the installation documentation for your operating system, you can create a user inside Postgres directly. You'll need to access the postgres schema, which you can usually do with psql like so:

```
$ psql postgres
```

Doing *this* could be tricky, as you may need to be the postgres user in your system. Again, the installation instructions for your operating system should show the way. Once you've done this, you can create a user inside psql:

```
$ psql postgres
postgres> CREATE USER shine PASSWORD 'shine';
```

Next, let's set up the database:

```
$ bundle exec rails db:create
$ bundle exec rails db:migrate
```

Depending on how you installed Postgres, these commands might fail with an error like PG::InsufficientPrivilege. If that happens, try accessing your database via psql and then executing the SQL alter role shine with superuser;.

You can now start the app to verify that everything worked. Although you don't have any database tables, Rails should complain if the database configuration is wrong, so this is a decent test of your configuration.

```
$ bundle exec rails server
```

You can now visit http://localhost:3000 and see the new Rails 5.1 welcome page, as shown in the following screenshot.

Last, let's make a page you can use to see the entire Rails view-rendering life cycle. This is needed to validate that you've installed Webpack properly, which we'll do after this. We'll call our page the *dashboard*, and our initial version will have a simple, static view.

Add the route to config/routes.rb:

```
1_setup/10-new-app/shine/config/routes.rb
Rails.application.routes.draw do
  root to: "dashboard#index"
end
```

Next, create app/controllers/dashboard_controller.rb:

```
1_setup/10-new-app/shine/app/controllers/dashboard_controller.rb
class DashboardController < ApplicationController
  def index
  end
end
```

Finally, create app/views/dashboard/index.html.erb with some basic content:

```
1_setup/10-new-app/shine/app/views/dashboard/index.html.erb
<header>
  <h1>
    Welcome to Shine!
  </h1>
  <h2>
    We're using Rails <%= Rails.version %>
  </h2>
</header>
<section>
  <p>
    Future home of Shine's Dashboard
  </p>
</section>
```

Restart your server, reload your app, and you should see the page we have created:

> **Welcome to Shine!**
>
> **We're using Rails 5.1.1**
>
> Future home of Shine's Dashboard

Now that you have a working Rails app, let's install Bootstrap. This requires first learning how to use Yarn to install Webpack, which will serve up our CSS and JavaScript for the rest of the book. (I'll explain why we aren't using Rails's asset pipeline as well.)

Setting Up Bootstrap with Yarn and Webpack

We want our users' experiences with Shine to be good, but we don't have hours and hours to spend styling and perfecting it. We also might not even have the *expertise* to do a good job. The reality of software development, especially for internal tools, is that there's rarely enough time or people to work on a great design.

Fortunately, there are now many *CSS frameworks* available that can help us produce a decent design that helps users get the most out of our software. A framework is a set of reusable classes that we can apply—without writing any actual CSS—to style our markup. For example, a framework might set up a set of font sizes that work well when used together. It may also provide classes we can apply to form fields to make them lay out effectively on the page.

Bootstrap[7] is one of the most popular and widely used CSS frameworks, and it gives programmers an immense amount of power to control the look and feel of their apps, without having to write any CSS themselves. Bootstrap is no replacement for an actual designer—its default visual style won't win any design awards. But, for an internal application like Shine, it's perfect. It will make our app look good.

To install Bootstrap, you're going to end up setting up Yarn to manage Shine's dependency on Bootstrap's code, and Webpack to serve it up. Webpack will eventually serve up Angular as well as the JavaScript you'll eventually write.

Although you could reference Bootstrap from a CDN[8] host, this is not common for production applications. In most cases, you want to control exactly what is bundled in your application, so you want Bootstrap to be part of the application. You could use RubyGems to achieve this; however, not all assets and JavaScript libraries you are going to want are available or up-to-date. (For example, as of this writing, Angular versions 2 and later are not available.)

This means we need another way to download Bootstrap's code and include it into our application. I would like to use a system like Bundler to manage it, but because Bundler only manages RubyGems, we will turn to the newest package management system for JavaScript (and the rest of the front-end ecosystem): Yarn.

Yarn[9] is a new package manager for JavaScript that uses the central NPM repository. It's the JavaScript equivalent of Bundler, and, as of this writing, Rails 5.1 includes support for it (which is why we aren't using NPM). Instead of a Gemfile, Yarn uses a file named package.json. Just as running bundle install updates the Ruby gems in our application, yarn install updates the front-end assets and libraries. This is the easy part. The hard part is figuring out how to serve up the assets downloaded with Yarn.

In theory, the Rails asset pipeline, powered by Sprockets, should be able to do this. In practice, it's not easy making this happen. In addition to the configuration difficulties this would involve, Sprockets is missing most modern features of front-end development. While we can do without many of them, when you start writing Angular code in Chapter 6, *Build a Dynamic UI with Angular*, on page 65, you'll need a few features Sprockets doesn't provide.

---

7. http://getbootstrap.com
8. http://en.wikipedia.org/wiki/Content_delivery_network
9. https://yarnpkg.com

So, while you might be able to get Bootstrap's CSS downloaded somewhere that Sprockets can serve it up, Sprockets won't work for code you'll write later on, and we don't want two systems to manage our assets—we just want one. That system is Webpack.[10]

Webpack is an asset pipeline that supports most modern features in front-end development, along with everything we were used to from Sprockets. It will allow us to serve up Bootstrap (once installed) and handle all the Java-Script needs we will have in later chapters. Unlike Sprockets, however, Webpack requires a substantial amount of up-front configuration to get working. That is what I will cover in the following section, but to do that, we have to first install Yarn.

Install Yarn

Yarn is a JavaScript application, so you'll need to install Node to get it to work. To install Node, visit http://nodejs.org and follow the instructions for your operating system. In particular, you may want to check out the page on installing Node via package managers,[11] because it has extensive documentation for various operating systems. The version of Node shouldn't matter too much, but this book was written using version 7.2.0.

Once you have Node installed, you'll need to install Yarn. Visit Yarn's install page[12] to find instructions for your operating system. This will install the yarn command-line application, which we'll use later to install Bootstrap. But next, we need to install Webpack.

Install and Configure Webpack

While we could install Webpack directly and set it up by hand, Rails 5.1 includes an optional gem called *Webpacker* that is the official way to use Webpack in a Rails application. Webpacker is a set of generators and helpers that creates a Webpack configuration. First, we'll add it to our Gemfile:

1_setup/20-install-webpack/shine/Gemfile
```
gem 'rails', '~> 5.1'
gem 'webpacker'
```

Then, we'll install it with Bundler:

```
> bundle install
```

---

10. https://webpack.github.io
11. https://nodejs.org/en/download/package-manager
12. https://yarnpkg.com/en/docs/install

We can now use Webpacker to install and configure Webpack for Shine by using the Rails task, webpacker:install:

```
> bundle exec rails webpacker:install
Copying webpack core config and loaders
      create  config/webpack
      create  config/webpack/configuration.js
      create  config/webpack/development.js
      create  config/webpack/development.server.js
      create  config/webpack/development.server.yml
      create  config/webpack/paths.yml
      create  config/webpack/production.js
      create  config/webpack/shared.js
      create  config/webpack/test.js
      create  config/webpack/loaders
      create  config/webpack/loaders/assets.js
      create  config/webpack/loaders/babel.js
      create  config/webpack/loaders/coffee.js
      create  config/webpack/loaders/erb.js
      create  config/webpack/loaders/sass.js
      create  .postcssrc.yml
Copying .babelrc to app root directory
      create  .babelrc
Creating javascript app source directory
      create  app/javascript
      create  app/javascript/packs/application.js
Copying binstubs
      create  bin/webpack-dev-server
      create  bin/webpack
Copying yarn
      create  bin/yarn
      append  .gitignore
Installing all JavaScript dependencies
         run  ./bin/yarn add webpack webpack-merge js-yaml…
yarn add v0.23.2
[1/4] Resolving packages...
[2/4] Fetching packages...
[3/4] Linking dependencies...
[4/4] Building fresh packages...
success Saved lockfile.
success Saved 216 new dependencies.

《Lots of output》

Done in 21.73s.
Installing dev server for live reloading
         run  ./bin/yarn add --dev webpack-dev-server from "."
yarn add v0.23.2
[1/4] Resolving packages...
[2/4] Fetching packages...
[3/4] Linking dependencies...
```

```
[4/4] Building fresh packages...
success Saved lockfile.
success Saved 7 new dependencies.
```

≪*More output*≫

```
Done in 4.45s.
Webpacker successfully installed
```

The output you see will be similar, but not identical (yours will likely include emoji . . . seriously). You should see that a lot of different files were created. Most of these configure Webpack, but you'll also see that you now have a file in the root of Shine called package.json. This file is analogous to the Gemfile in that it lists third-party libraries we need in our application. In this case, it's listing JavaScript (and, eventually, CSS) libraries. Webpacker has initialized it with what we need to run Webpack. Normally, you would install the libraries listed in this file using yarn install; however, Webpacker has also done that for us.

If this is the first time you've used Node, NPM, or Yarn, running yarn install is the JavaScript equivalent of bundle install. All the JavaScript dependencies were downloaded to the local directory node_modules. Generally, you don't want to check this into your version control system, but it depends on how you deploy.

Our development workflow with Webpack requires a second server to be run that serves up our JavaScript and CSS. Unlike with Sprockets, which executes inside our Rails app when we run rails new, Webpack runs outside of Rails. This means we need a way to run this server, but also a way to tell our Rails views to get JavaScript and CSS from this server.

The command to serve up our Webpack-managed code is bin/webpack-dev-server. While we could run this in another window alongside rails server, that's rather inconvenient. Instead, we can use a Ruby gem called *Foreman*.[13] Foreman allows us to specify any number of commands to run at the same time and in the same window.

First, let's install Foreman. Add it to your Gemfile:

1_setup/20-install-webpack/shine/Gemfile
```
gem 'jbuilder', '~> 2.5'
gem 'foreman'
```

Install it with bundle install as you did with Webpacker (we'll omit showing the output of bundle install from now on for brevity).

---

13. https://github.com/ddollar/foreman

To configure Foreman, list all the commands you want to run in a file called Procfile. The format of a Procfile is a series of lines, each having a name, followed by a colon, followed by the command to run. For our purposes, we want to run both rails server and bin/webpack-dev-server. Create Procfile in the root directory of your Rails app like so:

```
1_setup/20-install-webpack/shine/Procfile
rails:   bundle exec rails server
webpack: bin/webpack-dev-server
```

You can then run these commands with the single command-line invocation foreman start. For the rest of the book, this is how we'll run Shine, and we won't be doing bundle exec rails server any longer.

With this in place, we can now serve up JavaScript and CSS managed by Webpack to our Rails application. Before we bring in Bootstrap—our ultimate goal—let's see all the moving parts working for a simple case. Webpacker created the file app/javascript/packs/application.js, which includes a call to console.log. Webpacker also configured Webpack to serve up CSS files for us, but it didn't create a .css we can serve.

Create the file app/javascript/packs/application.css like so:

```
html {
  font-family: monospace;
}
```

With Webpack, all assets are managed from a JavaScript file. As odd as it sounds, to get Webpack to produce a CSS bundle like Sprockets does, we include our CSS in our JavaScript. That CSS won't actually end up in our JavaScript, but this is how Webpack is designed. To tell Webpack to manage a CSS file, we need to add a line of code to app/javascript/packs/application.js:

```
import "./application.css";
console.log('Hello World from Webpacker');
```

If you haven't seen import in a JavaScript file before, it's similar to Ruby's require: it brings in code from another file. In this case, Webpack knows that this file is a CSS file, not JavaScript. Instead, it creates a .css we can include in our views.

To do that, we'll use the helpers provided by the Webpacker gem: javascript_pack_tag and stylesheet_pack_tag. We'll put them in our main application layout, so we can see everything working.

```
1_setup/20-install-webpack/shine/app/views/layouts/application.html.erb
<!DOCTYPE html>
<html>
  <head>
    <title>Shine</title>
    <%= csrf_meta_tags %>

    <%= stylesheet_link_tag    'application', media: 'all' %>
    <%= javascript_include_tag 'application' %>
➤   <%= javascript_pack_tag "application" %>
➤   <%= stylesheet_pack_tag "application" %>
  </head>

  <body>
    <h1>Rails:<%= Rails.env %></h1>
    <%= yield %>
  </body>
</html>
```

Now, start Shine using foreman start (note that it will be running on port *5000* instead of 3000):

```
$ foreman start
« lots of output »
```

If you navigate to http://localhost:5000 you should see that your text is in a monospace font. This is our stylesheet in action. If you open the JavaScript console in your browser, you should see a "Hello World from Webpacker" message similar to what is shown in the following figure.

Before we move on, remove the contents of app/javascript/packs/application.css, but make sure the file is still there, empty. We don't want Shine to always use an ugly monospaced font.

With this in place, we can now bring in Bootstrap.

Download and Set Up Bootstrap

With Webpack's initial setup out of the way, bringing in Bootstrap is relatively straightforward. First, we'll add Bootstrap to package.json by using yarn add. Normally, you'd run something like yarn add bootstrap, but we don't want to accidentally bring in Bootstrap 4 when it gets released. The current alpha version has breaking changes, so we want to get the latest in the 3.x line of releases. We can do that by specifying bootstrap@3, like so:

```
> yarn add bootstrap@3
yarn add v0.20.3
warning No license field
[1/4] Resolving packages...
[2/4] Fetching packages...
[3/4] Linking dependencies...
[4/4] Building fresh packages...
success Saved lockfile.
success Saved 1 new dependency.
└ bootstrap@3.3.7
warning No license field
Done in 2.80s.
```

We've already seen how to bring in our custom CSS, so bringing in Bootstrap is a matter of using import with the right value. Webpacker has configured Webpack to look inside node_modules for files we pass to import. Previously, we imported "./application.css" and it looked in our current directory. Because we preceded our path name with ./, Webpack looked in the current directory.

Because Bootstrap was installed into node_modules, we won't use ./ in our path. Instead, we'll use a path relative to node_modules. You can poke around in there to find the right path if you like, but this is what you need to do:

```
1_setup/20-install-webpack/shine/app/javascript/packs/application.js
import "./application.css";
import "bootstrap/dist/css/bootstrap.css";
console.log('Hello World from Webpacker');
```

Before, we talked about the weird way the CSS that we import into our Java-Script made it into an actual .css file. By adding a second import of a CSS file, we can see more easily what Webpack is doing. It's merging the source files we write (or have brought in via Yarn) into a single file that gets included on the page via stylesheet_pack_tag.

With all of this completed, restart your app, navigate to the home page, and you should see that the font is now rendering in Helvetica, which is Bootstrap's default.

Rails:test

Welcome to Shine!

We're using Rails 5.1.1

Future home of Shine's Dashboard

Whew! That was a lot of setup. If you've ever used Webpack before, you'll appreciate Webpacker—it saved us from a *ton* of manual configuration. Although parts of it are weird, it's given us a development environment that works in a canonical Rails way, and will make it simple for us to add more complex features to Shine as we go through the book. Webpack will be particularly helpful when our JavaScript code gets complex and we need to write tests for it.

Next: Authentication with Devise, Styled by Bootstrap

Now that you are set up and ready to go, let's dive into Shine by setting up a basic authentication system using Devise. Devise does all the hard stuff for us, but it doesn't create usable or aesthetically pleasing views. That's where Bootstrap comes in.

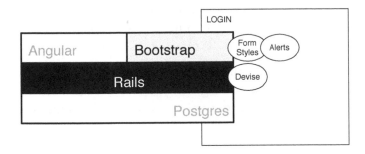

## CHAPTER 2

Create a Great-Looking Login with Bootstrap and Devise

Now that you have created and configured Shine, downloaded Bootstrap using Yarn, and have Webpack set to serve it all up, let's start adding features to Shine. In this chapter you'll set up a simple authentication system using Devise. Devise does all the hard work around authentication, but its default user interface leaves much to be desired. Bootstrap makes short work of this, and by the end of the chapter you'll have a secure Rails application with user-friendly views in no time, all without writing any CSS.

Adding Authentication with Devise

An authentication system is a great first step into thinking about problems as a full-stack developer—we want the user experience to be great, but we also want the back end to be secure, all the way down to the data layer. We'll use the *Devise*[1] gem to handle the middleware bits of authentication.

Creating an authentication system from scratch is rarely a good idea. It's difficult to get every part of it correct, because security controls can be subverted in unusual and counterintuitive ways. Devise is tried-and-true and handles all of this for us. It's also quite flexible and will totally suit our needs. Here are the rules we want for our authentication system:

---

1. https://github.com/plataformatec/devise

- Employees who need to use our app will sign up on their own.
- Employees must use their company email addresses when signing up.
- Employees' passwords must be at least 10 characters long.

Our app isn't going to require users to validate their email addresses, mostly to keep things simple by avoiding email configuration. You should consider it for a real app, and Devise makes it easy to use once you've fully configured your mailers.[2]

First, add Devise to your Gemfile:

```
2_bootstrap-login/10-install-devise/shine/Gemfile
gem 'jbuilder', '~> 2.5'
➤ gem 'devise'
```

Next, install it using Bundler:

```
$ bundle install
```

Devise includes several generators[3] you can use to simplify the setup and initial configuration. The devise:install generator is the first one you'll need to bootstrap Devise in the app.

```
$ bundle exec rails generate devise:install
    create  config/initializers/devise.rb
    create  config/locales/devise.en.yml
```

This command outputs a fairly lengthy message about further actions to take to set up Devise. I'll address all of that advice in this section, so don't worry about it for now.

Next, we need to tell Devise what model and database table we'll use for authentication. Even though our company's public website has a user authentication mechanism for our *customers*, we want to use a separate system for our internal users. This allows both systems to vary as needed for different parts of the business. It also creates a much more explicit wall between customers and users, and prevents customers from having access to our internal systems.

Devise is part of that separate system, but we also need a separate database table and model. Because we refer to our customers as "customers," we'll refer to our internal users as "users." Devise can create that table for us, using a generator called devise. It will create a User Active Record model and database table (called USERS) with the fields necessary for Devise to function.

---

2. http://guides.rubyonrails.org/action_mailer_basics.html#action-mailer-configuration
3. http://guides.rubyonrails.org/command_line.html#rails-generate

```
$ bundle exec rails generate devise user
    invoke   active_record
    create      db/migrate/20160714144446_devise_create_users.rb
    create      app/models/user.rb
    insert      app/models/user.rb
     route   devise_for :users
```

Have a look at what it created by examining the migration:

2_bootstrap-login/10-install-devise/shine/db/migrate/20160714144446_devise_create_users.rb

```ruby
class DeviseCreateUsers < ActiveRecord::Migration[5.0]
  def change
    create_table :users do |t|
      ## Database authenticatable
      t.string :email,              null: false, default: ""
      t.string :encrypted_password, null: false, default: ""

      ## Recoverable
      t.string   :reset_password_token
      t.datetime :reset_password_sent_at

      ## Rememberable
      t.datetime :remember_created_at

      ## Trackable
      t.integer  :sign_in_count, default: 0, null: false
      t.datetime :current_sign_in_at
      t.datetime :last_sign_in_at
      t.inet     :current_sign_in_ip
      t.inet     :last_sign_in_ip

      ## Confirmable
      # t.string   :confirmation_token
      # t.datetime :confirmed_at
      # t.datetime :confirmation_sent_at
      # t.string   :unconfirmed_email # Only if using reconfirmable

      ## Lockable
      # t.integer  :failed_attempts, default: 0,
      #            null: false # Only if lock
      #                        # strategy is :failed_attempts
      # t.string   :unlock_token # Only if unlock
      #                          # strategy is :email or :both
      # t.datetime :locked_at

      t.timestamps null: false
    end

    add_index :users, :email,                unique: true
    add_index :users, :reset_password_token, unique: true
    # add_index :users, :confirmation_token,   unique: true
    # add_index :users, :unlock_token,         unique: true
  end
end
```

Each section that's commented indicates which Devise modules the fields are relevant to. Don't worry about what those are for now. We also won't add any fields of our own at this point. If we need some later, we can always add them with a new migration.

There's one last step before you can finally see Devise in action. We need to indicate which controller actions require authentication. Without that, Devise won't do anything, since it will perceive all pages as being open to anonymous users.

Devise provides a controller filter called authenticate_user!, and you can use that in your ApplicationController, since we want *all* pages and actions to be restricted.

2_bootstrap-login/10-install-devise/shine/app/controllers/application_controller.rb

```
class ApplicationController < ActionController::Base
  protect_from_forgery with: :exception
➤ before_action :authenticate_user!
end
```

As a way to be certain you've actually authenticated the user, let's show the email address on the dashboard. Devise provides a helper method called current_user, which returns the User instance of the currently authenticated user. Because it's a helper, you can use it directly in your view.

2_bootstrap-login/10-install-devise/shine/app/views/dashboard/index.html.erb

```
<header>
  <h1>
➤   Welcome to Shine, <%= current_user.email %>
  </h1>
  <h2>
    We're using Rails <%= Rails.version %>
  </h2>
</header>
<section>
  <p>
    Future home of Shine's Dashboard
  </p>
</section>
```

Now, we're ready to see it working. We'll need to run migrations and then start our server.

```
$ bundle exec rails db:migrate
== 20160714144446 DeviseCreateUsers: migrating ================================
-- create_table(:users)
   -> 0.0321s
-- add_index(:users, :email, {:unique=>true})
   -> 0.0184s
-- add_index(:users, :reset_password_token, {:unique=>true})
```

```
      -> 0.0070s
== 20160714144446 DeviseCreateUsers: migrated (0.0577s) ========================
$ bundle exec foreman start
```

Navigating to http://localhost:5000 no longer shows the dashboard page, but instead asks us to log in or sign up, as shown in the following screen:

Rails:test

Log in

Email

Password

☐ Remember me

Log in

Sign up
Forgot your password?

Because we don't have a user account yet, let's create one by clicking the "Sign up" link. The Sign Up screen appears:

Rails:test

Sign up

Email

Password *(6 characters minimum)*

Password confirmation

Sign up
Log in

If you fill in the fields, your account will be created and you'll be automatically logged in. As shown in the following screen, you should be able to see your email address on the dashboard page, just as we wanted.

Rails:test

Welcome to Shine, user6658@example.com

We're using Rails 5.1.1

Future home of Shine's Dashboard

You can also see that Devise has created an entry in the USERS table by going into the database directly. Use the Rails dbconsole[4] command to access the database so that you can examine the USERS table:

---

4. http://guides.rubyonrails.org/command_line.html#rails-dbconsole

```
$ bundle exec rails dbconsole
postgres> \x on
Expanded display is on.
postgres> select * from users;
-[ RECORD 1 ]----------+------------------------------------------------
id                     | 1
email                  | user7722@example.com
encrypted_password     | $2a$11$JiBGEx3/TCx6SsQPmSp8/uWPdQHqy/LlBaZQ8wL4d2
reset_password_token   |
reset_password_sent_at |
remember_created_at    |
sign_in_count          | 1
current_sign_in_at     | 2016-07-14 14:56:52.245834
last_sign_in_at        | 2016-07-14 14:56:52.245834
current_sign_in_ip     | ::1
last_sign_in_ip        | ::1
created_at             | 2016-07-14 14:56:52.242083
updated_at             | 2016-07-14 14:56:52.246722
```

Note that you can exit dbconsole by typing \q and hitting Return.

This is an amazing amount of functionality just for installing a gem and adding a few lines of code to our application. And, because Devise is tried and tested, we know our authentication system is solid and dependable. But it's ugly.

You could open up app/assets/stylesheets/application.css and start trying to make it look better, but you don't have to. Bootstrap provides a ton of styles you can apply to your markup to make your login look great, and you won't have to write any CSS.

Styling the Login and Registration Forms

Bootstrap doesn't do much to naked elements in your markup. It sets the default font and makes a few color changes, but most of what Bootstrap does requires you to add classes to certain elements in a particular way. This means you'll need access to the markup before you get started.

You might recall that you didn't write any markup for the login screens—they were all provided by Devise. Devise is packaged as a Rails Engine,[5] so the gem itself contains the views. But it also contains a generator called devise:views that will extract those views into our application, allowing us to modify them.

```
$ bundle exec rails generate devise:views
  invoke  Devise::Generators::SharedViewsGenerator
  create    app/views/devise/shared
  create    app/views/devise/shared/_links.html.erb
```

---

5.   http://guides.rubyonrails.org/engines.html

```
invoke  form_for
create     app/views/devise/confirmations
create     app/views/devise/confirmations/new.html.erb
create     app/views/devise/passwords
create     app/views/devise/passwords/edit.html.erb
. . .
invoke  erb
create     app/views/devise/mailer
create     app/views/devise/mailer/confirmation_instructions.html.erb
create     app/views/devise/mailer/reset_password_instructions.html.erb
create     app/views/devise/mailer/unlock_instructions.html.erb
```

Now that you can edit these files, you can use Bootstrap's CSS classes to make them look how you'd like.

Since we'd like to style both the login screen *and* the registration screen, we need a way to log ourselves out so we can see them. Devise set up all the necessary routes for us, so we just need to create a link to the right path in app/views/dashboard/index.html.erb:

2_bootstrap-login/20-use-bootstrap/shine/app/views/dashboard/index.html.erb
```
<header>
  <h1>
    Welcome to Shine, <%= current_user.email %>
  </h1>
  <h2>
    We're using Rails <%= Rails.version %>
  </h2>
</header>
<section>
  <p>
    Future home of Shine's Dashboard
  </p>
➤ <%= link_to "Log Out", destroy_user_session_path, method: :delete %>
</section>
```

With that link in place, you can log out to see the screens you're going to style. You're just going to be using the styles Bootstrap provides—you aren't writing any CSS yourself. You'll be amazed at how much better our screens are with just these simple changes.

First, you need to make sure all of your markup is in one of Bootstrap's "containers," which will "unlock" many of the features you need. You can apply this to the body element in your application layout:

2_bootstrap-login/20-use-bootstrap/shine/app/views/layouts/application.html.erb
```
➤ <body class="container">
  <%= yield %>
</body>
```

Reloading the app, you can see that this class added some sensible margins and padding:

Welcome to Shine, user7247@example.com

We're using Rails 5.1.1

Future home of Shine's Dashboard

Log Out

Let's start with the login screen.

Style the Login Screen

Because Devise uses Rails's RESTful routing scheme, the resource around logging in is called a "user session." Therefore, the view for the login screen is in app/views/devise/sessions/new.html.erb.

For styling forms, Bootstrap's documentation[6] has several different options. We'll use the first, most basic one, which is perfect for our needs.

We'll wrap each label and input element in a div with the class form-group and then add the class form-control to each control. The check box requires slightly different handling. We put it inside its own label, which is inside an element with the class checkbox. We also need the submit tag to look like a button, so we'll use the btn class for that. We also want the button to be larger and more prominent. We can achieve that by using the classes btn-lg and btn-primary, respectively. These classes alter anything with the btn class, and this pattern is used throughout Bootstrap.

Here's what the revised template looks like:

```
2_bootstrap-login/20-use-bootstrap/shine/app/views/devise/sessions/new.html.erb
<header>
  <h1>Log in</h1>
</header>
<%= form_for(resource, as: resource_name,
                       url: session_path(resource_name)) do |f| %>
  <div class="form-group">
    <%= f.label :email %>
    <%= f.email_field :email, autofocus: true, class: "form-control" %>
  </div>
  <div class="form-group">
    <%= f.label :password %>
    <%= f.password_field :password, autocomplete: "off",
                                    class: "form-control" %>
  </div>
```

---

6.   http://getbootstrap.com/css/#forms

```
<% if devise_mapping.rememberable? -%>
  <div class="checkbox">
    <label>
      <%= f.check_box :remember_me %> Remember Me
    </label>
  </div>
<% end -%>
<%= f.submit "Log in", class: "btn btn-primary btn-lg" %>
<% end %>
<%= render "devise/shared/links" %>
```

If you reload your browser, the form (shown next) now looks *a lot* better than before:

The spacing and vertical rhythm of the elements is more pleasing. The form controls feel more spacious and inviting. The "Log in" button looks more clickable. You'll even notice a subtle animation and highlight when switching the active form field. And all we did was add a few classes to the markup!

Before moving on to the registration screen, there's one more thing to fix here. If you submit the form without providing an email address or password, Devise sets an error message in the Rails flash.[7] We're currently not displaying that anywhere.

We need to display it and style it in a way that allows users to easily see it. This will help users better understand when they've messed something up.

Style the Flash

In addition to classes designed to work with existing HTML entities like forms, Bootstrap provides *components*, which are a set of classes that, when applied to an element (or set of elements), create a particular effect. For the flash, Bootstrap provides a component called an alert.[8]

---

7. http://guides.rubyonrails.org/action_controller_overview.html#the-flash
8. http://getbootstrap.com/components/#alerts

Let's display the flash using this component, which just requires using the class alert and then either alert-danger or alert-info, for the alert and notice flash messages, respectively.

```
2_bootstrap-login/30-style-flash/shine/app/views/layouts/application.html.erb
  <body class="container">
➤   <% if notice.present? %>
➤     <aside class="alert alert-info">
➤       <%= notice %>
➤     </aside>
➤   <% end %>
➤   <% if alert.present? %>
➤     <aside class="alert alert-danger">
➤       <%= alert %>
➤     </aside>
➤   <% end %>
      <%= yield %>
  </body>
</html>
```

The markup got a bit more complex. We're using aside instead of div since it's more semantically correct. (Bootstrap doesn't generally care which type of element styles are applied to.) We've also had to wrap each alert component in code to check whether that message was actually set. This is because even without content, the Bootstrap alert component will still show up visually and look strange.

Also note the similarities between these classes and the ones we used to style the button on the login form. Here, alert declares our markup as an alert, and then alert-danger modifies it in the same way that btn-lg does for a btn.

With that done, you can navigate to a page requiring login, provide incorrect login details, and see that the flash messages are styled appropriately. Users can now easily see their mistakes and understand their successes, as shown in the screenshots on page 25.

The only thing left to do is to style the registration page.

Style the Registration Page

Devise refers to the resource for a user signing up as a *registration*, so the registration form is located in app/views/devise/registrations/new.html.erb. We'll apply the same classes to this page that we did to the previous.

```
2_bootstrap-login/40-style-registration/shine/app/views/devise/registrations/new.html.erb
<h2>Sign up</h2>
<%= form_for(resource, as: resource_name,
             url: registration_path(resource_name)) do |f| %>
```

Invalid Email or password.

Log in

Email

Password

☐ Remember Me

Log in

Sign up
Forgot your password?

Welcome! You have signed up successfully.

Welcome to Shine, user2266@example.com

We're using Rails 5.1.1

Future home of Shine's Dashboard

Log Out

```
<%= devise_error_messages! %>
<div class="form-group">
  <%= f.label :email %>
  <%= f.email_field :email, autofocus: true, class: "form-control" %>
</div>
<div class="form-group">
  <%= f.label :password %>
  <% if @minimum_password_length %>
    <em>(<%= @minimum_password_length %> characters minimum)</em>
  <% end %>
  <%= f.password_field :password,
                       autocomplete: "off",
                       class: "form-control" %>
</div>
<div class="form-group">
  <%= f.label :password_confirmation %>
  <%= f.password_field :password_confirmation,
                       autocomplete: "off",
                       class: "form-control" %>
</div>
  <%= f.submit "Sign up", class: "btn btn-primary btn-lg" %>
<% end %>
<%= render "devise/shared/links" %>
```

Reload the page and navigate to the Sign Up screen as shown on page 26.
You can see it's now styled similarly to the login page:

Sign up

Email

Password *(6 characters minimum)*

Password confirmation

Sign up

Log in

Devise also provides screens for resetting your password and for editing your login details. I'll leave that as an exercise for you to style those pages, but it will be just as simple as what you've seen already.

We now have a secure login system that looks great, and we've hardly written any code at all. We still have a few login requirements left to implement that aren't provided by Devise by default. In the next section, you'll see how to configure Devise to meet these requirements.

Validating Registration

If you look at the User model that Devise created, you can see that a Devise-provided method named devise is being used. This is how you can control the behaviors Devise uses for registration and authentication on a per-model basis. Note the :validatable symbol in the list.

2_bootstrap-login/50-validations/shine/app/models/user.rb
```
class User < ApplicationRecord
  devise :database_authenticatable,
         :registerable,
         :recoverable,
         :rememberable,
         :trackable,
         :validatable
end
```

This :validatable *module* is what we're interested in. By using this in our model, Devise sets up various validations for the model, namely that the password is at least eight characters and that the email address looks like an email address. These defaults are set in the initializer Devise created when you ran rails generate devise:install.

The initializer, located in config/initializers/devise.rb, has copious documentation about all of Devise's configuration options. If we search for the string "validatable," we can find the options we want to change, which are password_length and email_regexp. We'll change the minimum password length to 10 characters and require that emails end in our company's domain (which will be example.com).

2_bootstrap-login/50-validations/shine/config/initializers/devise.rb
```
# ==> Configuration for :validatable
config.password_length = 10..128
config.email_regexp = /\A[^@]+@example\.com\z/
```

Because we changed an initializer, you'll need to restart your server. Once you do that, if you try to register with a short password or an invalid email, you'll get an error message, as shown in the following screen:

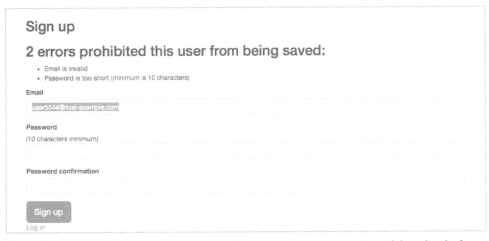

Note the unstyled error messages. These errors are produced by the helper method devise_error_messages!. You can override how this works by creating app/helpers/devise_helper.rb and implementing your own devise_error_messages! to output whatever markup you want. The details are on Devise's wiki[9] and, along with what you just learned about styling alerts with Bootstrap, you should be able to easily make those error messages look great.

This covers the user experience and, because this is implemented using Active Record validations, also covers most typical code paths that might modify the email column in the USERS table. Most, but not all.

---

9. https://github.com/plataformatec/devise/wiki/Override-devise_error_messages!-for-views

Next: Using Postgres to Make Our Login More Secure

Devise cannot absolutely prevent users from being added into our database that do not meet our security criteria. For example, Active Record provides the method update_attribute, which skips validations and could be used to insert a user with any email address into the USERS table. What we need is for the data layer itself to enforce our requirements. Postgres's *check constraints* can do this.

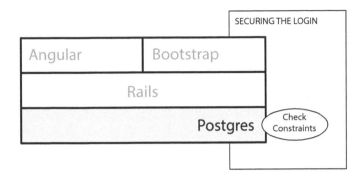

## CHAPTER 3

Secure the User Database with Postgres Constraints

Our registration and login system looks great, thanks to Bootstrap, and works great, thanks to Devise. But it's not as secure as it can be. As you recall from the previous chapter, we used validations to prevent users from registering with a non-company email address. Because this is done in Rails, it's easily circumventable using Rails's APIs or a direct database connection. Even something unintentional like bugs in our code could introduce vulnerabilities.

What we'd like is to prevent non-company email addresses from getting into the database entirely. Most SQL databases do not have powerful features for preventing bad data. With Postgres, however, we can, by using a feature called *check constraints*. This chapter is about setting up a check constraint for Postgres as part of our Rails database migrations.

Before you see how Postgres can solve our vulnerability, I'll explore it briefly, so you know exactly what problem we're solving.

Exposing the Vulnerability Devise and Rails Leave Open

You can easily verify the security hole in our application by creating a new user, signing out, changing that user's email in the database, and logging back in using the new email and previous password. This problem may seem academic, but it's more likely than you might think.

Even in a small company, there could be processes that access the database that aren't part of our application, and so won't benefit from the validations in our User model. Further, Rails itself provides methods like update_attribute that circumvent the validations, meaning a software bug could exist that used one of these methods and introduce a vulnerability.

How could this issue become a real problem? Consider a new employee named Sally. On Sally's first day, her company email wasn't set up properly, but she needed access to Shine. Sally was recruited by one of the engineers, Bob. Bob tries to help his friend Sally on her first day of work, and so creates a user for her using her personal email address so that she can start using Shine.

Months later, Sally leaves the company and Aaron in HR goes to deactivate her access to company systems. Aaron assumes that by deactivating Sally's email account, she won't have access to any more internal systems. Aaron doesn't know that Sally was using her personal email account to do that, so we are now in a situation where the company thinks Sally's access has been cut off, but it actually hasn't been.

Although this is all hypothetical, it now feels more possible than it might have seemed at first. When faced with security issues like this, you must weigh the cost of the security breach against the cost of preventing it. This means we need to figure out how much effort is required to prevent this vector of attack.

If preventing it required even a few days, it might not be worth it. Since we're using Postgres, it's a one-liner using *check constraints.*

Preventing Bad Data Using Check Constraints

If you've done any database work at all, you're no doubt familiar with a "not null" constraint that prevents inserting null into a column of the database:

```
CREATE TABLE people (
  id        INT          NOT NULL,
  name      VARCHAR(255) NOT NULL,
  birthdate DATE         NULL
);
```

In this table, id and name may not be NULL, but birthdate may be. Postgres takes the "null constraint" concept *much* further by allowing arbitrary constraints on fields. Postgres also has support for regular expressions. This means you can create a constraint on your email field that requires its value to match the same regular expression you used in our Rails code. This would prevent non-company email addresses from being inserted into the table entirely.

First, create a new migration where you can add this constraint:

```
$ bundle exec rails g migration add-email-constraint-to-users
    invoke  active_record
    create     db/migrate/20160718143725_add_email_constraint_to_users.rb
```

The *Domain-Specific Language* (DSL) for writing Rails migrations doesn't provide any means of creating this constraint, so you have to do it in straight SQL. Although Postgres *Data Definition Language* (DDL) looks different from what is normally used in migrations, it's still relatively straightforward and well documented online.[1]

The basic structure of our constraint is that we want to "alter" the USERS to "add" a constraint that will "check" the email column for invalid values. Here's what our migration will look like (see the following sidebar to learn why we're using the older up and down methods):

```
3_postgres-login/10-constraint/shine/db/migrate/20160718143725_add_email_constraint_to_users.rb
class AddEmailConstraintToUsers < ActiveRecord::Migration[5.0]
  def up
    execute %{
      ALTER TABLE
        users
      ADD CONSTRAINT
        email_must_be_company_email
      CHECK ( email ~* '^[^@]+@example\\.com$' )
    }
  end

  def down
    execute %{
      ALTER TABLE
        users
      DROP CONSTRAINT
        email_must_be_company_email
    }
  end
end
```

The ~* operator is how Postgres does regular expression matching. Therefore, this code means that the email column's value must match the regular expression we've given or the insert or update command will fail. The regular expression is more or less identical to the one we used when configuring Devise.

Let's see it in action by first running the migrations.

---

1. http://www.postgresql.org/docs/9.5/static/ddl-constraints.html

Why Aren't We Using change in Our Rails Migrations?

Rails 3.1 introduced the concept of *reversible migrations* via the method change in the migrations DSL. The Rails authors realized that most implementations of down were to reverse what was done inside up and Rails could figure out how to reverse the code in the up method automatically.

To make this work, programmers would need to constrain the contents of the change method to only those migration methods that Rails knows how to reverse, which are itemized in ActiveRecord::Migration::CommandRecorder.[a]

In most of the migrations we'll write in this book, we aren't using those methods, and are typically just using execute, because we need to run Postgres-specific commands. We could work within the Reversible Migrations framework by using reversible, but the resulting code is somewhat clunky:

```
class AddEmailConstraintToUsers < ActiveRecord::Migration[5.0]
  def change
    reversible do |direction|
      direction.up {
        execute %{
          ...
        }
      }
      direction.down {
        execute %{
          ...
        }
      }
    end
  end
end
```

Since up and down aren't deprecated, it ends up being easier to stick with the older syntax for the types of migrations we'll be writing.

---

a.   http://api.rubyonrails.org/classes/ActiveRecord/Migration/CommandRecorder.html

```
$ bundle exec rails db:migrate
== 20160718143725 AddEmailConstraintToUsers: migrating =============
-- execute("
    ALTER TABLE
      users
    ADD CONSTRAINT
      email_must_be_company_email
    CHECK ( email ~* '^[^@]+@example\\.com' )
  ")
  -> 0.0324s
== 20160718143725 AddEmailConstraintToUsers: migrated (0.0324s) ====
```

If you ran the migrations and saw something like the following error, you'd need to do a bit more work to apply this change.

```
$ bundle exec rails db:migrate
ActiveRecord::StatementInvalid: PG::CheckViolation: ERROR:
  check constraint "email_must_be_company_email" is violated by some row:
    ALTER TABLE
      users
    ADD CONSTRAINT
      email_must_be_company_email
    CHECK ( email ~* '[A-Za-z0-9._%-]+@example\.com' )
    ;
```

This means that at least one row in your development database has a value for the email column that violates our new constraint. Postgres is refusing to apply the constraint because it doesn't know what to do.

In your development environment, it's safe to manipulate the database or just blow it away. If you *are* seeing this issue, I recommend you just delete all the rows from the table since that's easy to do via delete from users;. If you were doing this to an active, production data set, you would not have that luxury. You would need to get more creative. There are several ways of handling this:

- Create a migration that deletes all users using a bad email address. This is drastic, but it would work.

- Create a migration to assign bogus company email addresses to the existing bad accounts. This would prevent those users from logging in but maintain their history. You could correct the accounts manually later on, but the constraint would be satisfied.

- You could also do something more complex where you demarcate active users with a new field and prevent inactive users from logging in. Your check constraint could then only check for active users—for example, active = true AND email ~* '[A-Za-z0-9._%-]@example\.com'.

In any case, if you're adding constraints to a running production system, you'll have to be more careful.

With the migration applied, let's see how it works. First, insert a user whose email is on our company's domain:

```
$ bundle exec rails dbconsole
shine_development> INSERT INTO
                      users (
                        email,
                        encrypted_password,
                        created_at,
                        updated_at
                      )
```

```
                        VALUES (
                          'foo@example.com',
                          '$abcd',
                          now(),
                          now()
                        );
INSERT 0 1
```

This works as expected. Now let's try to insert a user using a *different* domain:

```
shine_development> INSERT INTO
                        users (
                          email,
                          encrypted_password,
                          created_at,
                          updated_at
                        )
                        VALUES (
                          'foo@bar.com',
                          '$abcd',
                          now(),
                          now()
                        );
ERROR:  new row for relation "users" violates
        check constraint "email_must_be_company_email"
DETAIL: Failing row contains (4,
                          foo@bar.com,
                          $abcd,
                          null,
                          null,
                          null,
                          0,
                          null,
                          null,
                          null,
                          null,
                          '2015-03-03:12:12:14.000',
                          '2015-03-03:12:12:14.000'0).
```

You can see that Postgres refuses to allow invalid data into the table (and you get a pretty useful error message as well). This means that a rogue application, bug in the code, or even a developer at a production console will not be able to allow access to any user who doesn't have a company email address.

Given how little effort this was, and the peace of mind it gives us, it's a no-brainer to add this level of security. Postgres makes it simple, meaning the cost of securing our website is low.

There's one last thing we'll need to change because we're using a feature that's Postgres-specific. By default, Rails stores a snapshot of the database schema in db/schema.rb, which is a Ruby source file using the DSL for Rails migrations. Rails creates this by examining the database schema and creating what is essentially a single migration, in Ruby, to create the schema from scratch. This is what tests use to create a fresh database.

The problem is that Rails doesn't know about check constraints, so the one we just added won't be present in db/schema.rb. This is easily remedied by telling Rails to use SQL, rather than Ruby, for storing the schema. You can do this by adding one line to config/application.rb.

```
3_postgres-login/10-constraint/shine/config/application.rb
module Shine
  class Application < Rails::Application
    config.active_record.schema_format = :sql
  end
end
```

You'll then need to remove the old db/schema.rb file, create db/structure.sql by running migrations, and finally reset your test database by dropping it and re-creating it. You can do all this with rake:

```
$ rm db/schema.rb
$ bundle exec rails db:migrate
$ RAILS_ENV=test bundle exec rails db:drop
$ RAILS_ENV=test bundle exec rails db:create
```

You May Get Churn in db/structure.sql

Because db/structure.sql is a Postgres-specific dump of the schema, certain aspects of it are dependent on the local environment. For example, if you use add_foreign_key, the names Postgres auto-generates might be different on different machines.

It's not a big problem for your application's behavior, since db/structure.sql is not used in production, but it can make for unnecessary churn in your version control history. You can combat this by tightly controlling the versions of Postgres each developer is using, providing explicit names for constraints and indexes, and not committing spurious changes to the file.

Why Use Rails Validations?

Given the power of check constraints, why would you bother with Rails validations at all? The answer is part of why taking a full-stack view of development is so important—the user experience.

Rails validations are an elegant and powerful way to give users a great experience when providing data via web forms. The validations API is incredibly expressive, configurable, and extensible. If you remove the validations from our code and attempt to register with an invalid email, you'll get an exception—not a good user experience.

This *does* result in some duplication, which is a chance for inconsistency to creep into our app, but we can fight this by writing tests for each part of the stack (which you do in Chapter 7, *Test This Fancy New Code*, on page 91).

Next: Using Postgres Indexes to Speed Up a Fuzzy Search

The registration and login feature is now secure *and* pleasant to use. By using the best of both Postgres and Bootstrap, you've gotten a good taste of using the full application stack to deliver a great feature. The power of these tools allowed us to tackle an important part of any application—authentication—easily and quickly, without sacrificing security or user experience.

In the next chapter, you'll start on a new feature: customer search. Search is a great way to learn about all aspects of full-stack development. It's got everything: user input, complex output, and complex database queries. You'll start this feature by implementing a naive fuzzy search that you can then examine and optimize using special indexes Postgres provides.

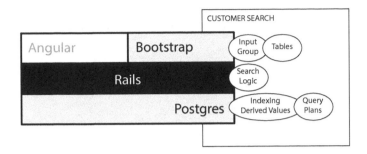

## CHAPTER 4

Perform Fast Queries with Advanced Postgres Indexes

Our users can now securely log in to Shine using a well-designed login form, which was a great way to get a taste of what Postgres and Bootstrap can offer. In the next few chapters, you'll implement a customer search feature, digging deeper into Postgres and Bootstrap. You'll also start learning Angular in Chapter 6, *Build a Dynamic UI with Angular*, on page 65.

In this chapter, you'll implement the basics of our search, which will perform poorly. This allows you to learn about the advanced indexing features of Postgres that will speed this search up without changing any code or setting up new infrastructure. You'll also learn how to understand query performance in Postgres, so you can be sure that the indexes you create have the performance improvements you want.

Because this is the first bit of code you're writing for this feature, you'll also need some UI and middleware logic. Although this chapter is mostly about Postgres, you'll be working in all parts of the stack. Specifically, you'll write the basics of our search logic in Rails, and you'll learn how to style forms in Bootstrap using input groups, as well as how Bootstrap styles tables. In Chapter 5, *Create Clean Search Results*, on page 55, you'll spend more time on the search results themselves.

First, you'll implement a naive fuzzy search that allows our users to locate customers based on first name, last name, or email. It'll look something like the figure on page 38.

After that, you'll look at the performance of Active Record's SQL query using Postgres's *query plan*. You'll then use a special type of index on our tables to speed up our search, which you'll then verify by reexamining the new query plan. This all might feel really low-level, but you'll be surprised just how easy it is to get great performance out of Postgres with just a few lines of code.

Let's get to it by implementing a naive version of the search.

Implementing a Basic Fuzzy Search with Rails

As mentioned in the *Introduction*, on page xi, Shine will be sharing a database with an existing customer-facing application. The customer-search feature we're building will search one of the tables in that database.

In the real world, our database would already exist and you'd hook up to it directly. Since that's not the case, you'll need to simulate its existence by creating the table in Shine's database. And, because you'll use Postgres query performance optimization, our table is going to need a lot of data in it.

Set Up the New Table and Data

If you were using an existing table, you wouldn't need a migration—you could just create the Customer model and be done. That's not the case (since this is an example in a book), so we'll create the table ourselves. It will ultimately look like the schema on page 39.

A customer has first and last names, an email address, a username, and creation and last update dates. None of the fields allow null and the data in the username and email fields must both be unique (that's what the "index_customers_on_email" UNIQUE, btree (email) bit is telling us). This is more or less what we'd expect from a table that stores information about our customers.

The Final Customer Table Schema

```
                              Table "public.customers"
     Column     |              Type              |          Modifiers
 ---------------+--------------------------------+-----------------------------
  id            | integer                        | not null default
                |                                | nextval('customers_id_seq')
  first_name    | character varying              | not null
  last_name     | character varying              | not null
  email         | character varying              | not null
  username      | character varying              | not null
  created_at    | timestamp without time zone    | not null
  updated_at    | timestamp without time zone    | not null
 Indexes:
     "customers_pkey" PRIMARY KEY, btree (id)
     "index_customers_on_email" UNIQUE, btree (email)
     "index_customers_on_username" UNIQUE, btree (username)
```

Because this table doesn't exist yet in our example, you can create it using Rails's model generator. This creates both the database migration that will create this table as well as the Customer class that allows us to access it in our code.

```
$ bundle exec rails g model customer first_name:string \
                            last_name:string \
                            email:string \
                            username:string
   invoke  active_record
   create    db/migrate/20160718151402_create_customers.rb
   create    app/models/customer.rb
```

The migration file Rails created will define our table, column names, and their types, but it won't include the not null and unique constraints. You can add those easily enough by opening up db/migrate/20160718151402_create_customers.rb.

```
4_postgres-index/10-setup-customer-data/shine/db/migrate/20160718151402_create_customers.rb
class CreateCustomers < ActiveRecord::Migration[5.0]
  def change
    create_table :customers do |t|
➤     t.string :first_name , null: false
➤     t.string :last_name  , null: false
➤     t.string :email      , null: false
➤     t.string :username   , null: false
➤
➤     t.timestamps          null: false
    end
➤   add_index :customers, :email, unique: true
➤   add_index :customers, :username, unique: true
  end
end
```

With that created, you can go ahead and run the migrations.

```
$ bundle exec rails db:migrate
== 20160718151402 CreateCustomers: migrating ===========
-- create_table(:customers)
   -> 0.0257s
-- add_index(:customers, :email, {:unique=>true})
   -> 0.0026s
-- add_index(:customers, :username, {:unique=>true})
   -> 0.0019s
== 20160718151402 CreateCustomers: migrated (0.0303s) ==
```

You should be able to verify that the schema created matches the schema on page 39 via

```
> bundle exec rails dbconsole
shine_development=> \d customers
```

Next, you need some customer data. Rather than provide you with a download of a giant database dump to install (or include it in the code downloads for this book), I'll have you generate data algorithmically. We'll aim to make 350,000 rows of "real-looking" data. To help, we'll use a gem called *faker*,[1] which is typically used to create test data. First, add that to the Gemfile:

4_postgres-index/10-setup-customer-data/shine/Gemfile
```
gem 'devise'
➤ gem 'faker'
```

Then, install it:

```
$ bundle install
Installing faker 1.6.5
```

You can now use faker to create real-looking data, which will make it much easier to use Shine in our development environment, since you'll have real-sounding names and email addresses. We'll create this data by writing a small script in db/seeds.rb. Rails's seed data[2] feature is intended to prepopulate a fresh database with reference data, like a list of countries, but it'll work for creating our sample data.

4_postgres-index/10-setup-customer-data/shine/db/seeds.rb
```
350_000.times do |i|
  Customer.create!(
    first_name: Faker::Name.first_name,
    last_name: Faker::Name.last_name,
     username: "#{Faker::Internet.user_name}#{i}",
        email: Faker::Internet.user_name + i.to_s +
```

---

1.   https://github.com/stympy/faker

2.   http://guides.rubyonrails.org/active_record_migrations.html#migrations-and-seed-data

```
                "@#{Faker::Internet.domain_name}")
  print '.' if i % 1000 == 0
end
puts
```

The reason we're appending the index to the username and email is to ensure these values are unique. As you added unique constraints to those fields when creating the table, faker would have to have over 350,000 variations, selected with perfect random distribution. Rather than hope that's the case, you'll ensure uniqueness with a number. Note the final line in the loop where you use print if the current index is a multiple of 1000. This will output a dot on the command line to give you a sense of progress. With the seed file created, we'll run it (this may take up to 30 minutes depending on the power of your computer).

```
$ bundle exec rails db:seed
```

With data filling the table, you can implement the basics of the search feature.

Build the Search UI

When starting a new feature, it's best to start from the user interface, especially if you didn't have a designer design it in advance. Recall that our requirements are to allow searching by first name, last name, and email address. Rather than require users to specify which field they're searching by, we'll provide one search box and do an inclusive search of all fields on the back end. We'll also display the results in a table, since that is fairly typical for search results.

The search will be implemented as the index action on the customers resource. First, add a route to config/routes.rb:

```
4_postgres-index/20-search-ui/shine/config/routes.rb
root to: "dashboard#index"
resources :customers, only: [ :index ]
```

That route expects an index method on the CustomersController class, which doesn't exist yet. You could use a Rails generator, but it's just as easy to create the file from scratch. You'll create app/controllers/customers_controller.rb and add the definition of the CustomersController there. You'll implement the index method to just grab the first ten customers in the database, so you have some data you can use to style the view.

```
4_postgres-index/20-search-ui/shine/app/controllers/customers_controller.rb
class CustomersController < ApplicationController
  def index
    @customers = Customer.all.limit(10)
  end
end
```

You can now start building the view in app/views/customers/index.html.erb (which won't exist yet). You'll need two main sections in your view: a search form and a results table. First, you should make a header letting users know what page they're on.

```
4_postgres-index/20-search-ui/shine/app/views/customers/index.html.erb
<header>
  <h1 class="h2">Customer Search</h1>
</header>
```

Next, create the search form. Because there's just going to be one field, you don't need an explicit label (though you'll include markup for one that's only visible to screen readers). The design we want is a single row with both the field and the submit button, filling the horizontal width of the container (a large field will feel inviting and easy to use).

Bootstrap provides CSS for a component called an *input group*. An input group allows you to attach elements to form fields. We'll use it to attach the submit button to the right side of the text field. This, along with the fact that Bootstrap styles input tags to have a width of 100%, will give us what we want.

```
4_postgres-index/20-search-ui/shine/app/views/customers/index.html.erb
<section class="search-form">
  <%= form_for :customers, method: :get do |f| %>
    <div class="input-group input-group-lg">
      <%= label_tag :keywords, nil, class: "sr-only" %>
      <%= text_field_tag :keywords, nil,
            placeholder: "First Name, Last Name, or Email Address",
              class: "form-control input-lg" %>
      <span class="input-group-btn">
        <%= submit_tag "Find Customers",
              class: "btn btn-primary btn-lg" %>
      </span>
    </div>
  <% end %>
</section>
```

The sr-only class on our label is provided by Bootstrap and means "Screen Reader Only." You should use this on elements that are semantically required (like form labels) but that, for aesthetic purposes, you don't want to be visible. This makes your UI as inclusive as possible to users on all sorts of devices.

With our search form styled (you'll see what it looks like in a moment), we'll now create a simple table for the results. Applying the class table to any table causes Bootstrap to style it appropriately for the table's contents. Adding the class table-striped will create a striped effect where every other row has a light gray background. This helps users visually navigate a table with many rows.

4_postgres-index/20-search-ui/shine/app/views/customers/index.html.erb

```erb
<section class="search-results">
  <header>
    <h1 class="h3">Results</h1>
  </header>
  <table class="table table-striped">
    <thead>
      <tr>
        <th>First Name</th>
        <th>Last Name</th>
        <th>Email</th>
        <th>Joined</th>
      </tr>
    </thead>
    <tbody>
      <% @customers.each do |customer| %>
        <tr>
          <td><%= customer.first_name %></td>
          <td><%= customer.last_name %></td>
          <td><%= customer.email %></td>
          <td><%= l customer.created_at.to_date %></td>
        </tr>
      <% end %>
    </tbody>
  </table>
</section>
```

Now that the table is styled, you can see the entire view in the following figure. It looks pretty good, and you still haven't had to write any actual CSS.

With the UI built, all you need to do to implement our search is replace the implementation of index in CustomersController with the actual search.

Implement the Search Logic

At a high level, our search should accept a string and do the right thing. Because our users are interacting with customers via email, we want to search by email, but because customers sometimes use multiple email addresses, we also want to search by first name and last name. To more strictly state our requirements:

- If the search term contains a "@" character, search email by that term.

- Use the *name* part of the email to search first and last name (for example, we'd search for "pat" if given the term "pat123@example.com").

- If the search term does *not* contain an "@" character, don't search by email, but *do* search by first and last name.

- The search should be case-insensitive.

- The first and last name search should match names that start with the search term, so a search for "Pat" should match "Patty."

- The results should be ordered so that exact email matches are listed first, and all other matches are sorted by last name.

This isn't the most amazing search algorithm, but it's sufficient for our purposes here, which is to implement the feature and demonstrate the performance problems present in an even moderately complex query.

There are two tricky things about the search we're running. The first is that we want case-insensitive matches, and Active Record has no API to do that directly. The second is that we want exact email matches first. Fortunately, Postgres provides a means to do both of these things. You can use SQL like lower(first_name) LIKE 'pat%' and you can use complex expressions in the order by clause. Ultimately, you'll want a query that looks like this:

```
SELECT
  *
FROM
  customers
WHERE
  lower(first_name) LIKE 'pat%' OR
  lower(last_name)  LIKE 'pat%' OR
  lower(email)      =    'pat@example.com'
ORDER BY
  email = 'pat@example.com' DESC,
  last_name ASC
```

The order by in Postgres can take a wide variety of expressions. According to documentation, it can "be any expression that would be valid in the query's select list."[3] In our case, we can order fields based on the results of matching the email column value to pat@example.com. This evaluates to true or false for each row.

Note that semantically, we could use an expression such as first_name ILIKE 'pat%', which uses a case-insensitive LIKE. This will not use the index we'll create later and can't be as easily optimized. As you learn more about indexing and databases, you'll find that you need to write SQL in a particular way to trigger the use of an index. This is a great example of that.

Because Postgres considers false less than true, an ascending sort would sort rows that *don't* match pat@example.com first, so we use desc to sort email matches first.

To execute this query using Active Record, you'd need to write the following code:

```
Customer.where("lower(first_name) LIKE :first_name OR " +
               "lower(last_name)  LIKE :last_name  OR " +
               "lower(email)      =    :email", {
                 first_name: "pat%",
                 last_name: "pat%",
                 email: "pat@example.com"
               }).order("email = 'pat@example.com' desc, last_name asc")
```

Note that you're appending % to the name search term and using like so that you meet the "starts with" requirement. You have to do this because Active Record has no direct API for doing this. To create this query in our code, let's create a class called CustomerSearchTerm that can parse params[:keywords] and produce the arguments you need to where and order.

Our class will expose three attributes: where_clause, where_args, and order. These values will be different depending on the type of search being done. If the user's search term included an @, we'll want to search the email column, in addition to last_name and first_name. If there's no @, we'll just search first_name and last_name.

First, let's create app/models/customer_search_term.rb and add the three attributes as well as an initializer. Let's assume that two private methods exist called build_for_email_search and build_for_name_search that will set the attributes appropriately, depending on the type of search as dictated by the search term. We'll see their implementation in a minute, but here's how we'll use them in the constructor of CustomerSearchTerm:

---

3.   http://www.postgresql.org/docs/9.5/static/queries-order.html

```
4_postgres-index/30-naive-search/shine/app/models/customer_search_term.rb
class CustomerSearchTerm
  attr_reader :where_clause, :where_args, :order
  def initialize(search_term)
    search_term = search_term.downcase
    @where_clause = ""
    @where_args = {}
    if search_term =~ /@/
      build_for_email_search(search_term)
    else
      build_for_name_search(search_term)
    end
  end
end
```

We're converting our term to lowercase first, so that we don't have to do it later, and we're also initializing @where_clause and @where_args under the assumption that they will be modified by our private methods.

Let's implement build_for_name_search first. We'll create a helper method case_insensitive_search that will construct the SQL fragment we need and use that to build up @where_clause inside build_for_name_search. We'll also create a helper method called starts_with that handles appending the % to our search term.

```
4_postgres-index/30-naive-search/shine/app/models/customer_search_term.rb
private

  def build_for_name_search(search_term)
    @where_clause << case_insensitive_search(:first_name)
    @where_args[:first_name] = starts_with(search_term)

    @where_clause << " OR #{case_insensitive_search(:last_name)}"
    @where_args[:last_name] = starts_with(search_term)

    @order = "last_name asc"
  end

  def starts_with(search_term)
    search_term + "%"
  end

  def case_insensitive_search(field_name)
    "lower(#{field_name}) like :#{field_name}"
  end
```

Next, we'll implement build_for_email_search, which is slightly more complex. Given a search term of "pat123@example.com" you want to use that exact term for the email part of our search. But because we want rows where first_name or last_name starts with just "pat" we'll create a helper method called extract_name that uses regular expressions in gsub to remove everything after the @ as well as any digits.

4_postgres-index/30-naive-search/shine/app/models/customer_search_term.rb
```ruby
def extract_name(email)
  email.gsub(/@.*$/,'').gsub(/[0-9]+/,'')
end
```

There's one last bit of complication, which is the ordering. To create the order by clause we want, it may seem you'd have to do something like this:

```ruby
@order = "email = '#{search_term}' desc, last_name asc"
```

If building a SQL string like this concerns you, it should. Because search_term contains data provided by the user, it could create an attack vector via SQL injection.[4] To prevent this, you need to SQL-escape search_term before you send it to Postgres for querying. Active Record provides a method quote, available on ActiveRecord::Base's connection object.

Armed with this knowledge, as well as our helper method extract_name_from_email, you can now implement build_for_email_search.

4_postgres-index/30-naive-search/shine/app/models/customer_search_term.rb
```ruby
def build_for_email_search(search_term)
  @where_clause << case_insensitive_search(:first_name)
  @where_args[:first_name] = starts_with(extract_name(search_term))

  @where_clause << " OR #{case_insensitive_search(:last_name)}"
  @where_args[:last_name] = starts_with(extract_name(search_term))

  @where_clause << " OR #{case_insensitive_search(:email)}"
  @where_args[:email] = search_term

  @order = "lower(email) = " +
    ActiveRecord::Base.connection.quote(search_term) +
    " desc, last_name asc"
end
```

Note that you don't need to use quote when creating your SQL fragment in case_insensitive_search, because the strings involved there are from literals in our code and not user input. Therefore, you know they are safe.

Now that CustomerSearchTerm is implemented, you can use it in CustomersController to implement the search.

4_postgres-index/30-naive-search/shine/app/controllers/customers_controller.rb
```ruby
class CustomersController < ApplicationController
  def index
    if params[:keywords].present?
      @keywords = params[:keywords]
      customer_search_term = CustomerSearchTerm.new(@keywords)
      @customers = Customer.where(
```

---

4. http://en.wikipedia.org/wiki/SQL_injection

```
          customer_search_term.where_clause,
          customer_search_term.where_args).
          order(customer_search_term.order)
      else
        @customers = []
      end
    end
  end
end
```

This may have seemed complex, but it's important to note that this search is quite simplified from what you might actually want. You might really need something more complex; for example, a search term of "Pat Jones" would result in a first name search for "pat" and a last name search for "jones." The point is that our simplistic search is still too complex for Active Record's API to handle. You had to create your own where clause and your own order by.

Now that our search is implemented, you can see the results by starting our server (via forman start) and navigating to http://localhost:5000/customers. As you see in the following figure, the email match is listed first, while the remaining ones are sorted by last name.

Customer Search

First Name, Last Name, or Email Address   Find Customers

Results

First Name	Last Name	Email	Joined
Jacky	Kling	pat@somewhere.com	2017-05-25
pat	Cremin	darryl@wunschfranecki.net	2017-05-25
patrick	Framl	eden@kihnschmeler.biz	2017-05-25
PATTY	Hyatt	brittany_franecki@rau.io	2017-05-25
Pat	King	rickie@altenwerthsipes.biz	2017-05-25
Rudy	Patrice	davon@vonrueden.org	2017-05-25
Florine	Patt	braeden@turcottegerhold.com	2017-05-25
Shanelle	Patton	brice@walsh.name	2017-05-25
Sibyl	paterson	otho.ankunding@harber.co	2017-05-25
Belle	patrica	rosalind@schimmel.net	2017-05-25

Depending on the computer you're using, the search might seem fast enough. Or it might seem a bit slow. If customers had more rows in it, or our database were under the real stress of production, the search might be unacceptably slow. It's popular to solve this problem by caching results in a NoSQL[5] database like Elasticsearch.

---

5.   http://en.wikipedia.org/wiki/NoSQL

While there may be a case made for caching, Postgres gives more options than your average SQL database to speed up searches, which means we can get a lot more out of a straightforward implementation before complicating our architecture with additional data stores. In the next section, you'll learn about the powerful indexing features Postgres provides. You'll see that they're much more powerful than the indexes you get from most SQL databases.

Understanding Query Performance with the Query Plan

If you aren't familiar with database indexes, Wikipedia has a pretty good definition,[6] but in essence, an index is a data structure created inside the database that speeds up query operations. Usually, databases use advanced data structures like B-trees to find the data you're looking for without examining every single row in a table.

If you *are* familiar with indexes, you might only be familiar with the type of indexes that can be created by Active Record's Migrations API. This API provides a "lowest common denominator" approach. The best we can do is create an index on last_name, first_name, and email. Doing so won't actually help us because of the search we are doing. We need to match values that *start* with the search term and ignore case.

Postgres allows much more sophisticated indexes to be created. To see how this helps, let's ask Postgres to tell us how our existing query will perform. This can be done by preceding a SQL statement with EXPLAIN ANALYZE. The output is somewhat opaque, but it's useful. We'll walk through it step by step.

```
$ bundle exec rails dbconsole
shine_development> EXPLAIN ANALYZE
                    SELECT *
                    FROM    customers
                    WHERE
                      lower(first_name) like 'pat%' OR
                      lower(last_name)  like 'pat%' OR
                      lower(email)      = 'pat@example.com'
                    ORDER BY
                      email = 'pat@example.com' DESC,
                      last_name ASC ;

                    QUERY PLAN
----------------------------------------------------------------------------
① Sort  (cost=13930.19..13943.25 rows=5225 width=79)
        (actual time=618.065..618.103 rows=704 loops=1)
     Sort Key: (((email)::text = 'pat@example.com'::text)) DESC, last_name
     Sort Method: quicksort  Memory: 124kB
```

---

6. http://en.wikipedia.org/wiki/Database_index

```
  ❷    ->  Seq Scan on customers  (cost=0.00..13607.51 rows=5225 width=79) #
                                    (actual time=0.165..612.380 rows=704 loops=1)
  ❸           Filter: ((lower((first_name)::text) ~~ 'pat%'::text) OR
                       (lower((last_name)::text) ~~ 'pat%'::text)  OR
                       (lower((email)::text) = 'pat@example.com'::text))
               Rows Removed by Filter: 349296
       Planning time: 1.223 ms
  ❹  Execution time: 618.258 ms
```

This gobbledegook is the *query plan* and is quite informative if you know how to interpret it. There are four parts to it that will help you understand how Postgres will execute our query.

❶ Here, Postgres is telling us that it's sorting the results, which makes sense since we're using an order by clause in our query. The details (for example, cost=15479.51) are useful for fine-tuning queries, but we're not concerned with that right now. Just take from this that sorting is part of the query.

❷ This is the most important bit of information in *this* query plan. "Seq Scan on customers" means that Postgres has to examine every single row in the table to satisfy the query. This means that the bigger the table is, the more work Postgres has to do to search it. Queries that you run frequently should not require examining every row in the table for this reason.

❸ This shows us how Postgres has interpreted our where clause. It's more or less what was in our query, but Postgres has annotated it with the internal data types it's using to interpret the values.

❹ Finally, Postgres estimates the runtime of the query. In this case, it's more than half a second. That's not much time to you or me, but to a database, it's an eternity.

EXPLAIN vs. EXPLAIN ANALYZE

EXPLAIN ANALYZE actually runs the query, whereas EXPLAIN (without ANALYZE) will just show the query plan. This means that repeatedly executing EXPLAIN ANALYZE on the same query could produce different timings, because Postgres could cache the query's results. The query plan (everything up to "Execution time" in the output shown earlier) will always be the same. It's not easy to control the caches Postgres uses, but if you vary the search string or ID in your WHERE clauses, you can often prevent it from using the cache.

Given all of this, it's clear that our query will perform poorly. It's likely that it performs poorly on our development machine, and will certainly not scale in a real-world scenario.

In most databases, because of the case-insensitive search and the use of like, there wouldn't be much we could do. Postgres, however, can create an index that accounts for this way of searching.

Indexing Derived and Partial Values

Postgres allows you to create an index on *transformed* values of a column. This means you can create an index on the lowercased value for each of our three fields. Further, you can configure the index in a way that allows Postgres to optimize for the "starts with" search you are doing. Here's the basic syntax:

```
CREATE INDEX
  customers_lower_last_name
ON
  customers (lower(last_name) varchar_pattern_ops);
```

If you're familiar with creating indexes, the varchar_pattern_ops might look odd. This is a feature of Postgres called *operator classes*. Specifying an operator class isn't required; however, the default operator class used by Postgres will only optimize the index for an exact match. Because you're using a like in your search, you need to use the nonstandard operator class varchar_pattern_ops. You can read more about operator classes in Postgres's documentation.[7]

Now that you've seen the SQL needed to create these indexes, you need to adapt them to a Rails migration. Previous versions of Rails didn't provide a way to do this, and you'd have to use execute to directly execute SQL, but as of Rails 5, we can pass custom SQL to add_index, making our migration a bit cleaner. Let's create the migration file using Rails's generator.

```
$ bundle exec rails g migration add-lower-indexes-to-customers
    invoke  active_record
    create    db/migrate/20160721030725_add_lower_indexes_to_customers.rb
```

Next, edit the migration to add the indexes. Rails 5 added the ability to create these Postgres-specific indexes using add_index. Previous versions of Rails required using execute and typing the CREATE INDEX SQL directly.

4_postgres-index/40-add-indexes/shine/db/migrate/20160721030725_add_lower_indexes_to_customers.rb
```
class AddLowerIndexesToCustomers < ActiveRecord::Migration[5.0]
  def change
    add_index :customers, "lower(last_name) varchar_pattern_ops"
    add_index :customers, "lower(first_name) varchar_pattern_ops"
    add_index :customers, "lower(email)"
  end
end
```

---

7.   http://www.postgresql.org/docs/9.5/static/indexes-opclass.html

Note that we aren't using the operator class on the email index since we'll always be doing an exact match. Sticking with the default operator class is recommended if we don't have a reason not to. Next, let's run this migration (it may take several seconds due to the volume of data being indexed).

```
$ bundle exec rails db:migrate
== 20160721030725 AddLowerIndexesToCustomers: migrating ===========
-- add_index(:customers, "lower(last_name) varchar_pattern_ops")
   -> 0.5506s
-- add_index(:customers, "lower(first_name) varchar_pattern_ops")
   -> 0.4963s
-- add_index(:customers, "lower(email)")
   -> 7.1292s
== 20160721030725 AddLowerIndexesToCustomers: migrated (8.1763s) ==
```

Before you try the app, let's run the EXPLAIN ANALYZE again and see what it says. Note the highlighted lines.

```
$ bundle exec rails dbconsole
shine_development> EXPLAIN ANALYZE
                    SELECT *
                    FROM    customers
                    WHERE
                      lower(first_name) like 'pat%' OR
                      lower(last_name)  like 'pat%' OR
                      lower(email)      = 'pat@example.com'
                    ORDER BY
                      email = 'pat@example.com' DESC,
                      last_name ASC
                    ;
                    QUERY PLAN
-----------------------------------------------------------------
 Sort  (cost=5666.10..5679.16 rows=5224 width=79)
       (actual time=14.467..14.537 rows=704 loops=1)
   Sort Key: (((email)::text = 'pat@example.com'::text)) DESC, last_name
   Sort Method: quicksort  Memory: 124kB
   -> Bitmap Heap Scan on customers
          (cost=145.31..5343.49 rows=5224 width=79)
          (actual time=0.387..8.650 rows=704 loops=1)
       Recheck Cond: ((lower((first_name)::text) ~~ 'pat%'::text) OR
                     (lower((last_name)::text) ~~ 'pat%'::text)  OR
                     (lower((email)::text) = 'pat@example.com'::text))
        Filter: ((lower((first_name)::text) ~~ 'pat%'::text) OR
               (lower((last_name)::text) ~~ 'pat%'::text)  OR
               (lower((email)::text) = 'pat@example.com'::text))
       Heap Blocks: exact=655
       -> BitmapOr  (cost=145.31..145.31 rows=5250 width=0)
                     (actual time=0.263..0.263 rows=0 loops=1)
          -> Bitmap Index Scan on
             index_customers_on_lower_first_name_varchar_pattern_ops
```

```
                    (cost=0.00..41.92 rows=1750 width=0)
                    (actual time=0.209..0.209 rows=704 loops=1)
➤                  Index Cond: (
➤                     (lower((first_name)::text) ~>=~ 'pat'::text) AND
➤                     (lower((first_name)::text) ~<~ 'pau'::text))
             -> Bitmap Index Scan on
                  index_customers_on_lower_last_name_varchar_pattern_ops
                    (cost=0.00..41.92 rows=1750 width=0)
                    (actual time=0.007..0.007 rows=0 loops=1)
➤                    Index Cond: (
➤                       (lower((last_name)::text) ~>=~ 'pat'::text) AND
➤                       (lower((last_name)::text) ~<~ 'pau'::text))
             -> Bitmap Index Scan on index_customers_on_lower_email
                    (cost=0.00..57.55 rows=1750 width=0)
                    (actual time=0.046..0.046 rows=0 loops=1)
➤                    Index Cond: (
➤                       lower((email)::text) = 'pat@example.com'::text)
➤  Planning time: 0.193 ms
➤  Execution time: 14.732 ms
```

This time, there is *more* gobbledegook, but if you look closely, Seq Scan on customers is gone, and you can see a lot of detail around our where clause. The highlighted lines indicate *index scans*, in contrast to the Seq Scan you saw before. And the index scan is using our index and thus *not* examining each row in the table to find the correct results. You can see that it's doing three lookups, one for each field, using our indexes, and then or-ing the results together.

Setting aside the details of how Postgres does this, you can see that the results are about 40 times faster—the query should complete in under 15 milliseconds!

If you try our search in Shine now, the results come back almost instantly. We've improved the performance of our search by more than a factor of 40, all with just a few lines of SQL in a migration. *And* you didn't have to change a line of code in the Rails application. If you were using a less powerful database, you'd need to set up new infrastructure for making this search fast, and that could have a significant cost to development, maintenance, and production support.

This sort of index is just the tip of the iceberg—Postgres has many advanced features.

With our search performing better, let's take a final pass at the user interface. Bootstrap's default table styling made it a snap to create a reasonable user interface in no time. This then enabled us to focus on the Rails application's behavior and performance. If you stopped now and shipped what you have, you'd be shipping a feature you could be proud of. But, because you haven't spent *that* much time on this feature, let's see if there's any way to make the UI better for our users.

Next: Better-Looking Results with Bootstrap's List Group

You've got a solid back end going for our search. It's now really fast and you didn't have to do anything other than add a few indexes to your database. The user interface actually isn't too bad, either, considering we didn't spend much time on it. But it could be better.

The next chapter will bring you back to the front end as you redesign the results. You'll see that Bootstrap's many helper classes and components can make it easy to try out new designs. This means you can provide better software for your users without investing huge amounts of time in writing CSS.

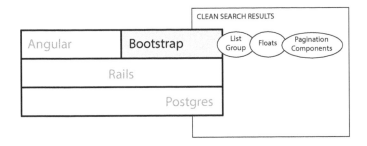

## CHAPTER 5

Create Clean Search Results with Bootstrap Components

The customer search you've implemented is using tables to display the results. Tables are a common design component to use, but they aren't always the best. The reason they are so common isn't because the results are necessarily tabular, but because tables look decent by default. Everything lines up reasonably well, and the rows and columns nature of tables tends to be usable by default.

Bootstrap provides a lot more options than tables to get great-looking results. That's what you'll learn in this chapter. You're going to restyle your results to do two things. First, you're going to get rid of the tables and create a more Google-like result that formats each customer in a *component* style, rather than as a row in a table.

This will demonstrate how easy it is to build a seemingly complex design by using Bootstrap's *list group*, its typographic styles, and CSS floats. Second, you're going to paginate the results using one of Bootstrap's custom components. And you aren't going to write *any* CSS.

The UI you'll build will look like the figure on page 56. Let's start by removing the table and replacing it with component-based results.

Creating Google-Style Search Results Without Tables

If you were styling this application on your own, the prospect of building a customized, nontabular search results page (like Google's, for example) would not be very appealing. You'd need to figure out the layout, design, and CSS

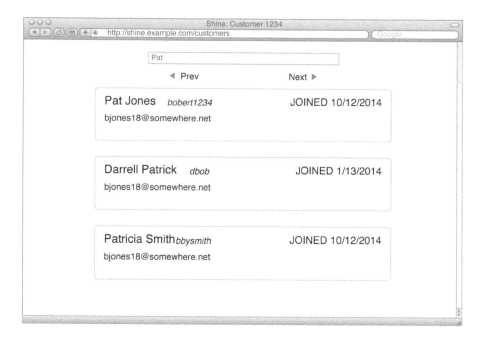

to get it just right. But because you're probably always under pressure to ship your software and move on to the next feature, you might not be able to spend the time to give the user a better experience.

Bootstrap provides many components that make it easy to at least *attempt* something different, without a huge time investment. Let's try using Bootstrap's list group component. This component renders information in a list, but allows us to format what is in each list item with more flexibility than a table.

You'll recall the original motivation for this feature—users want to search customers by name or email to see if they signed up before a certain date. That means that the sign-up date is fairly important. It's also worth considering that our users will be getting emails from customers that will likely contain their full name written out, such as Pat Jones. Finally, our users might include their usernames in their email.

Perhaps the user interface would be better served with a mini-component for each user, like the following, instead of a row in a table?

Robert Jones bobby_reina   JOINED **2017-05-25**
bob123@somewhere.net

Unless you write a lot of CSS, this layout might appear to be somewhat tricky to pull off, especially if you consider how well aligned all the subcomponents are. Fortunately, Bootstrap makes this simple. You'll use three features of Bootstrap to do this: the list group component, the behavior of typography inside a small HTML element, and some floating-element helper classes.

The list group component styles a list of elements so that the contents of each element are set inside a bordered box, with appropriate spacing and padding to work well in a list of similar elements. To use it, you'll replace our table with an ordered list that has the class list-group and give each list item the class list-group-item. Inside each list element, you'll put each bit of information inside the appropriate "H" element, based on how important it is to the task at hand.

5_bootstrap-components/10-simple-list-group/shine/app/views/customers/index.html.erb
```
  <!-- Existing header and search form -->
<section class="search-results">
  <header>
    <h1 class="h3">Results</h1>
  </header>
  <ol class="list-group">
    <% @customers.each do |customer| %>
      <li class="list-group-item">
        <h2><%= customer.first_name %> <%= customer.last_name %></h2>
        <h3>Joined <%= l customer.created_at.to_date %></h3>
        <h4><%= customer.email %></h4>
        <h5><%= customer.username %></h5>
      </li>
    <% end %>
  </ol>
</section>
```

The results are a bit mixed, but as you can see in the figure on page 58, our design is starting to form, because Bootstrap's list group does a reasonable job formatting the information.

Next, you want to change the position of the elements to match our earlier design. The main challenge is getting the customer's join date aligned to the right side of the component. To do that, you'll use some helper classes Bootstrap provides for floats.

Floats in CSS are a way to shift content to the right or left and allow other content to flow around it. For example, if you float some content to the left, the markup that follows that float will render to the right of the floated content. Floats are the basis of many advanced layout techniques in CSS.

Getting this working can be tricky, especially if you aren't familiar with how floats behave in various contexts. Bootstrap provides two classes that you'll

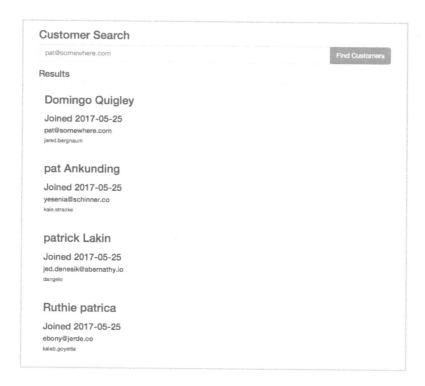

use to help achieve our design: pull-right and clearfix (there's also a pull-left, but you don't need it for this design).

5_bootstrap-components/20-list-group-positioned/shine/app/views/customers/index.html.erb

```
  <!-- Existing header and search form -->
<section class="search-results">
  <header>
    <h1 class="h3">Results</h1>
  </header>
  <ol class="list-group">
    <% @customers.each do |customer| %>
      <li class="list-group-item clearfix">
        <h3 class="pull-right">
          Joined <%= l customer.created_at.to_date %>
        </h3>
        <h2><%= customer.first_name %> <%= customer.last_name %></h2>
        <h4><%= customer.email %></h4>
        <h5><%= customer.username %></h5>
      </li>
    <% end %>
  </ol>
</section>
```

We moved the h3 that contains the join date above the h2 containing the customer's name because we want the name to flow to the left of the joined date. If you kept the join date in its original position, only the username and email would flow to the left.

The clearfix class is provided by Bootstrap to reset the floats. Because of the way floats are implemented, our page will explode to the right if you don't reset them (it's hard to explain, but try removing the clearfix class and see what happens). Now, take a look at the following figure. Our design is pretty close to what we want to achieve.

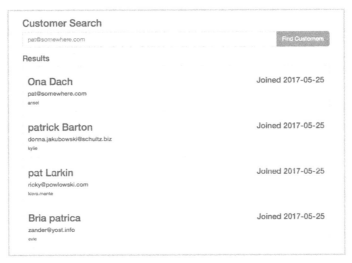

The last thing you need to do is reduce the visual weight of both the username as well as the label "Joined." This allows the other information to be highlighted in a subtle way. To do that, you'll put both elements inside small tags, which will trigger alternate typography from Bootstrap. You'll also use the class text-uppercase on the "Joined" label so that it has a subtle, yet distinct visual appearance from the more dynamic parts of our component.

5_bootstrap-components/30-better-ui/shine/app/views/customers/index.html.erb

```
<!-- Existing header and search form -->

<section class="search-results">
  <header>
    <h1 class="h3">Results</h1>
  </header>
  <ol class="list-group">
    <% @customers.each do |customer| %>
      <li class="list-group-item clearfix">
        <h3 class="pull-right">
          <small class="text-uppercase">Joined</small>
          <%= l customer.created_at.to_date %>
```

```
        </h3>
        <h2 class="h3">
          <%= customer.first_name %> <%= customer.last_name %>
          <small><%= customer.username %></small>
        </h2>
        <h4><%= customer.email %></h4>
      </li>
    <% end %>
  </ol>
</section>
```

Note that you've also added the h3 class to the user's name. This will render it visually identical to the h3 containing the join date. Doing this will ensure that both elements' text is horizontally aligned properly. It's a subtle difference, but polish like this will make Shine *feel* better to its users.

Now, the search looks pretty darn good!

This layout is much trickier than you've seen before, but Bootstrap made it simple to achieve, and you *still* haven't written any CSS. This is the power of a CSS framework like Bootstrap: if you have a design in mind, even if you just want to quickly try it out, Bootstrap provides a lot of tools, at every level of abstraction, to implement it.

There's one last thing you should take care of before moving on. Ordinary searches are returning a *lot* of results. This could be because our fake data only had so many fake usernames to choose from, but even in a real data set, common names could generate more results than a user will want to scroll through. Let's paginate the results, so our users can see only ten results at a time, under the assumption the result they want is in the first ten.

Paginating the Results Using Bootstrap's Components

Adding pagination can be done in just two steps: adjusting the query to find the right "page," and adding pagination controls to the view. There are several RubyGems out there that can help us, but it's not that much code to just do it ourselves. Since you'll be porting our view over to Angular in the next chapter, there's little benefit to integrating a gem at this point.

We'll take it one step at a time. First, we'll adjust the controller to handle pagination.

Handle Pagination in the Controller

For simplicity, let's hard-code the size of a page to ten results, and look for a new parameter, :page, that indicates which page the user wants, with a default of 0.

```
5_bootstrap-components/40-pagination/shine/app/controllers/customers_controller.rb
class CustomersController < ApplicationController
  PAGE_SIZE = 10

  def index
    @page = (params[:page] || 0).to_i

    # ...
```

Next, use both PAGE_SIZE and @page to construct parameters to Active Record's offset and limit methods. Because our results are sorted, you can rely on these two methods to allow us to reliably page through the results without the order changing between pages.

```
5_bootstrap-components/40-pagination/shine/app/controllers/customers_controller.rb
if params[:keywords].present?
  @keywords = params[:keywords]
  customer_search_term = CustomerSearchTerm.new(@keywords)
  @customers = Customer.where(
    customer_search_term.where_clause,
    customer_search_term.where_args).
    order(customer_search_term.order).
    offset(PAGE_SIZE * @page).limit(PAGE_SIZE)
else
  @customers = []
end
```

That's all there is to our controller. Now, let's adjust the view to allow paging.

Add Pagination Controls to the View

To keep things simple, we'll go with previous/next pagination. This means you'll need two links on the page, which you can create by adding or subtracting 1 to @page and passing that to the Rails-provided customers_path helper.

To style the links, Bootstrap provides a component you can use, called a *pager*. Let's set it up in a partial, which you'll then use to place the pager before *and* after the results list. (This allows the user to always have the pager handy.) You'll need to create app/views/customers/_pager.html.erb, and I've highlighted the markup and classes Bootstrap requires to style the pager. Note that I'm omitting the previous link if the user is on the first page. Bootstrap includes a disabled class you could use to render the button in a disabled state, but it requires more complexity on the Rails side to make it work, so I'll just omit the link entirely to make it simpler. (Omitting the "Next" link when we've reached the end of the results is even more complex, since you have to do a separate count of the number of results or otherwise pass a flag to the front end to indicate that there aren't any more results.)

```
5_bootstrap-components/40-pagination/shine/app/views/customers/_pager.html.erb
<nav>
➤  <ul class="pager">
      <% if page > 0 %>
➤        <li class="previous">
          <%= link_to "&larr; Previous".html_safe,
                customers_path(keywords: keywords, page: page - 1),
                title: "Previous Page" %>
        </li>
      <% end %>
➤      <li class="next">
        <%= link_to "Next &rarr;".html_safe,
              customers_path(keywords: keywords, page: page + 1),
              title: "Next Page" %>
      </li>
    </ul>
</nav>
```

Now, let's include the partial in app/views/customers/index.html.erb.

```
5_bootstrap-components/40-pagination/shine/app/views/customers/index.html.erb
  <header>
    <h1 class="h3">Results</h1>
  </header>
➤  <% if @customers.present? %>
➤    <%= render partial: "pager",
➤              locals: { keywords: @keywords, page: @page } %>
➤  <% end %>
  <ol class="list-group">
```

```
    <!-- ... -->
  </ol>
➤ <% if @customers.present? %>
➤   <%= render partial: "pager",
➤               locals: { keywords: @keywords, page: @page } %>
➤ <% end %>
  </section>
```

If you start your server and search, you'll now only see ten results. You can see our pager control at the top and bottom and, because this is the first page, the "Prev" link is missing:

Customer Search

pat123@somewhere.net   Find Customers

Results

                                                        Next →

Pat Jones patty_dustin   JOINED **2017-05-25**
pat123@somewhere.net

Pat Bahringer janae9   JOINED **2017-05-25**
audreanne.mayer9@rodriguez.info

Pat Borer tyrel_prosacco12   JOINED **2017-05-25**
willow12@johnson.io

Pat Connelly alexie_funk6   JOINED **2017-05-25**
tavares.haag6@dooleykuhlman.com

Pat Donnelly deja8   JOINED **2017-05-25**
elisha_schiller8@heidenreich.net

Pat Durgan concepcion4   JOINED **2017-05-25**
elnora4@sawayn.net

Pat Gerhold agustin1   JOINED **2017-05-25**
gwen1@pfannerstillrunolfsdottir.org

Pat Harvey antwan.lynch13   JOINED **2017-05-25**
susan13@nikolaus.com

Pat Johnston al.schultz5   JOINED **2017-05-25**
adelbert5@rodriguezveum.name

Pat Kassulke emerald7   JOINED **2017-05-25**
jerome7@ruecker.io

                                                        Next →

If you click "Next," you'll see the second page of results:

Because of our indexes, Postgres's powerful implementation of order by, and Bootstrap's premade components, you were able to add performant pagination in just a few lines of code.

Next: Angular!

In the next chapter, you'll add a third tool to our toolbox: Angular. Angular is a full-fledged Model-View-Controller (MVC) framework for JavaScript. Unlike libraries like jQuery, Angular provides a higher level of abstraction for designing interactive user interfaces.

Even though Angular might feel heavyweight for the features Shine currently has, it's not. Angular can be applied lightly, on a screen-by-screen basis, to make interactive behavior far easier than it would using jQuery. Angular also scales with the complexity of your views—where your jQuery code would start to get messy, Angular keeps things simple.

Getting Angular working with Rails requires a bit more setup than simply installing a gem, so in the next chapter, you'll set up Angular and learn how it works by implementing a "typeahead" search. Instead of requiring our users to type a search term and click a search button, we'll fetch results in real time, as they type. Because our search is so fast now—thanks to our Postgres-specific indexes—the user interface will feel snappy, and the code that powers it will be clean, clear, and maintainable.

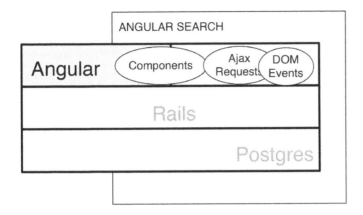

## CHAPTER 6

Build a Dynamic UI with Angular

You've seen some of what Postgres and Bootstrap can do, but our user interface is still fairly static. It's now time to see what Angular is all about and how it can improve the experience for our users.

In this chapter you're going to rework our search feature so that the system searches as our users type, dynamically changing the results as they type out a user's name. For example, if a user wants to find a customer named Patricia Smith, a search for just Pat may return more results than needed. The user would have to search again with a more refined query. If the results were visible while typing, the user could keep typing Patricia and potentially get the desired record right away, without having to wait for the browser to re-render the view. The figure on page 66 shows a mock-up of how it will work.

Angular makes it easy to implement this feature. Since you've already set up Webpack in *Setting Up Bootstrap with Yarn and Webpack*, on page 6, we can focus here on getting Angular configured in Shine. Because this will use features of Rails that are new to Rails (and new to you!), we'll take small, verifiable steps. That way, if something goes wrong, you'll know where.

You'll do this by using Webpacker to generate a bare-bones Angular configuration and place the example component it creates onto the search page. This will validate that our configuration is good so we can proceed to our search feature. We'll first make it work the same way it does now, but using Angular, before removing the search button entirely and to support the search-as-you type interaction described earlier.

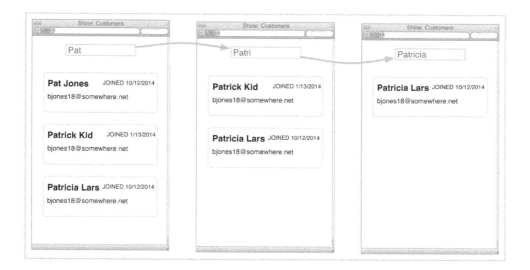

"App" vs. "Application"

One thing to keep in mind is that an Angular *app* is the front-end code and templates, whereas a Rails *application* refers to our entire Rails codebase, in this case Shine. Put another way, our Rails application can (and will) power multiple Angular apps. We'll stick to this convention throughout the book.

Configuring Rails and Angular

As I mentioned earlier, using Angular with the Rails asset pipeline is difficult. In the previous edition of this book, I used Bower to download Angular, and Sprockets (the library that powers Rails's asset pipeline) automatically brought it in. Angular is not available via Bower, so we have to use Yarn (that's why we set it up in Chapter 2, *Create a Great-Looking Login with Bootstrap and Devise*, on page 15). Configuring the asset pipeline to use Yarn-based libraries and packages is not simple, mainly due to the assumptions the NPM modules Yarn downloads make about the JavaScript environment they are running in. Fortunately, Rails 5.1 introduced Webpacker and that *can* interoperate with modern JavaScript tools. We used it to set up Bootstrap in Chapter 1, *Set Up the Environment*, on page 1, and we can use it again to set up Angular.

Install Angular

Installing Angular requires adding a *lot* of modules to package.json and doing some tricky configuration of Webpack. Fortunately, Webpacker includes generators for various front-end frameworks, including Angular. We can do this setup by running bin/rails webpacker:install:angular:

```
> bin/rails webpacker:install:angular
Webpacker is installed
Using /Users/davec/Projects/rails-book/shine/config/webpa…
Copying angular loader to /Users/davec/Projects/rails-boo…
      create  config/webpack/loaders/angular.js
Copying angular example entry file to /Users/davec/Projec…
      create  app/javascript/packs/hello_angular.js
Copying hello_angular app to /Users/davec/Projects/rails-…
      create  app/javascript/hello_angular
      create  app/javascript/hello_angular/app/app.compon…
      create  app/javascript/hello_angular/app/app.module…
      create  app/javascript/hello_angular/index.ts
      create  app/javascript/hello_angular/polyfills.ts
Copying tsconfig.json to the Rails root directory for typ…
      create  tsconfig.json
Installing all angular dependencies
         run  ./bin/yarn add typescript ts-loader core-js…
yarn add v0.23.3
[1/4]  Resolving packages...
[2/4]  Fetching packages...
[3/4]  Linking dependencies...
[4/4]  Building fresh packages...
success Saved lockfile.
success Saved 13 new dependencies.
├─ @angular/common@4.1.3
├─ @angular/compiler@4.1.3
├─ @angular/core@4.1.3
├─ @angular/platform-browser-dynamic@4.1.3
├─ @angular/platform-browser@4.1.3
├─ colors@1.1.2
├─ core-js@2.4.1
├─ rxjs@5.4.0
├─ semver@5.3.0
├─ symbol-observable@1.0.4
├─ ts-loader@2.0.3
├─ typescript@2.3.2
└─ zone.js@0.8.11
Done in 52.87s.
Webpacker now supports angular and typescript
```

We also will need the optional Angular forms module as well as the Http
module, neither of which Webpacker includes by default. We can add them
with yarn add:

```
> yarn add @angular/forms @angular/http
yarn add v0.24.5
[1/4] Resolving packages...
[2/4] Fetching packages...
[3/4] Linking dependencies...
[4/4] Building fresh packages...
```

```
success Saved lockfile.
success Saved 1 new dependency.
└─ @angular/forms@4.1.3
Done in 6.76s.
```

As we saw before, this both modifies package.json and runs yarn install for us. You'll note that there are a few mentions of TypeScript[1] in the output above. Angular is written in TypeScript, and the developers assume that you'll be writing TypeScript, too. We'll be using JavaScript as much as we can, to reduce the conceptual overload, but it's worth understanding what TypeScript is and what's been set up.

TypeScript is a superset of JavaScript that provides additional features that can make working in a large codebase more predictable. TypeScript works by *transpiling* the TypeScript code into JavaScript that a browser can understand. This transpilation is performed by Webpack, and the configuration necessary to do this was set up by Webpacker.

Angular will introduce many new concepts, and having to also learn TypeScript, which itself introduces many *other* new concepts, will be difficult. So, we'll be writing our Angular code in the hopefully familiar JavaScript you're used to. While we'll need to learn a few new things about modern JavaScript, the goal is to keep that code as familiar as possible.

The good news is that because TypeScript is a superset of JavaScript, you can start using TypeScript whenever you like. In fact, we'll write all of our code in .ts files to make that transition easier. The downloadable code for the book includes a version translated into TypeScript if you are curious to learn it after you've gone through everything in JavaScript.

The sample component that Webpacker generated *is* in TypeScript, but we don't have to worry about it to validate our setup. We simply need to use it somewhere and see it all working, so let's do that.

Validate the Angular Install Using The Demo Component

Before jumping into a new piece of technology, it's always a good idea to write something simple with it so that you can validate that all the configuration and plumbing is hooked up properly. Webpacker has mostly done that for us. It's created a simple component that inserts "Hello Angular!" into an h1 tag on the page. We just need to add the component to the page where we want to see it.

---

1. https://www.typescriptlang.org/

In *Install and Configure Webpack*, on page 8, we used javascript_pack_tag to validate our Webpack configuration. What this help does is to bring in a file that's inside app/javascript/packs. If you look in that directory know, you'll see the file hello_angular.js. It looks like so:

```
6_angular/10-install-angular/shine/app/javascript/packs/hello_angular.js
// Run this Angular example by adding the following HTML markup to your view:
//
// <hello-angular>Loading...</hello-angular>
//
// <%= javascript_pack_tag 'hello_angular' %>

require('../hello_angular')
```

The comment at the top of the file tells you what to do to see this demo component in action. We need to add <hello-angular></hello-angular> to a page, and then call javascript_pack_tag with "hello_angular" as an argument. We'll explain later what's happening, but for now, let's do that on the search results page.

```
6_angular/10-install-angular/shine/app/views/customers/index.html.erb
<header>
  <h1 class="h2">Customer Search</h1>
➤ <hello-angular></hello-angular>
➤ <%= javascript_pack_tag "hello_angular" %>
</header>
```

Now, when you run the app and navigate to the customer search page, you should see, in a big font, the string "Hello Angular!":

This validates that everything is working and configured properly. You can remove the code you just added before we move on to building out our new search component.

Porting Our Search to Angular

Although Angular works best when you have a dynamic user interface, it's often easier to introduce new technology by using it to solve an existing problem. That way, you aren't wrestling to understand both the new feature and the technology. To that end, we'll rewrite our existing search feature in Shine using Angular. As before, the user will still type in a keyword and hit a submit button to perform the search. The difference is that the search will be powered by Angular, not by a browser submitting a form.

We'll write JavaScript code that grabs the search term the user entered, submits an Ajax request to the server, receives a JSON response, and updates the DOM with the results of the search, all without the page reloading.

This feels straightforward, at least conceptually. Again, this isn't the best demonstration of Angular's power, but it's enough to get your feet wet with some of Angular's concepts. You'll need this grounding to see more powerful features later. So, despite how simple this example seems, we're going to take things step by step.

The most important concept in Angular is *components*. Previous versions of Angular (as well as many other front-end frameworks) view the JavaScript app as a series of models, views, and controllers (much like how a Rails application is organized). Angular, however, views the app as a series of components. A component can be thought of as a model, view, and controller all wrapped up into one. In Angular, a component is, at the very least, a view template and a class. The class contains data and functions available to the view template. The component can then be used anywhere its selector is written.

In the previous section, when you put <hello-angular></hello-angular> in your markup, that was using the demo component Webpacker installed. Here, you'll create a component for our customer search.

First, you'll set up an empty component that just renders markup. Next, you'll write some JavaScript that shows us how to respond to a click event generated by clicking the search button. Then, you'll update that JavaScript to put canned data into the view when the user does a search, thus demonstrating how to manipulate the DOM. Finally, you'll change our code to get real results from the server by making an Ajax call.

Set Up the Empty Component

Since the view for our search will be managed by Angular, you need to replace the entire contents of the Rails-based view with just the markup needed to bring in our new component, as well as a call to javascript_pack_tag, which will make sure our Angular component's code is available on the page. We'll use the selector shine-customer-search.

```
6_angular/20-angularized-search/shine/app/views/customers/index.html.erb
<section>
  <shine-customer-search></shine-customer-search>
</section>
<%= javascript_pack_tag "customers" %>
```

Prefixing Selector Names

Angular recommends all selector names have a prefix to ensure that there are no name clashes when you bring in other components or when the HTML spec evolves. We'll use shine- as the prefix to our selector names.

Next, we'll create our component, which will require peeking under the hood at how Webpacker configured Angular for us. Angular requires a lot of Java-Script modules to be loaded. These modules produce side-effects merely by being loaded, and we need those side-effects to happen.

To load a module in Webpack-managed JavaScript, we use the import statement. import is similar to require in Ruby, in that it loads code located in other files, but it's a bit more sophisticated. We'll learn about the difference in a moment, but for our immediate need to load Angular's various modules, we can meet that by writing code like import "«module name»";.

There are a lot of modules to load, however Webpacker has already taken care of that for us. After all, the demo "Hello Angular!" component was able to work, so it must already be loading the right modules. It does this inside app/javascript/hello_angular/polyfills.ts. We can re-use this file by importing it! This is the first line in our new component's file, in app/javascript/packs/customers.js

6_angular/20-angularized-search/shine/app/javascript/packs/customers.js
```
import "hello_angular/polyfills";
```

Next, we need to import some specific classes and functions we'll need to create our component. Unlike Ruby, where require'ing a file creates classes we can access, JavaScript requires us to explicitly name anything we want out of a file we import. To do that, we use a different form of import that uses curly braces to name the classes or functions to require out of a given module. Here's what it looks like (and these are the next few lines you need in app/javascript/packs/customers.js):

6_angular/20-angularized-search/shine/app/javascript/packs/customers.js
```
import { Component, NgModule     } from "@angular/core";
import { BrowserModule           } from "@angular/platform-browser";
import { FormsModule             } from "@angular/forms";
import { platformBrowserDynamic } from "@angular/platform-browser-dynamic";
```

The first line means "import the @angular/core module and make available both Component and NgModule to my code." The other lines have similar meanings, and after these lines are executed, Component, NgModule, BrowserModule, FormsModule, and platformBrowserDynamic are all pulled in from Angular's libraries and available for our use. You will see their use—and learn what they are—as we build our component.

Let's create a shell for our component. We can do this by calling the Component function we imported. It takes an object that accepts various pieces of configuration. For our current needs, we must specify the selector and the template. We must then call Class on the return value of Component to declare a class for our component's logic. The basic outline looks like so:

```
var CustomerSearchComponent = Component({
  selector: "shine-customer-search",
  template: «to be added in a moment»
}).Class({
  constructor: function() {
  }
});
```

What this code does is declare a class that has been annotated with additional information that makes it considered a component by the Angular internals. You will see this pattern again several times as you work your way through the book.

Next, copy the markup from our Rails view into the template: key of the object passed to Component. Note that I've removed all Rails helpers and converted everything to plain HTML, hard-coding a single search result. I also removed the pagination, which, by the end of the chapter, you will be able to add back as an exercise if you like. Also note that each line ends with a backslash (\ ) so that you can have a multi-line string (we'll get rid of this slight annoyance in Chapter 8, *Create a Single-Page App*, on page 127).

```
6_angular/20-angularized-search/shine/app/javascript/packs/customers.js
var CustomerSearchComponent = Component({
  selector: "shine-customer-search",
  template: '\
<header> \
  <h1 class="h2">Customer Search</h1> \
</header> \
<section class="search-form"> \
  <form> \
    <div class="input-group input-group-lg"> \
      <label for="keywords" class="sr-only">Keywords></label> \
      <input type="text" id="keywords" name="keywords" \
             placeholder="First Name, Last Name, or Email Address"\
             class="form-control input-lg">\
      <span class="input-group-btn"> \
        <input type="submit" value="Find Customers"\
               class="btn btn-primary btn-lg">\
      </span> \
```

```
      </div> \
    </form> \
  </section> \
  <section class="search-results"> \
    <header> \
      <h1 class="h3">Results</h1> \
    </header> \
    <ol class="list-group"> \
      <li class="list-group-item clearfix"> \
        <h3 class="pull-right"> \
          <small class="text-uppercase">Joined</small> \
          2016-01-01\
        </h3> \
        <h2 class="h3"> \
          Pat Smith\
          <small>psmith34</small> \
        </h2> \
        <h4>pat.smith@example.com</h4> \
      </li> \
    </ol> \
  </section> \
    '
}).Class({
  constructor: function() {
  }
});
```

In addition to creating our component, we also need to bootstrap the Angular app. When you're done with the book you'll have created many different components, but they'll all be part of a single Angular app that is called "customers" (thus, customers.js). Angular needs to know about this top-level app. We tell it by creating an app module (using NgModule that we imported) and by then *bootstrapping* that module into the DOM.

It's not terribly important what this means—it's just a few lines of boilerplate that every Angular app has to have. First, create the app module using NgModule. Like Component, NgModule accepts some configuration in the form of an object, and then requires that we call Class on the result to ultimately create a class.

6_angular/20-angularized-search/shine/app/javascript/packs/customers.js
```
var CustomerAppModule = NgModule({
  imports:      [ BrowserModule, FormsModule ],
  declarations: [ CustomerSearchComponent ],
  bootstrap:    [ CustomerSearchComponent ]
})
.Class({
  constructor: function() {}
});
```

Note that we're passing BrowserModule and FormsModule to imports: and our existing CustomerSearchComponent to both declarations: and bootstrap:. Angular doesn't work like Rails, by making smart guesses about conventional behavior. Instead, Angular likes to know what code it should manage in a very explicit way.

Since our app is going to be run in a browser and will use the Angular forms library, we need to tell Angular that explicitly. Similarly, we need to tell Angular about all of our components (of which there is currently just one) by declaring them. We also need to tell Angular which component is the top-most component responsible for rendering the app (which is a process it calls *bootstrapping*).

With that setup, you can now explicitly bootstrap your app by calling platform-BrowserDynamic().bootstrapModule:

6_angular/20-angularized-search/shine/app/javascript/packs/customers.js
```
platformBrowserDynamic().bootstrapModule(CustomerAppModule);
```

We must do this because Angular doesn't assume it's always running in a browser. Because of this, we have to tell it by calling the bootstrapModule function.

If you run our Rails application (remember to use foreman start) and navigate to http://localhost:5000/customers, you should now see our search form and one result, all rendered by Angular:

Now that you've got Angular rendering our markup, let's make it dynamic. You'll write code to respond to a click event in our search form and have that populate the results list with some canned results.

Respond to Click Events

If you've written dynamic user interfaces with JavaScript before, the overall mechanics of what we're doing will be familiar. You'll add a click handler to the "Find Customers" button in our search form, and you'll then arrange to render the results template once for each result you get back. For now, the results will be a hard-coded array in our JavaScript code.

First, you need to set the click event. The way Angular does this (and, in fact, the way all of our interactions with the DOM work) is by providing a way to set a *property* on a DOM element. Many of these properties are part of the JavaScript specification and are implemented by your browser. Angular adds some of its own properties as well, but the overall model is the same: the markup in your view template uses attributes to set properties.

In the case of responding to clicks, you want to connect the standard click[2] property to a function you write that fetches the search results. Let's assume that function is called search(). You'd then modify the <input type="submit" ... > in our search form like so:

```
<input type="submit" value="Find Customers"\
       class="btn btn-primary btn-lg" \
       on-click="search()"> \
```

Note that you didn't write click="search()", but instead used the prefix on-. This tells Angular exactly *how* you want to connect the click property to your code. Said another way, this is how you tell Angular what functions in your code to call on the click event.

This arrangement is called a *binding*, and this type of binding is called *one-way* from the "view target to data source," to use Angular's parlance.[3] Practically speaking, this means that when the user clicks the submit button, Angular calls the search function (which you'll see in a moment). Also note that there is a more compact syntax for bindings that we're not using in order to make our code clear. See *Why Are We Using on-, bind-, and bindon?*, on page 79 for an explanation.

This also demonstrates that the HTML we're writing isn't *exactly* HTML. You could think of it more as configuring Angular's representation of the DOM. The attributes we set, like type or on-click, set properties of Angular's internal data structures that ultimately render HTML in the browser. You don't often need to worry about this detail, but it can help you form a correct mental model of what's going on.

Our search function can't work without the search term the user has entered, so you'll need to find a way to access that. Angular provides such a way via a custom property called ngModel. You need to bind that property to a value you have access to.

You can't write ngModel="keywords" since this would not establish a dynamic binding (instead this would render the initial value of keywords in the text field only). Further, on-ngModel also won't work, due to the implementation details

---

2. https://developer.mozilla.org/en-US/docs/Web/API/HTMLElement/click
3. https://angular.io/docs/ts/latest/guide/template-syntax.html#binding-syntax

of ngModel. Instead, you need a *two-way binding* so that our code is updated when the value changes, and the view updates if the code changes the value. You can do that by using bindon-ngModel like this:

```
<input type="text" id="keywords" name="keywords" \
       placeholder="First Name, Last Name, or Email Address"\
       class="form-control input-lg" \
       bindon-ngModel="keywords"> \
```

Now, our markup is in place to make the current value of the user's search term available via keywords and to call the function search whenever the "Find Customers" button is clicked. Let's see where those two things are defined.

If you recall when you set up our CustomerSearchComponent, you wrote this code using the Class function:

```
}).Class({
  constructor: function() {
  }
})
```

This created a class to go along with our component, and it's this class where properties and functions can be defined so that they can be referenced in the view template. In other words, this is where you define search as well as where you define keywords.

```
  }).Class({
    constructor: function() {
➤      this.keywords = null;
    },
➤    search: function() {
➤      alert("Searched for: " + this.keywords);
➤    }
  })
```

Because the version of JavaScript we can safely use in a browser has no official way to define a class, you're using the mechanism Angular provides. The previous code would be similar to the following Ruby code:

```
class CustomerSearchComponent
  def initialize
    @keywords = nil
  end

  def search
    puts "Searched for " + @keywords
  end
end
```

With this definition of search, you should be able to reload the app, type in a search term, click "Find Customers," and see a JavaScript alert with your search terms in them. All in all, this wasn't that much code to write. You specified the backing model for the text field and wrote a small function to use that value.

All that's left is to populate the search results. Currently, you've hard-coded one result in our template. What we want is to render the search result markup (the content inside and include the li) once for each result. You saw that in Rails where you used a call to each inside our ERB template. In Angular, you do this with ngFor.

Populate the DOM Using ngFor

Manipulating the DOM for our results requires two things. First, you need to iterate over the results and render an li for each one. Second, you need to render properties of our customer objects inside our template. We'll start with iterating over the results.

The syntax you're about to see is quite verbose. Although you'll be using a much more compact version in the end, it's important to see what the full, explicit, and expanded version looks like. This will provide insight into how Angular works, which may help make future concepts seem less complicated.

Angular uses the standard template element[4] to implement control structures like loops. Inside the template tag, you'll set the ngFor property, which tells Angular the contents of the template should be rendered in a loop. You'll bind the ngForOf property to the list of results using a one-way binding from "data source to view target" (the opposite of what you did with the click property). This is done by prefixing the property with bind-:

```
<template ngFor bind-ngForOf="customers">
  <!-- template -->
</template>
```

The ngFor property tells Angular that you are creating a loop, and the bind-ngForOf tells it what you're looping over. Whatever markup is inside the template tags will be rendered once for each element in customers. Of course, you need access to the element during each iteration so you can render its data in the template. You can do that by telling Angular what name you'd like, much how you use the pipes in a call to each in Ruby:

```
@customers.each do |customer|
end
```

---

4. https://developer.mozilla.org/en-US/docs/Web/HTML/Element/template

In Angular, you can do that by setting an attribute for our variable name, prefixed with let-. This is one of the special prefixes Angular looks for, much like the way you used bind-, on-, and bindon- earlier. The reason it's "let" is because this is the keyword[5] introduced in the latest version of JavaScript that declares a block-scoped variable (which is basically what you are doing here). Putting it all together, here is our loop:

```
<template ngFor bind-ngForOf="customers" let-customer> \
  <!-- template --> \
</template> \
```

As I said, this loop is verbose, but it's important to know how it actually works. Angular provides a much more compact syntax for this. Instead of using a templates element and several different properties, you can use this syntax:

```
<li *ngFor="let customer of customers" \
    class="list-group-item clearfix"> \
    \
    <!-- REST OF MARKUP --> \
    \
</li> \
```

The asterisk is what Angular uses to enable this syntactic sugar. Note that the contents of *ngFor are *not* a programming language, so what you are allowed to do in there is limited. The documentation[6] has more details, but also see the following sidebar for information on this type of symbolic syntactic sugar.

With our loop sorted out, you just need to render the various parts of each customer in the results template. In ERB, you would use something like <%= customer.first_name %>. In Angular, you use double braces: {{customer.first_name}}. These work just like their counterparts in ERB, by evaluating the contents and converting the result to a string. Here is what our complete loop looks like:

```
<li *ngFor="let customer of customers" \
    class="list-group-item clearfix"> \
  <h3 class="pull-right"> \
    <small class="text-uppercase">Joined</small> \
    {{customer.created_at}} \
  </h3> \
  <h2 class="h3"> \
    {{customer.first_name}} {{customer.last_name}} \
    <small>{{customer.username}}</small> \
  </h2> \
  <h4>{{customer.email}}</h4> \
</li> \
```

---

5. https://developer.mozilla.org/en-US/docs/Web/JavaScript/Reference/Statements/let
6. https://angular.io/docs/ts/latest/api/common/index/NgFor-directive.html

Why Are We Using on-, bind-, and bindon?

If you've explored Angular on your own, you might not have seen much code that uses the prefixes we're using. Instead, you might see code similar to this:

```
<input [(ngModelChange)]="keywords" >
<input type="submit" value="Find Customers"
       class="btn btn-primary btn-lg"
       (click)="search()">
```

This is syntactic sugar for the prefixes we've been using. Instead of writing on-click=, you can write (click)=. bind-name= can be written as [name]= and bindon-ngModelChange= can be replaced with [(ngModelChange)].

You may prefer this syntax, but you should always use the style adopted by your team. I chose to use the more verbose syntax to make it easier to understand what was going on. I personally find symbolic notation difficult to understand, hard to search for, and easy to mess up. In particular, if you were to reverse the brackets and parentheses in a bindon-, such as by writing ([ngModelChange]), the binding silently doesn't work.

I can't speculate why the Angular team added a second syntax that saves so few characters of typing, but you are likely to see this syntax in wide use, as it's promoted by the documentation and tutorials. My hope was that, while learning a lot of new things, using the more intuitive prefixes would smooth the learning curve for you (it certainly did for me!).

The last thing to do is implement search() so it sets the customers property, which will cause Angular to re-render the view and display the results. To do this, you need to establish that property in our class, and then set it inside search. You'll initialize customers to null in the constructor function, the same as you did with keywords. You'll implement search to set customers to some canned results if the search term is "pat" and to an empty list otherwise.

6_angular/30-canned-results/shine/app/javascript/packs/customers.js

```
constructor: function() {
  this.customers = null;
  this.keywords  = "";
},
search: function() {
  if (this.keywords == "pat") {
    this.customers = RESULTS;
  }
  else {
    this.customers = [];
  }
}
```

This references a hard-coded array of results called RESULTS:

6_angular/30-canned-results/shine/app/javascript/packs/customers.js
```
var RESULTS = [
  {
    first_name: "Pat",
    last_name: "Smith",
    username: "psmith",
    email: "pat.smith@somewhere.net",
    created_at: "2016-02-05",
  },
  {
    first_name: "Patrick",
    last_name: "Jones",
    username: "pjpj",
    email: "jones.p@business.net",
    created_at: "2014-03-05",
  },
  {
    first_name: "Patricia",
    last_name: "Benjamin",
    username: "pattyb",
    email: "benjie@aol.info",
    created_at: "2016-01-02",
  },
  {
    first_name: "Patty",
    last_name: "Patrickson",
    username: "ppat",
    email: "pppp@freemail.computer",
    created_at: "2016-02-05",
  },
  {
    first_name: "Jane",
    last_name: "Patrick",
    username: "janesays",
    email: "janep@company.net",
    created_at: "2013-01-05",
  },
];
```

Now, you can reload our app, type in "pat," click the "Find Customers" button, and see our hard-coded results, as shown in the figure on page 81.

With all the pieces of our Angular app wired together, you can re-implement search so that it gets real results from our Rails application, instead of the canned ones.

Customer Search

pat	Find Customers

Results

Pat Smith psmith
pat.smith@somewhere.net
JOINED **2016-02-05**

Patrick Jones pjpj
jones.p@business.net
JOINED **2014-03-05**

Patricia Benjamin pattyb
benjie@aol.info
JOINED **2016-01-02**

Patty Patrickson ppat
pppp@freemail.computer
JOINED **2016-02-05**

Jane Patrick janesays
janep@company.net
JOINED **2013-01-05**

Get Data from the Back End

The logic for searching customers in CustomersController is sound; you just need
it to return JSON. Rails makes that easy by using respond_to. We'll add this to
the end of the index method:

6_angular/40-backend/shine/app/controllers/customers_controller.rb
```ruby
class CustomersController < ApplicationController

  PAGE_SIZE = 10

  def index

    # method as it was before

➤    respond_to do |format|
➤      format.html {}
➤      format.json {
➤        render json: { customers: @customers }
➤      }
➤    end
  end
end
```

To call it from our Angular app, you'll use the Angular Http class. Like almost all JavaScript libraries that make network calls, Angular's Http operates asynchronously. This means you'll make an HTTP request to our Rails application and set up a function that will be called back when the HTTP request is complete.

In Angular, the mechanism to achieve this is via *observables*, specifically the Reactive Extensions for JavaScript (RxJS) library (see *Reactive Programming with RxJS [Man15]* for a deep dive on this library).[7] The way an observable works is that you *subscribe* to the *events* being observed by passing a function to the observable's subscribe function.

In our case, the event you want to observe is the HTTP request you'll make to our Rails application. When you get a response, you'll set the customers property to what you get back, and Angular will re-render our results. Making this work requires both writing the new search function to use Http, but also bringing in and setting up the Http module. In your day-to-day coding, you'd do the setup first, but this will require a slight digression into how Angular manages such classes, so let's see the code for search first:

```
6_angular/40-backend/shine/app/javascript/packs/customers.js
search: function() {
❶   var self = this;
❷   self.http.get(
❸     "/customers.json?keywords=" + self.keywords
    ).subscribe(
❹     function(response) {
❺       self.customers = response.json().customers;
      },
❻     function(response) {
        window.alert(response);
      }
    );
}
```

Let's go through each line.

❶ Ultimately, you need to modify this.customers with the data you get back from our Rails application. Since you'll be doing that inside a function, the value of this in that function will be different, so if you wrote this.customers = «response»;, it wouldn't work. (Yehuda Katz wrote an excellent blog post[8] explaining this in detail.) For our purposes, we'll save it as self, a local

---

7.   https://github.com/Reactive-Extensions/RxJS
8.   http://yehudakatz.com/2011/08/11/understanding-javascript-function-invocation-and-this

variable we can refer to later (a common technique among JavaScript programmers).

❷ Here's where you set up the HTTP request to the Rails application. Note that you're assuming the existence of an Http object available via self.http. You'll see how that gets set up later. Also note that you are using self here instead of this. Because you've saved this in the variable self, it makes the code easier to follow if you consistently use self (even if this might work in some cases).

❸ This is the URL to our Rails controller you modified earlier. Note that you are using .json in the URL so that Rails knows to send us back JSON instead of rendering HTML.

❹ This is where you set up our function to be notified when the HTTP request is completed. The value passed to our function is a Response[9] object.

❺ Finally, you extract the results out of the response and set the value of customers. Note the use of our local variable self here. To reiterate, if you had used this here, this would not have referred to the right object and our code wouldn't work.

❻ Last, you pass a second function to subscribe that will be called if there was an error talking to the server. You're simply alerting the user with whatever the response is for now. In a real production application, you'd need to make some design decisions around the user experience when an error happens and implement that here.

With search implemented, you just need to find out where this.http came from. This requires learning about how Angular does *dependency injection.*

Dependency injection refers to a way of structuring code so that when one piece of code depends on another, a third piece of code will wire the two together, *injecting* the first with the second. In our case, instead of creating an instance of Http ourselves, you want Angular to do that and then inject that instance into CustomerSearchComponent.

Angular is built entirely using the concept that code should be injected with its dependencies instead of creating them itself. This is the complete opposite of how Rails works and how you write Rails code. Part of why Angular does this is philosophical, but a practical upside is that it simplifies writing unit tests, which you'll see in Chapter 7, *Test This Fancy New Code*, on page 91.

---

9. https://angular.io/docs/ts/latest/api/http/index/Response-class.html

The way you will set this up in your Angular app is to modify our constructor in a way that describes to Angular that you wouldd like an instance of Http passed when CustomerSearchComponent is first created. You do that by changing the value of the constructor property from a single function to an array with a special form.

The way this special array works is that the last element is our constructor function, and it will take, as arguments, all the objects you want Angular to pass to it. The remaining elements are the classes representing the instances you need. For example, you'll pass Http (the location of the Http class based on how you used function) as the first argument, and our constructor accepting an instance of that class as the second argument. (It's weird, but you get used to it.)

6_angular/40-backend/shine/app/javascript/packs/customers.js
```
constructor: [
  Http,
  function(http) {
    this.customers = null;
    this.http     = http;
    this.keywords = "";
  }
],
```

If you later need another object, say Angular's router, you'd add it to the array, and then add it to the constructor function:

```
constructor: [
  Http,
  Router,
  function(http, router) {
    this.customers = null;
    this.keywords  = null;
    this.http     = http;
    this.router   = router;
  }
],
```

Angular doesn't keep a list of every possible dependency that could be injected into other code, so you have to take one more step to tell Angular that you want Http to be injectable into your classes. We do this by adding HttpModule to the import key of our NgModule we configured earlier.

6_angular/40-backend/shine/app/javascript/packs/customers.js
```
var CustomerAppModule = NgModule({
  imports:     [
    BrowserModule,
    FormsModule,
```

```
    HttpModule ],
  declarations: [ CustomerSearchComponent ],
  bootstrap:    [ CustomerSearchComponent ]
})
.Class({
  constructor: function() {}
});
```

Understanding why you have to do this requires knowing a bit about Angular's internal design, which we will not get into here. Suffice it to say, when you want access to classes provided by an Angular library, you need to take explicit steps to make those classes available—they will not just show up because you required the library. The high-level advantage of all this is that our code never has to create instances of Angular's classes. Because we write our code assuming Angular will hand them to us, when we go to test this code (in Chapter 7, *Test This Fancy New Code*, on page 91), it will be much easier.

The last step is to bring in the Http module so that Http and HttpModule properly refer to Angular's Http class and HttpModule constant, respectively. You do this by adding a new import at the top of our file:

```
6_angular/40-backend/shine/app/javascript/packs/customers.js
import { Component, NgModule     } from "@angular/core";
import { BrowserModule           } from "@angular/platform-browser";
import { FormsModule             } from "@angular/forms";
import { platformBrowserDynamic } from "@angular/platform-browser-dynamic";
import { Http,HttpModule         } from "@angular/http";
```

Let's recap the steps. They are listed here in the order you'd normally do them once you understand the concepts in play.

1. Bring in the Http and HttpModule using import.

2. Configure our NgModule to import HttpModule to provide an implementation of Http.

3. Change the constructor to indicate that it's the piece of code that needs an instance of Http by using a specially formed array.

4. Modify the constructor *function*—which is in the last position of the specially formed array—to accept an argument that, at runtime, will be an instance of Http, configured by one of Angular's providers.

If you reload the page, enter a search term, and click "Find Customers," you can see real results come back. It will behave just as it did before, but now it's all in Angular!

Converting our search to use Angular is just a step toward our goal of making the search feature work better for our users. By keeping the functionality the same while converting to Angular, you were able to focus just on the Angular-based aspects of the feature. Now that you've done that, you can change the search so that it searches as you type.

Changing Our Search to Use Typeahead

Given everything you've done up to this point, changing the search from one where you must click a button to one where the search happens as you type will actually be fairly straightforward. Because Angular has allowed us to separate our concerns, you have all the code you need in place. You'll just need to connect it to the user interface in a different way.

Currently, when the user modifies the contents of the text field, Angular updates the value of keywords in our CustomerSearchComponent class. You can't directly see it, but it does it as the user types. If you can hook into that behavior, you can perform your search as the user is typing.

Angular provides a way to do this by binding to the ngModelChange property. The code you have now is

```
<input bindon-ngModel="keywords" ... >
```

which is equivalent to this:

```
<input bind-ngModel="keywords"
       on-ngModelChange="keywords=$event" ... >
```

Recall that on- creates a one-way binding from the view to our code (you used this for the click event earlier in *Respond to Click Events*, on page 74). As part of sending the event back to our code for ngModelChange, Angular sets the global variable $event. This means that instead of assigning it to keywords, as happens by default, you can send $event to our search function:

```
<input type="text" id="keywords" name="keywords" \
       placeholder="First Name, Last Name, or Email Address"\
       class="form-control input-lg" \
       bind-ngModel="keywords" \
       on-ngModelChange="search($event)"> \
```

Note that because you've replaced Angular's default behavior, you need to set this.keywords inside search yourself. Right after you do that, however, you can use the updated value to perform the search just as before (though you're only going to do a search for three or more characters so you don't do too broad a search):

```
6_angular/50-actual-typeahead/shine/app/javascript/packs/customers.js
➤ search: function($event) {
    var self = this;
➤   self.keywords = $event;
➤   if (self.keywords.length < 3) {
➤     return;
➤   }
    self.http.get(
      "/customers.json?keywords=" + self.keywords
    ).subscribe(
      function(response) {
        self.customers = response.json().customers;
      },
      function(response) {
        window.alert(response);
      }
    );
  }
```

Finally, let's remove the "Find Customers" button since it's no longer needed. Removing this means you can remove the span surrounding the button as well as the div you used to make the button group. Our search form now looks like so:

```
<section class="search-form"> \
  <form> \
    <label for="keywords" class="sr-only">Keywords</label> \
    <input type="text" id="keywords" name="keywords" \
           placeholder="First Name, Last Name, or Email Address"\
           bind-ngModel="keywords" \
           on-ngModelChange="search($event)" \
           class="form-control input-lg">\
  </form> \
</section> \
```

Now, reload the page and type in "pat." You'll see some search results like those shown in the figure on page 88.

Customer Search

pat

Results

Pat Bogisich mathilde4
wilton.altenwerth4@marvin.biz

JOINED **2017-05-25T13:51:31.994Z**

Pat Considine haskell2
rachelle.keeling2@jacobson.name

JOINED **2017-05-25T13:51:31.990Z**

Patricia Hegmann dallin66
gabriel66@streich.co

JOINED **2017-05-25T13:51:31.997Z**

Pat Hermann unique1
harley_jast1@lebsack.org

JOINED **2017-05-25T13:51:31.989Z**

Pat Jones patty_valentin
pat123@somewhere.net

JOINED **2017-05-25T13:51:32.000Z**

Patricia Koelpin desiree.goodwin99
leonardo99@hane.info

JOINED **2017-05-25T13:51:31.995Z**

Pat Reichert kamryn0
madilyn0@collinsmoriette.com

JOINED **2017-05-25T13:51:31.984Z**

Pat Ritchie friedrich.buckridge3
eileen3@heathcotelittel.org

JOINED **2017-05-25T13:51:31.992Z**

If you keep typing out "patricia," the results automatically reduce to only those that match, as shown in the next figure.

Customer Search

patricia

Results

Patricia Hegmann dallin66
gabriel66@streich.co

JOINED **2017-05-25T13:51:31.997Z**

Patricia Koelpin desiree.goodwin99
leonardo99@hane.info

JOINED **2017-05-25T13:51:31.995Z**

The typeahead works! The entire feature required little code (once you installed and configured Angular—a one-time cost), and instead of implementing typeahead with a special-purpose library, you have set up a framework for implementing any user interface you might need. Because of how Angular works, you aren't wrestling with how to attach our JavaScript to our DOM elements or how to interact with the back end. Because of how Rails works, our back end is almost identical to the original back end.

In other words, by using what Rails gives us, and using what Angular gives us, you were able to create a fairly sophisticated feature quickly and without a lot of code. And it's fast, thanks to Postgres's sophisticated indexing and ordering features.

Next: Testing

It's one thing to get code working in a browser, but it's another to have confidence in that code to ship it to your users. To get that confidence, you need automated tests. We've completely avoided writing tests up to this point because it would complicate the tasks of learning about Angular, Bootstrap, and Postgres. But now that you've got a bit of confidence with these new technologies, we're at a point where we can turn our attention to tests.

In the next chapter, you'll build on the testing tools that Rails provides and learn how to test database constraints, write unit tests for our Angular code, and write acceptance tests that execute our Angular app in a real browser.

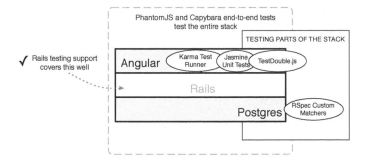

CHAPTER 7

Test This Fancy New Code

To be confident with new libraries and technologies, you need to do more than just write working code—you have to be able to test it. Rails has a long history of supporting and encouraging testing, providing many useful features for testing every part of your application. You want the same experience testing Angular and database constraints that you get with Rails models and controllers. You also want a seamless experience testing end to end in a browser.

Rails has no built-in support for testing JavaScript, nor does it provide a direct way to test database constraints. And, up until Rails 5.1, there was no Rails Way for running an end-to-end test in a browser. But Rails is configurable enough to allow us to set it up ourselves. That's what we'll focus on in this chapter.

You'll learn how to write a clean and clear test of the database constraint you created in *Exposing the Vulnerability Devise and Rails Leave Open*, on page 29. You'll then learn how to create acceptance tests that run in a real browser, executing our client-side code the same way a user's browser would, using Capybara, PhantomJS, and Poltergeist.

Finally, I'll show you how to write a unit test for the Angular code you wrote in Chapter 6, *Build a Dynamic UI with Angular*, on page 65 using the Java-Script-based test library Jasmine, executed in a browser by a JavaScript-based test runner called Karma. This will allow you to write small, focused tests for the individual pieces of our Angular app, without relying entirely on the browser-based acceptance tests.

For the tests you'll write in Ruby, you'll use RSpec instead of Test::Unit, and this requires some additional setup to our Rails application. So, before we get into our actual tests, let's get that set up, and understand *why* we want to use RSpec.

Installing RSpec for Testing

Rails ships with Test::Unit as the default testing framework. Test::Unit is a fine choice, and demonstrates the concepts of testing in Rails quite well. Despite that, RSpec is quite popular among Ruby developers.

While this is a good reason to become familiar with RSpec, it's not the main reason we want to use it here. When you get to *Writing Unit Tests for Angular Components*, on page 111, you'll be using Jasmine for testing our JavaScript, and both Jasmine and RSpec share a similar syntax. Here's an RSpec test:

```
describe "a simple test" do
  it "should test something" do
    expect(number).to eq(10)
  end
end
```

Here's that same test in Jasmine:

```
describe("a simple test", function() {
  it("should test something", function() {
    expect(number).toEq(10);
  });
});
```

As you can see, both tests have a similar shape and structure. This means that when you're bouncing between Ruby and JavaScript tests, the mental overload will be less, since you'll be looking at the same overall way of structuring and organizing your tests. So, while RSpec has many virtues, our reason for using it here is to reduce friction as we test throughout the stack of our application.

With that said, setting it up is easy. First, add *rspec-rails* to the Gemfile:

```
group :development, :test do
  gem "rspec-rails", '~> 3.4'
end
```

This gem includes tight Rails integration for RSpec and will bring in the base RSpec gems as dependents.

Now, bundle install:

```
$ bundle install
```

RSpec comes with a generator that will add the necessary configuration to get RSpec working.

```
$ bundle exec rails g rspec:install
create   .rspec
create   spec
create   spec/spec_helper.rb
create   spec/rails_helper.rb
```

The majority of RSpec's configuration is in spec/spec_helper.rb. It includes a set of defaults, commented out, that it recommends you uncomment. We're going to uncomment most of them so you can use them, but also add a few non-default configuration options. Here's what the file should look like, with our additions highlighted:

7_testing/10-install-rspec/shine/spec/spec_helper.rb

```
RSpec.configure do |config|
  config.expect_with :rspec do |expectations|
    expectations.include_chain_clauses_in_custom_matcher_descriptions = true
➤   expectations.syntax = [:expect]
  end

  config.mock_with :rspec do |mocks|
    mocks.verify_partial_doubles = true
➤   mocks.verify_doubled_constant_names = true
  end
  config.shared_context_metadata_behavior = :apply_to_host_groups

➤ config.expose_dsl_globally = true

  if config.files_to_run.one?
    config.default_formatter = 'doc'
  end

  config.profile_examples = 10

  config.order = :random

  Kernel.srand config.seed
end
```

We're explicitly requiring the expect(..) syntax—you don't want to use the .should assertions because this would be counter to our desire for our Ruby and JavaScript tests to be similar. We're setting verify_doubled_constant_names as an extra safety measure if you should need to mock class behavior (this warns you if you mock classes that don't exist). Finally we're setting expose_dsl_globally, which will allow our tests to just use RSpec's DSL methods like describe without prefixing them with RSpec.

The Rails-specific configuration in spec/rails_helper.rb is fine as is for now. Let's create a basic spec file to verify everything's working in spec/canary_spec.rb.

```
require 'rails_helper'

describe "rspec is configured properly" do
  it "should pass" do
    expect(true).to eq(true)
  end

  it "can fail" do
    expect(false).to eq(true)
  end
end
```

When you run bin/rails spec, it will run this spec, and you should see one test pass and the other fail.

```
$ bin/rails spec
rspec is configured properly
  should pass
  can fail (FAILED - 1)

Failures:

  1) rspec is configured properly can fail
     Failure/Error: expect(false).to eq(true)

       expected: true
            got: false

       (compared using ==)
     # ./spec/canary_spec.rb:8:in `block (2 levels) in <top (required)>'

Finished in 0.00388 seconds (files took 4.06 seconds to load)
2 examples, 1 failure

Failed examples:

rspec ./spec/canary_spec.rb:7 # rspec is configured properly
```

This looks good, and you're ready to test the new features and technologies we've discussed. Note that we won't be going over the sorts of tests you'd typically write for a Rails app. This isn't because you shouldn't write them (you should), but because I want to focus on the new types of tests you need for what we're discussing. The Rails code you've seen *is* tested, and you can refer to the source included with the book if you want to see how I've done that.

Let's start by writing tests of our User model that exercise the database constraints you created in *Exposing the Vulnerability Devise and Rails Leave Open*, on page 29.

Testing Database Constraints

When treating your SQL database as a "dumb store" (or when using an RDBMS that lacks the sophisticated features of Postgres), you'd typically use various features of Active Record to ensure database integrity and you'd naturally want to test that code. Although we're using constraints to enforce database integrity (like the check constraint from *Exposing the Vulnerability Devise and Rails Leave Open*, on page 29), we'd still like to have test coverage that the constraint is doing what we want.

You can easily test this constraint in RSpec, but it requires a somewhat cumbersome assertion mechanism using exceptions. First, you'll see how this works, and then you'll create an RSpec matcher to abstract the awkward syntax away so our tests can be cleaner and clearer.

Assert That Constraints Exist Using RSpec's Matchers

To test our database constraint, you'll need to force Active Record to insert bad data into the database so that *Postgres* is generating the error about bad data, not Active Record. Recall that you added Active Record validations to assist in the registration process, which means it will be difficult to use Active Record to insert bad data into the database. Difficult, but not impossible.

The method update_attribute is available on all Active Record instances and it circumvents validations. You can use this in our test to attempt to insert bad data and simulate a rogue agent that's not using Active Record. It will attempt to write to the database immediately, so invoking it with a non-example.com email address should fail. Here's what it looks like in the Rails console:

```
$ bundle exec rails c
2.2.0 :002 > User.first.update_attribute(:email,"foo@somewhere.com")
  User Load (0.7ms)  SELECT  "users".* FROM "users"
                       ORDER BY "users"."id" ASC LIMIT 1
   (0.1ms)  BEGIN
  SQL (1.8ms)  UPDATE "users" SET "email" = $1,
                                  "updated_at" = $2
             WHERE "users"."id" = $3
                  [
                    ["email", "foo@somewhere.com"],
                    ["updated_at", "2015-03-18 15:33:08.091547"],
                    ["id", 2]
                  ]
➤ PG::CheckViolation: ERROR:  new row for relation "users" violates
➤                             check constraint "email_must_be_company_email"
➤ ActiveRecord::StatementInvalid: PG::CheckViolation: ERROR:
➤          new row for relation "users" violates
➤            check constraint "email_must_be_company_email"
```

I've reformatted the error message to show only what we're interested in, but you can see that the internals of Rails raised a PG::CheckViolation, which Active

Record wrapped inside an ActiveRecord::StatementInvalid exception. To test that this error occurs, you'll need to use RSpec's expect { ... }.to raise_error(...) form.

The raise_error matcher accepts two arguments: the exception we're expecting, and the message it should contain (or a regular expression it should match). Since ActiveRecord::StatementInvalid is so generic, if you just check that you've received that exception, our test might pass if there are different errors happening. We want the test to pass *only* when our constraint is violated. So, we'll expect both that an ActiveRecord::StatementInvalid is raised and that the error message names our constraint. This isn't as precise as we'd like, but it's the best we can do, and it's a reasonable compromise.

Create the file spec/models/user_spec.rb and add the following code (the use of raise_error is highlighted):

```
7_testing/10-install-rspec/shine/spec/models/user_spec.rb
require 'rails_helper'

describe User do
  describe "email" do
    let(:user) {
      User.create!(email: "foo@example.com",
                   password: "qwertyuiop", password_confirmation: "qwertyuiop")
    }
    it "absolutely prevents invalid email addresses" do
      expect {
        user.update_attribute(:email, "foo@bar.com")
      }.to raise_error(ActiveRecord::StatementInvalid,
                       /email_must_be_company_email/i)
    end
  end
end
```

Note that you're using a regular expression as the second argument to raise_error so that you aren't too tightly coupled to the specific error message. Let's run our tests.

```
$ bin/rails spec SPEC=spec/models/user_spec.rb
Randomized with seed 16383
User
  email
    absolutely prevents invalid email addresses

Finished in 0.09785 seconds (files took 4.91 seconds to load)
1 example, 0 failures
```

Our test passes. This gives us a way to drive the addition of sophisticated database constraints with tests. But it's pretty ugly catching exceptions and asserting that their messages match a regular expression. Unfortunately, there's not a better way to do it, but you *can* make the test code a bit cleaner and more intention revealing by creating a custom RSpec matcher.

Use RSpec Matchers to Make the Test Code Cleaner

RSpec uses the term *matcher* to describe the constructs it provides to evaluate assertions. In a line of code like expect(2 + 2).to eq(4), the method eq is a matcher. It's matching the result of 2 + 2 against the constant 4.

You can create your own custom matchers to test attributes of your code that are more particular to what you're doing. This saves us test code and can make our tests clearer. Ideally, you'd be able to write your test like so:

```
7_testing/20-custom-matcher/shine/spec/models/user_spec.rb
it "absolutely prevents invalid email addresses" do
  expect {
    user.update_attribute(:email, "foo@bar.com")
  }.to violate_check_constraint(:email_must_be_company_email)
end
```

If you could create the matcher violate_check_constraint, it would not only make your tests clearer, but also would allow you to abstract the method you're using to test: catching an exception and checking its message. This means if you could devise a better way of testing the constraint, you'd have to change it in only one place—our matcher.

RSpec makes it easy to create such a matcher. The code to do so is quite dense, but once you see how it works, you'll find it's straightforward to create your own custom matchers.

We'll create our custom matcher in spec/support/violate_check_constraint_matcher.rb. It's customary to put code that supports your specs in spec/support. Naming the file violate_check_constraint_matcher.rb will make it easy to know what's in there and where to find it, since it uses the name of the matcher with a _matcher suffix. Let's look at the code:

```
7_testing/20-custom-matcher/shine/spec/support/violate_check_constraint_matcher.rb
RSpec::Matchers.define :violate_check_constraint do |constraint_name|
  supports_block_expectations
  match do |code_to_test|
    begin
      code_to_test.()
      false
    rescue ActiveRecord::StatementInvalid => ex
      ex.message =~ /#{constraint_name}/
    end
  end
end
```

Like I said, this code is dense, so let's take it one step at a time.

❶ Here, you define your matcher and state its name. Since RSpec has an English-like syntax, you'll want your matcher to follow from the word "to." In this case we expect our code "to violate check constraint email_must_ be_company_email." Any arguments given to the matcher are passed to the block as arguments. We've named the argument we're expecting constant_name.

❷ By default, custom matchers don't support the block syntax you're using. In that case, the match method (discussed next) would be given the result of the code under test. Since you need to actually *execute* the code under test ourselves—so you can detect the exception that was thrown—you must use the block syntax. The supports_block_expectations method tells RSpec that this is the case.

❸ This is where you define what passing or failing means. match takes a block that is expected to evaluate to true or false if the actual value matches the expected one, or not, respectively. Since you used supports_block_expectations, the argument passed is the block used, unexecuted. Our job is to execute it and see what happens.

❹ Here, you run the code under test.

❺ If you didn't get an exception, this is where the flow of control will end up. Since you *want* an exception, getting here means our test failed, so you return false.

❻ Here, you catch the exception you're expecting. If you get any other exception, the test will fail. Catching the exception is only part of the test.

❼ The final part of the test is to examine the message of the caught exception. Just as you did before, you'll assert that it contains the name of the constraint you're expecting should be violated.

You're almost ready to use your custom matcher. The last thing to do is to bring it into our spec file. While it's possible to configure RSpec to auto-require everything in spec/support, doing so can make your specs much harder to understand. Because RSpec plays so fast and loose with Ruby's syntax, it can be challenging to look at the use of a matcher and figure out where it's defined.

To that end, we'll explicitly require our customizations, like so:

```
7_testing/20-custom-matcher/shine/spec/models/user_spec.rb
require 'rails_helper'
➤  require 'support/violate_check_constraint_matcher'
```

```
describe User do
  describe "email" do

    # rest of the spec...

  end
end
```

Running our spec, you can see it still passes.

```
$ bundle exec rake rspec SPEC=spec/models/user_spec.rb
Randomized with seed 2818
User
  email
    absolutely prevents invalid email addresses

Finished in 0.15076 seconds (files took 5.78 seconds to load)
1 example, 0 failures
```

You've now seen how RSpec can allow you to test your database constraints and, by using custom matchers, do so with clean and clear test code.

Now, let's head to the total opposite end of our application stack and learn how to write end-to-end acceptance tests that run in a real browser, thus executing the Angular code you've written and simulating user behavior.

Running Headless Acceptance Tests in PhantomJS

Acceptance tests are the way in which we assure that our application meets the needs of the users. In most Rails applications, an acceptance test performs a *black box test* against the HTTP endpoints and routes.

When our application uses a lot of JavaScript—as our Angular-powered typeahead search does—it's often necessary for our acceptance tests to execute the downloaded HTML, CSS, and JavaScript in a running browser, so you can be sure that all of the DOM manipulation you are doing is actually working.

Typically, developers would use Selenium, which would launch an instrumented instance of Firefox, running it on your desktop during the acceptance testing phase. This is quite cumbersome and slow, and for running tests on remote continuous integration servers, it requires special configuration to allow a graphical app like Firefox to run.

Ideally, we'd want something that executes our front-end code in a real browser—complete with a JavaScript interpreter—but that can run *headless*, that is, without popping up a graphical application. *PhantomJS*[1] is such a browser.

---

1. http://phantomjs.org

PhantomJS describes itself as "a headless WebKit, scriptable with a JavaScript API." WebKit is the browser engine that powers Apple's Safari (and was the basis of Google's Chrome). The "scriptable JavaScript API" means that you can interact with it in your tests.

Most Rails acceptance tests use *Capybara*,[2] which provides an API for interacting with such an instrumented browser. To allow Capybara to talk to PhantomJS, you're going to use *Poltergeist*,[3] which is analogous to Selenium if you were using Firefox.

This may sound like a *ton* of new technologies and buzzwords, but it's all worth it to get the kind of test coverage you need. You need to add the PhantomJS and Poltergeist gems to the Gemfile, do a bit of configuration, and start writing acceptance tests as you normally would. Let's get to it.

Install and Set Up PhantomJS and Poltergeist

First, you'll need to download and install PhantomJS. The specifics of this depend on your operating system, but the details for Mac, Windows, and Linux are on PhantomJS's download page.[4] You'll need the latest version, which is 2.1.1 as of this writing. Pay particular attention to this since version 1.9 is still in wide use and will *not* work for our purposes here.

You can verify your install by running phantomjs and issuing some basic JavaScript:

```
$ phantomjs --version
2.1.1
$ phantomjs
phantomjs> console.log("HELLO!");
HELLO!
undefined
phantomjs>
```

This is the only time you'll need to interact with PhantomJS in this way, but it's enough to validate your install.

Now, we'll install Poltergeist, which is an adapter between the Ruby code you'll write for our acceptance tests and the "scriptable JavaScript API" PhantomJS provides. To do this, add it to the testing group in your Gemfile and then do bundle install to install it.

---

2. https://github.com/jnicklas/capybara
3. https://github.com/teampoltergeist/poltergeist
4. http://phantomjs.org/download.html

```
7_testing/30-acceptance-tests/shine/Gemfile
group :development, :test do

  # other gems...

  gem 'database_cleaner'
  gem 'rspec-rails', '~> 3.4'
➤ gem 'poltergeist'
end
```

Installing Poltergeist will bring in Capybara as a dependency. If you aren't familiar with it, I'll explain more when we see the acceptance tests.

To use Poltergeist to run acceptance tests in a browser, you have to do three things: (1) you have to configure Capybara to use it during test runs; (2) you must configure RSpec to handle the testing database differently for acceptance tests than for our unit tests; and (3) you have to make sure webpack-dev-server is running so that our JavaScript and CSS are served up during the tests.

Configuring Capybara

To connect Poltergeist and Capybara, you just need a few lines in spec/rails_helper.rb. You'll need to require Poltergeist and then set Capybara's drivers to use it. Capybara has two different drivers: one default and one for JavaScript. This is handy if you don't have a lot of JavaScript and want our acceptance tests to normally run using a special in-process driver that won't execute JavaScript on the page. That's not the case for Shine, so we'll use Poltergeist (which is powering PhantomJS) for all acceptance tests.

Here are the changes to spec/rails_helper.rb:

```
ENV['RAILS_ENV'] ||= 'test'
require 'spec_helper'
require File.expand_path('../../config/environment', __FILE__)
require 'rspec/rails'
➤ require 'capybara/poltergeist'

➤ Capybara.javascript_driver = :poltergeist
➤ Capybara.default_driver    = :poltergeist

ActiveRecord::Migration.maintain_test_schema!

RSpec.configure do |config|

  # rest of the file ...

end
```

Note that you're using spec/rails_helper.rb and not spec/spec_helper.rb because these tests require the full power of Rails to execute (namely, access to Active Record and the path helpers).

Next, we need to deal with how we manage our test data during acceptance test runs. We'll do that using a gem called *DatabaseCleaner*.

Using DatabaseCleaner to Manage Test Data

In a normal Rails unit test, the testing database is maintained using *database transactions*.[5] At the start of a test run, Rails opens a new transaction. Our tests would then write data to the database to set up the test, run the test (which might make further changes to the database), and then assert the results, which often require querying the database. When the test is complete, Rails will *roll back* the transaction, effectively undoing all the changes you made, restoring the test database to a pristine state.

This works because the process that starts the transaction can see all of the changes made to the database inside that transaction, even though no other process can. Because Rails runs our tests in the same process that it uses to execute them, using transactions is a clever and efficient way to manage test data. But our acceptance tests will actually run *two* processes: our application and our test code (which will use PhantomJS to access our application).

Because of the way database transactions work, our test code can see the data it's inserting for the test (since it opened the transaction), but the application we're testing—running in another process—cannot. Only if we commit that transaction in our test process can the server process see the data. We need to arrange to do that inside our acceptance tests.

Doing this creates a new problem, which is that we now need a way to restore the test database to a pristine state between test runs. For example, if we are testing our search by populating the database with four users named "Pat," but we are also testing our registration by signing up a user named "Pat," our search test might fail if the registration test runs first, since there would be *five* users named "Pat."

Fortunately, this is a common problem and has a relatively simple solution: the *DatabaseCleaner*[6] gem.

DatabaseCleaner works with RSpec and Rails to reset the database to a pristine state without using transactions (although it can—it provides several strategies). RSpec allows us to customize the database setup and teardown by test type. This means you can keep the fast and efficient transaction-based approach for our unit tests, but use a different approach for our acceptance tests.

---

5. http://en.wikipedia.org/wiki/Database_transaction
6. https://github.com/DatabaseCleaner/database_cleaner

First, add DatabaseCleaner to the Gemfile and bundle install:

`7_testing/30-acceptance-tests/shine/Gemfile`

```ruby
group :development, :test do

  # other gems...

  gem 'database_cleaner'
end
```

Now, configure it in spec/rails_helper.rb. To do this, disable RSpec's built-in database handling code by setting use_transactional_fixtures to false (note that the generated rails_helper.rb will have it set to true). Then use RSpec's hooks[7] to allow DatabaseCleaner to handle the databases. By default, use DatabaseCleaner's :transaction strategy, which works just like RSpec and Rails's default. But for our acceptance tests (which RSpec calls "features"), we'll use :truncation, which means DatabaseCleaner will use the SQL truncate keyword to purge data that's been committed to the database.

Here's what we'll add to spec/rails_helper.rb, with the most relevant parts highlighted:

`7_testing/30-acceptance-tests/shine/spec/rails_helper.rb`

```ruby
RSpec.configure do |config|
➤   config.use_transactional_fixtures = false
➤   config.infer_spec_type_from_file_location!

    # rest of the file...

➤   config.before(:suite) do
➤     DatabaseCleaner.clean_with(:truncation)
➤   end

➤   config.before(:each) do
➤     DatabaseCleaner.strategy = :transaction
➤   end

➤   config.before(:each, :type => :feature) do
➤     DatabaseCleaner.strategy = :truncation
➤   end

➤   config.before(:each) do
➤     DatabaseCleaner.start
➤   end

➤   config.after(:each) do
➤     DatabaseCleaner.clean
➤   end

  end
```

---

7.   https://www.relishapp.com/rspec/rspec-core/v/3-2/docs/hooks/before-and-after-hooks

Now that you've set up PhantomJS, Poltergeist, and DatabaseCleaner, you're ready to write an acceptance test.

Test the Typeahead Search

There are two parts of the typeahead search we can test. The first is that merely typing in the search field will perform the search. The second is that our results are ordered according to our original specification from Chapter 4, *Perform Fast Queries with*, on page 37.

To test the search, you'll write two tests: one that searches by name, and a second that searches by email. This will allow us to validate that matching emails are listed first. Both tests will assert that merely typing in the search term returns results.

In addition to the one-time setup we just did, we also need to do more setup per test. First, all pages in Shine require a login, so we'll need a valid user in the database we can use to log in. Second, we'll need test customers in our database tos earch for. The basic flow of our test will be: create a test user, create test customers, log in as the test user, navigate to the customer page, and perform a search.

RSpec calls acceptance tests *feature specs*, and expects the tests to be in spec/features. Locating our tests files there is signal to RSpec to use Capybara and to run our tests as full-on acceptance tests. The first step, then, is to create spec/features/customer_search_spec.rb like so:

7_testing/30-acceptance-tests/shine/spec/features/customer_search_spec.rb
```
require 'rails_helper'

feature "Customer Search" do

  # setup and tests will go here...

end
```

Note the use of feature instead of describe. This is purely aesthetic, but provides useful context when editing test files on larger projects. First, let's create a method that will create a test user for us.

Way back in Chapter 3, *Secure the User Database*, on page 29, we talked about how Devise properly secures our user information, including passwords. This means it'll be difficult to write a valid encrypted password from our tests. Fortunately, the additions Devise made to our User model allow us to do this directly.

```
User.create!(email: "pat@example.com"
             password: "password123",
             password_confirmation: "password123")
```

This is what happens when a user registers, so we can just call code like this in our test. Create a helper method to do this (so we don't clutter up our actual test):

```
7_testing/30-acceptance-tests/shine/spec/features/customer_search_spec.rb
def create_test_user(email: , password: )
  User.create!(
    email: email,
    password: password,
    password_confirmation: password)
end
```

This method requires email and password as arguments because we'll need those in our test to fill out the login form. The way to manage data like this in an RSpec test is to use let, which defines we can use in both setup and tests. There's no need to use Faker, so just hard-code some valid values:

```
7_testing/30-acceptance-tests/shine/spec/features/customer_search_spec.rb
let(:email)    { "pat@example.com" }
let(:password) { "password123" }
```

To create customers, we're going to create them manually inside our test file. Although Rails provides *test fixtures*[8] to do this, we're not going to use them here. Because tests related to search require meticulous setup of many different rows, we want that setup to be in our test file so that we (and future maintainers of our code) can clearly see what we're setting up for our test.

To help create customers, you'll define a helper method, create_customer, that will allow you to specify only those fields of a customer you want, using Faker to fill in the remaining required fields.

```
7_testing/30-acceptance-tests/shine/spec/features/customer_search_spec.rb
def create_customer(first_name:, last_name:, email: nil)
  username = "#{Faker::Internet.user_name}#{rand(1000)}"
  email  ||= "#{username}#{rand(1000)}@" +
             "#{Faker::Internet.domain_name}"

  Customer.create!(
    first_name: first_name,
    last_name: last_name,
    username: username,
    email: email
  )
end
```

With create_customer, email, and password in place, you can create the test data you need to run the tests. You can do this inside a *before block*, which we saw inside

---

8. http://guides.rubyonrails.org/testing.html#the-low-down-on-fixtures

our RSpec configuration when setting up DatabaseCleaner. That syntax works in our test files as well, and defines code to run before each test:

7_testing/30-acceptance-tests/shine/spec/features/customer_search_spec.rb

```
before do
  create_test_user(email: email, password: password)

  create_customer first_name: "Chris"    , last_name: "Aaron"
  create_customer first_name: "Pat"      , last_name: "Johnson"
  create_customer first_name: "I.T."     , last_name: "Pat"
  create_customer first_name: "Patricia" , last_name: "Dobbs"

  # This user is the one we'll expect to be listed first
  create_customer first_name: "Pat",
                  last_name: "Jones",
                  email: "pat123@somewhere.net"
end
```

Now we can start writing tests. Our first test will search by name. If we search for the string "pat", given our test data, we should expect to get four results back. Further, we should expect that the test user named "Patricia Dobbs" will be sorted first, whereas the test user "I.T. Pat" will be last (since our search sorts by last name).

To assert this, we'll use the all method of the page object Capybara provides in our tests. all returns all DOM nodes on the page that match a given selector. In our case, we can use a CSS selector to count all list items with the class list-group-item (you'll recall from Chapter 5, *Create Clean Search Results*, on page 55 that we designed our results using Bootstrap's List Group component). You can also dereference the value returned by all to make assertions about the content of a particular list item.

Here's what our test looks like (note the use of scenario instead of it—this is purely stylistic, but most RSpec acceptance tests use this for readability).

7_testing/30-acceptance-tests/shine/spec/features/customer_search_spec.rb

```
scenario "Search by Name"do
  visit "/customers"

  # Login to get access to /customers
  fill_in "Email",    with: email
  fill_in "Password", with: password
  click_button "Log in"

  within "section.search-form" do
    fill_in "keywords", with: "pat"
  end

  within "section.search-results" do
    expect(page).to have_content("Results")
    expect(page.all("ol li.list-group-item").count).to eq(4)
```

```
    list_group_items = page.all("ol li.list-group-item")

    expect(list_group_items[0]).to have_content("Patricia")
    expect(list_group_items[0]).to have_content("Dobbs")
    expect(list_group_items[3]).to have_content("I.T.")
    expect(list_group_items[3]).to have_content("Pat")
  end
end
```

Before we run the test, there's one more thing we have to do the code we're testing. Our test makes logical sense, but if you think about it more deeply, it's assuming that the back end will respond (and results will be rendered) between the time *after* the fill_in, but *before* the first expect. This is likely not enough time, meaning we'll start expecting results in our test before they've been rendered in the browser (this is a form of *race condition*). Worse, if you try to debug it (see the following sidebar for some tips), the test will pass, because debugging will introduce enough of a delay that the DOM will render and make the test pass. This is a recipe for a flaky test.

What you want to do is have the test wait for the back end to complete. There are many ways to do this, but the cleanest way, and the way Capybara is designed, is to write the markup and tests so that a change in the DOM signals the completion of the back end.

For the Capybara part, we are actually already set up to wait for the DOM. within is implemented by using find,[9] which is documented to wait a configured amount of time for an element to appear in the DOM—exactly what we want!

The problem is that the markup we're waiting on (<section class='search-results'>) is always shown, even before we have results. This means that the within won't have to wait, since the element is there, and it will proceed with the expectations, which fail. So, we'll change our template to only show this markup if there are search results by using *ngIf like so:

```
➤ <section class="search-results" *ngIf="customers"> \

    <!-- Rest of the template -->

</section> \
```

*ngIf is similar to *ngFor in that the special leading asterisk is syntactic sugar for a much longer construct using the <template> element. I won't show the expansion here, since you learned how this concept generally works already in *Populate the DOM Using ngFor*, on page 77.

---

9. http://www.rubydoc.info/github/jnicklas/capybara/master/Capybara/Node/Finders#find-instance_method

The way *ngIf works is to remove elements from the DOM if the expression given to it evaluates to false. This means that until you have results, there won't be any element that matches section.search-results, which means that within will wait on that element to appear. As long as our back end returns in three seconds (Capybara's default wait time), our test will pass. If you find that adding calls to sleep makes your tests pass, consider reexamining your use of within and find and see if you can change your markup to use this approach.

Debugging Browser-Based Tests

In a Selenium-based testing setup, you can observe the browser during the tests. This makes it possible to debug tests that are failing for features that are working when executed manually. For headless tests, it's much more difficult. Here are two techniques I've used to help debug these tests.

Printing the HTML   Capybara's page object has a method called html that will dump the HTML of the current browser. A simple call to puts page.html right before a failing expectation can often be quite illuminating as to what the state of the page is. If you combine this with debugging information in your view code, the answer to your test woes often reveals itself.

Taking a Screenshot   Capybara can also take screenshots via the save_screenshot[a] method (in fact, this feature is what has created most of the screenshots in this book). You can give it a filename and it will show what the browser would render at that moment—for example, save_screenshot("/tmp/screenshot.png").

---

a.   http://www.rubydoc.info/github/jnicklas/capybara/master/Capybara/Session#save_screenshot-instance_method

---

With this in place, we can now run our test and get a bizarre failure:

```
> bin/rails spec SPEC=spec/features/customer_search_spec.rb

Randomized with seed 21046

Customer Search
  Search by Name (FAILED - 1)

Failures:

  1) Customer Search Search by Name
     Failure/Error: <%= javascript_pack_tag 'application' %>
     ActionView::Template::Error:
       Can't find application.js in public/packs/manifest-test.json.
       Is webpack still compiling?
     # ./app/views/layouts/application.html.erb:12:in
       `_app_views_layouts_application_html_erb___127481630256380…
     # ------------------
     # --- Caused by: ---
     # Webpacker::FileLoader::NotFoundError:
```

```
#    Can't find application.js in public/packs/manifest-test.json.
#      Is webpack still compiling?
#    ./app/views/layouts/application.html.erb:12:in
  `_app_views_layouts_application_html_erb___127481630256380623…
Top 1 slowest examples (1.63 seconds, 94.7% of total time):
  Customer Search Search by Name
    1.63 seconds ./spec/features/customer_search_spec.rb:56

Finished in 1.73 seconds (files took 2.03 seconds to load)
1 example, 1 failure

Failed examples:

rspec ./spec/features/customer_search_spec.rb:56 # Customer Search Search by Name

Randomized with seed 21046
```

When developing our features, we were running webpack-dev-server to serve up
our compiled JavaScript and CSS. That server isn't running when we run our
tests, so it makes sense that our JavaScript and CSS can't be found. To make
this work, we can run bin/webpack manually in the test environment:

```
> RAILS_ENV=test bin/webpack
```

≪lots of output≫

And now, our test passes:

```
> bin/rails spec SPEC=spec/features/customer_search_spec.rb

Randomized with seed 51846

Customer Search
  Search by Name

Top 1 slowest examples (2.25 seconds, 97.3% of total time):
  Customer Search Search by Name
    2.25 seconds ./spec/features/customer_search_spec.rb:56

Finished in 2.31 seconds (files took 1.72 seconds to load)
1 example, 0 failures

Randomized with seed 51846
```

Having to remember to run Webpack before each test is a pain. We can arrange
for it to run before all of our tests by augmenting the RSpec-provided spec
task. Create the file lib/tasks/features.rake like so:

7_testing/30-acceptance-tests/shine/lib/tasks/features.rake
```
task :run_webpack_in_test_env do
  unless ENV["SKIP_WEBPACK"] == 'true'
    system({ "RAILS_ENV" => "test"}, "bin/webpack")
  end
end
task :spec => :run_webpack_in_test_env
```

The test for the environment variable SKIP_WEBPACK allows us to avoid running Webpack when we are just testing one test that doesn't need it. For example, to run the tests for User, we'd execute:

```
> SKIP_WEBPACK=true bin/rails spec SPEC=spec/models/user_spec.rb

Randomized with seed 6438

User
  email
    absolutely prevents invalid email addresses

Top 1 slowest examples (0.0591 seconds, 36.5% of total time):
  User email absolutely prevents invalid email addresses
    0.0591 seconds ./spec/models/user_spec.rb:18

Finished in 0.16194 seconds (files took 2.22 seconds to load)
1 example, 0 failures

Randomized with seed 6438
```

This way, when we run all of our tests with bin/rails spec, Webpack will run and our acceptance tests will have the latest version of our Angular code and CSS. When we are doing focused TDD on one unit test, we can skip Webpack. This setup isn't ideal, but a more sophisitcated solution is quite complex, and this will be good enough to get us working for now.

Now that you understand the importance of within, let's see our test for searching by email. It will be structured similarly to our previous test, but we want to check that the user with the matching email is listed first. We'll then check that the remaining results are sorted by last name, using a similar technique to what you saw in our search-by-name test.

7_testing/30-acceptance-tests/shine/spec/features/customer_search_spec.rb
```ruby
scenario "Search by Email" do
  visit "/customers"

  # Login to get access to /customers
  fill_in "Email",    with: email
  fill_in "Password", with: password
  click_button "Log in"

  within "section.search-form" do
    fill_in "keywords", with: "pat123@somewhere.net"
  end
  within "section.search-results" do
    expect(page).to have_content("Results")
    expect(page.all("ol li.list-group-item").count).to eq(4)

    list_group_items = page.all("ol li.list-group-item")

    expect(list_group_items[0]).to have_content("Pat")
    expect(list_group_items[0]).to have_content("Jones")
```

```
    expect(list_group_items[1]).to have_content("Patricia")
    expect(list_group_items[1]).to have_content("Dobbs")
    expect(list_group_items[3]).to have_content("I.T.")
    expect(list_group_items[3]).to have_content("Pat")
  end
end
```

Now, let's run our tests.

```
$ bin/rails spec SPEC=spec/features/customer_search_spec.rb
```

```
Customer Search
  Search by Email
  Search by Name

Finished in 3.63 seconds (files took 7.08 seconds to load)
2 examples, 0 failures
```

They pass! We now have a way to test our features the way a user would use them: using a real browser. Our tests can properly handle our extensive use of JavaScript, but they don't need to pop up a web browser, which makes them easy to run in a continuous integration environment.

Of course, testing Angular code purely in the browser is somewhat cumbersome, especially if it becomes complex with a lot of edge cases. To help get good test coverage without always having to go through a browser, you need to be able to unit test your Angular code.

Writing Unit Tests for Angular Components

Browser-based acceptance tests are slow and brittle. Even though you've eschewed starting an actual browser for each test by using PhantomJS, you still have to start our server and have it serve pages to the headless browser. Further, our tests rely on DOM elements and CSS classes to locate content used to verify behavior. You may need (or want) to make changes to the view that don't break functionality, but break our tests.

Although we don't want to abandon acceptance tests—after all, they are the only tests we have that exercise the system end to end—we need a way to test isolated bits of functionality (commonly called *unit tests*). In Rails, you have model tests and controller tests that allow you to do that for our server-side code. Unfortunately, Rails doesn't provide any help for unit testing our client-side code.

In a classic Rails application, there isn't much client-side code, so we are comfortable not explicitly testing it. In our more modern app, where a nontrivial amount of logic is written in JavaScript, the lack of unit testing will be a problem. For example, in the Angular app that powers the typeahead search you built in Chapter 6, *Build a Dynamic UI with Angular*, on page 65, the search function has logic to prevent doing a search if the search term is fewer than three characters. It's simple code, but there should be a test for it.

In this section, you'll set up a means of writing and running unit tests for your Angular code. You'll use *Karma* to run the tests, which you'll write using *Jasmine*.[10] Both are common tools in the JavaScript testing ecosystem. You'll also use the *Testdouble.js*[11] library to stub the various functions and objects Angular is providing to our code so that you can test in isolation. Because of how Angular is structured, this will be surprisingly straightforward.

First, let's get set up for testing by installing Karma, Jasmine, and Testdouble.js, and then arranging to run our unit tests with Rake.

Set Up Karma, Jasmine, Testdouble.js, and the Rake Tasks

Setup instructions are always prescriptive, but it's good to know why we are installing so many tools. Karma is a *test runner* that is agnostic of both how we write our tests and how we assemble our JavaScript. Jasmine is a *testing library* that contains various functions we can use to write our tests. In Rails, RSpec is both test runner and testing library. While Jasmine does include a basic test runner, it cannot use Webpack to assemble our dependencies. Karma can.

Karma has another advantage over Jasmine as a test runner. Jasmine's test runner uses Node to execute our JavaScript, whereas Karma uses a browser. Since our Angular code is destined to run in a browser, it would be a better test of it to use a browser. Fortunately, we've already seen the advantages of PhantomJS as a headless browser, and we can use it with Karma as well.

Our setup has a lot of moving parts: Karma uses Webpack to assemble our JavaScript, which it combines with our testing code before sending it to PhantomJS to execute. But, it will all work and be the closest simulation of the real-world execution environment as possible. Let's get installing!

Karma, Jasmine, and Testdouble.js are only needed for development and testing. If these were Ruby gems, we'd put them in the development group in our *Gemfile*. We can accomplish the same thing by using devDependencies in our package.json. But, rather than edit the file ourselves, we can manage it with yarn by using the --dev flag to yarn add.

---

10. https://jasmine.github.io
11. https://github.com/testdouble/testdouble.js

```
> yarn add jasmine \
          jasmine-core \
          karma \
          karma-jasmine \
          karma-phantomjs-launcher \
          karma-webpack \
          testdouble \
          --dev
```

«command output»

Because yarn add also installs the library being added, we are now ready to get our testing environment set up. First, we'll need a basic configuration file for Karma. As you are coming to learn about the JavaScript ecosystem, there are very few defaults, so basic things must be explicitly specified. In the case of Karma, we have to tell it what testing library we are using, where our JavaScript tests are located, and what browser to use to execute them. We must also point karma-webpack at our Webpack configuration so it can use Webpack to preprocess the files.

Create the directory spec/javascript and file spec/javascript/karma.conf.js like so:

```
7_testing/40-setup-karma/shine/spec/javascript/karma.conf.js
module.exports = function(config) {
  config.set({
    frameworks: ['jasmine'],
    files: [
      '**/*.spec.js'
    ],
    preprocessors: {
      '**/*.spec.js': [ 'webpack' ]
    },
    webpack: require('../../config/webpack/test.js'),
    browsers: ['PhantomJS'] })
}
```

You'll also need to make a small change to the Webpack configuration generated by Webpacker. In config/webpack/shared.js, you'll need to change how the ManifestPlugin is configured. This plugin generates a JSON file at runtime so that Rails knows where all the Webpack-generated content is. Because of various incompatibilities with Karma and Webpack, we need to configure this plugin to not write the manifest file during tests.

```
7_testing/40-setup-karma/shine/config/webpack/shared.js
plugins: [
  new webpack.EnvironmentPlugin(JSON.parse(JSON.stringify(env))),
  new ExtractTextPlugin(
    env.NODE_ENV === 'production' ? '[name]-[hash].css' : '[name].css'),
  new ManifestPlugin({
```

```
    publicPath: output.publicPath,
    writeToFileEmit: env.NODE_ENV !== 'test'
  })
],
```

To validate this configuration, let's create a basic test that always passes in spec/javascript/canary.spec.js. Don't worry about the Testdouble stuff in there for the moment—I'll explain that shortly. We want to make sure our tests can pull in third-party dependencies to validate our configuration.

```
7_testing/40-setup-karma/shine/spec/javascript/canary.spec.js
import td from "testdouble/dist/testdouble";

describe("JavaScript testing", function() {
  it("works as expected", function() {
    var mockFunction = td.function();

    td.when(mockFunction(42)).thenReturn("Function Called!");

    expect(mockFunction(42)).toBe("Function Called!");
  });
});
```

We can run that test using the karma command-line application, which is installed in node_modules/.bin. Yarn provides a simpler way to execute command-line applications installed via Yarn, which is to use $(yarn bin)/karma, like so:

```
        > $(yarn bin)/karma --version
Karma version: 1.7.0
```

Let's try running our test:

```
> NODE_ENV=test $(yarn/bin)/karma start spec/javascript/karma.conf.js \
                    --single-run \
                    --log-level=error \
                    --fail-on-empty-test-suite
PhantomJS 2.1.1 (Mac OS X 0.0.0): Executed 1 of 1 SUCCESS (0.004 secs…
```

Your version numbers might not match mine, but you should see the message, "Executed 1 of 1 SUCCESS," which indicates our test was executed and passed. The --single-run switch means we want Karma to execute our tests and exit. (By default, it starts a web server that runs our tests in a browser.) --log-level makes an attempt to reduce the output of the command, and --fail-on-empty-test-suite is a sanity check that Karma has actually found our tests. Note that we explicitly set NODE_ENV to test, which triggers some test-only configuration in Webpack.

As mentioned earlier, let's put this into a rake task so we don't have to remember this long invocation. Doing so will also allow us to include our JavaScript tests as part of our build when someone types rake. Create the file lib/tasks/karma.rake like so:

```
7_testing/40-setup-karma/shine/lib/tasks/karma.rake
desc "Run unit tests of JavaScript code with Karma"
task :karma do
  ENV["NODE_ENV"] = "test"
  mkdir_p "spec/fake_root"
  sh("$(yarn bin)/karma start spec/javascript/karma.conf.js " +
     "--single-run --log-level=error --fail-on-empty-test-suite")
end
task :default => :karma
```

This does exactly what we were doing on the command line: ensures we are in our app's root directory and runs karma from node_modules/.bin. You can try it by running rake karma and if you just run rake, you should see that these tests are run as a part of that.

With our testing libraries installed, let's write a unit test of our existing Angular code.

Write a Unit Test for the Angular Code

We're going to write a complete unit test for CustomerSearchComponent, which will test its behavior when created and the behavior of the search function. Let's create spec/javascript/CustomerSearchComponent.spec.js and just write out what we want to test using describe and it.

```
7_testing/40-setup-karma/shine/spec/javascript/CustomerSearchComponent.spec.js
describe("CustomerSearchComponent", function() {
  describe("initial state", function() {
    it("sets customers to null");
    it("sets keywords to the empty string");
  });

  describe("search", function() {
    describe("A search for 'pa', less than three characters", function() {
      it("sets the keywords to be 'pa'");
      it("does not make an HTTP call");
    });
    describe("A search for 'pat', three or more characters", function() {
      describe("A successful search", function() {
        it("sets the keywords to be 'pat'");
        it("sets the customers to the results of the HTTP call");
      });
      describe("A search that fails on the back-end", function() {
        it("sets the keywords to be 'pat'");
        it("leaves customers as null");
        it("alerts the user with the response message");
      });
    });
  });
});
```

This roughly describes the behavior of CustomerSearchComponent, so all we need to do is fill in each of the it calls with our tests. To do *that*, we'll need access to CustomerSearchComponent, which is currently defined inside app/javascript/packs/customer.js. You could try to require that file in our tests, but doing so won't give us access to CustomerSearchComponent because it's not being exported. In Java-Script, unlike Ruby, you have to explicitly export anything you want visible outside a file.

app/javascript/packs/customer.js also has code we don't want to deal with for a unit test, such as the NgModule configuration. Let's extract the code for CustomerSearch-Component out of this file, so we can load only that class for our unit test. This is much more like how we manage our Ruby files and will seem natural. After we do that, we'll write our first tests, and then learn about mocking Customer-SearchComponent's dependencies using TestDouble.js.

Extracting CustomerSearchComponent Into Its Own File

Webpacker's intent is for each pack to have a file in app/javascript/packs, which we are doing now, but to put the meat of any code into app/javascript. The idea is that each pack is a separate .js file that the browser will include. Webpack constructs each of those files for us, and the construction of those files might include re-usable modules we write, which are stored in app/javascript.

This is a big difference from how Sprockets works—Sprockets just creates a single file that has everything in it. Webpack produces multiple files that we include only when needed. What this means for us is that we need to move some code around into this structure, which meshes perfectly with our desire to extract code for testing.

Since the code in app/javascript/packs/customers.js that *isn't* our CustomerSearchCompo-nent is just about setting up the Angular app itself, we'll leave that in there and only extract the code for CustomerSearchComponent. This is a good rule of thumb for Angular apps with Webpacker: component code should go in app/javascript and app-wide setup should stay in app/javascript/packs.

This means that our app/javascript/packs/customers.js should look like so:

```
7_testing/50-angular-unit-test/shine/app/javascript/packs/customers.js
import { NgModule              } from "@angular/core";
import { BrowserModule        } from "@angular/platform-browser";
import { FormsModule          } from "@angular/forms";
import { platformBrowserDynamic } from "@angular/platform-browser-dynamic";
import { HttpModule           } from "@angular/http";
import { CustomerSearchComponent } from "CustomerSearchComponent";
```

Note that we've slightly changed our imports. customers.js no longer needs Component or Http, so we can remove those from our import. We've also added an import for CustomerSearchComponent.

The Webpack configuration that Webpacker set up for us means that code like import { CustomerSearchComponent} from "CustomerSearchComponent" will look for the file app/javascript/CustomerSearchComponent/index.js or index.ts. This might seem odd, but as we'll see in *Storing View Templates in HTML Files*, on page 129, we can further extract our component into files, and having them in a directory will make it easy to keep everything organized.

Given this convention, let's create the directory app/javascript/CustomerSearchComponent and create index.ts in there like so:

```
7_testing/50-angular-unit-test/shine/app/javascript/CustomerSearchComponent/index.ts
➤ import { Component } from "@angular/core";
➤ import { Http     } from "@angular/http";

  var CustomerSearchComponent = Component({

    // Same code as before...

  });

➤ export { CustomerSearchComponent };
```

I've highlighted the two bits of new code you'll need to add. The first bit probably looks familiar—it brings in the Angular components our code needs. This feels like duplication compared to how things work with Ruby, and it highlights a difference in how JavaScript treats modules. In JavaScript, everything is isolated to the file, and there isn't really any global state. This is great for encapsulation and code management, but it does require us to be explicit about what external libraries and functions any given file needs.

The second bit of highlighted code is at the end and shows how we export our code to other files that require this file. module.exports is special to JavaScript and Webpack. It's the glue between our extracted code and what is set up by the import statement in app/javascript/packs/customers.js.

One last oddity is that we named our file with a .ts extension, which is for files containing TypeScript, instead of a .js one. I mentioned briefly in *Install Angular*, on page 66 that we were not going to use TypeScript, and generally we aren't. Since many examples online *are* in TypeScript, you may want to learn it and start using it after you get through this book. Because TypeScript is a superset of JavaScript, you can start using it whenever you want, since the configuration Webpacker created already supports TypeScript. By using .ts files now, your switch to TypeScript later will be much easier.

Now that we've extracted CustomerSearchComponent into its own class, we can run our browser-based tests to make sure we haven't broken anything and then move on to writing some tests for it.

Writing Simple Unit Tests

Let's start with the tests around the initial state of the component. This allows us to see how we create the component and inspect it. First, we'll use import to bring in CustomerSearchComponent:

7_testing/50-angular-unit-test/shine/spec/javascript/CustomerSearchComponent.spec.js

```
➤ import "./SpecHelper";
➤ import { CustomerSearchComponent } from "CustomerSearchComponent";
```

Note that we've required SpecHelper.js. We're borrowing this pattern from RSpec, and this file, which we'll create in a moment, can handle cross-cutting set up which, unfortunately, we need. If you recall, we had to import a bunch of libraries to set up a shared global state. Those are currently in app/javascript/hello_angular/polyfills.ts. We need those in our tests, too, but rather than have that inside each test, we'll centralize them in one file called SpecHelper.js.

One thing that's not obvious now, however, is that one of the polyfills—zone.js —cannot be imported more than once. Since we cannot conditionally import a file, we need to make it easy to import the polyfills that are safe to import multiple times. To that end, we'll create app/javascript/polyfills/no_zonejs.ts that has all the polyfills save for zone.js's. We'll then import that file in app/javascript/polyfills/index.ts, where we'll also import zone.js. Finally, our SpecHelper.js can import only polyfills/no_zonejs.ts. Whew! Let's see the code changes.

First, here's what app/javascript/polyfills/index.ts should look like:

7_testing/50-angular-unit-test/shine/app/javascript/polyfills/index.ts

```
import './no_zonejs';
import 'zone.js/dist/zone';
```

Next is app/javascript/polyfills/no_zonejs.ts:

7_testing/50-angular-unit-test/shine/app/javascript/polyfills/no_zonejs.ts

```
import 'core-js/es6/symbol';
import 'core-js/es6/object';
import 'core-js/es6/function';
import 'core-js/es6/parse-int';
import 'core-js/es6/parse-float';
import 'core-js/es6/number';
import 'core-js/es6/math';
import 'core-js/es6/string';
import 'core-js/es6/date';
import 'core-js/es6/array';
import 'core-js/es6/regexp';
```

```
import 'core-js/es6/map';
import 'core-js/es6/set';
import 'core-js/es6/reflect';
import 'core-js/es7/reflect';
```

You should remove app/javascript/hello_angular/polyfills.ts and update both app/java-script/hello_angular/index.ts and app/javascript/packs/customers.js to reference the new file. Here's hello_angular's:

7_testing/50-angular-unit-test/shine/app/javascript/hello_angular/index.ts

```
import 'polyfills';

import { platformBrowserDynamic } from '@angular/platform-browser-dynamic';
import { AppModule } from './app/app.module';

platformBrowserDynamic().bootstrapModule(AppModule);
```

And here's customers.js:

7_testing/50-angular-unit-test/shine/app/javascript/packs/customers.js

```
import "polyfills";
```

And *finally*, we can create spec/javascript/SpecHelper.js to only import those polyfills that can be safely imported more than once:

7_testing/50-angular-unit-test/shine/spec/javascript/SpecHelper.js

```
import "polyfills/no_zonejs";
```

To write your test, you need an instance of your component. I didn't talk much about what the Component and Class functions actually do. Under the covers, they create a JavaScript class, meaning you can create an instance of CustomerSearchComponent by using new, and anything you pass to the constructor will be sent along to the constructor function you defined.

Right now we don't need to worry about the constructor arguments, so we'll create our instance via new CustomerSearchComponent(). In order to only do that once, we'll use Jasmine's beforeEach function, which works just like RSpec's before method. Because of JavaScript's scoping rules, we need the variable for our component to be declared outside our describe function, so we'll declare it at the top of the file, and then assign it inside beforeEach:

7_testing/50-angular-unit-test/shine/spec/javascript/CustomerSearchComponent.spec.js

```
var component = null;

describe("CustomerSearchComponent", function() {
  beforeEach(function() {
    component = new CustomerSearchComponent();
  });
```

Now, we can fill in our two tests. All they'll do is access the customers and key-words properties of our instance and make sure they are set to their initial values (note this code appears right after the beforeEach code we just wrote):

7_testing/50-angular-unit-test/shine/spec/javascript/CustomerSearchComponent.spec.js

```
describe("initial state", function() {
  it("sets customers to null", function() {
    expect(component.customers).toBe(null);
  });
  it("sets keywords to the empty string", function() {
    expect(component.keywords).toBe("");
  });
});
```

If you run rake karma, you'll see that our two assertions ran and our test passed:

```
> bin/rails karma
«tons of output»
PhantomJS 2.1.1 (Mac OS X 0.0.0):
  Executed 3 of 10 (skipped 7) SUCCESS (0.011 secs / 0.005 secs)
```

Now, let's test the search function of our component. This requires setting up some test doubles for Angular's HTTP library.

Using Test Doubles to Stub Dependencies

Because we're writing unit tests, we want to test in isolation, meaning we don't want to actually make HTTP calls in our test. To avoid that, we'll stub out the Http class we're using at runtime. Because of how Angular components are designed, we can easily pass in our own implementation of Http to the constructor of CustomerSearchComponent. The question, then, is where do we get our test implementation?

Although Angular provides a system for mocking out HTTP calls, it is highly complex and will make our job of testing in isolation quite difficult, as we'll need to do fairly extensive setup work in our tests to make it work. Even if we used TypeScript, we'd still have a lot of conceptual overhead in getting this working, so let's instead use generic test doubles. This won't be simple, but it will be simpler.

The test double library is called Testdouble.js and you installed it earlier. It provides everything you need to make a mock HTTP object. Let's start with our first test of search, which will do a search for "pa" and assert that we don't make any HTTP calls. In our case, our code would execute http.get() if it *did* perform a search, so we want a test double that responds to get() and a way to check that it wasn't called.

First, we'll bring in the Testdouble.js library:

```
7_testing/50-angular-unit-test/shine/spec/javascript/CustomerSearchComponent.spec.js
import td from "testdouble/dist/testdouble";
```

Note the slight change in syntax for import: we aren't using curly braces. This is because we want to import everything that is exported, and not just a particular function or class.

Next, we'll create a beforeEach block for our tests that creates a test double for Angular's HTTP and passes it into our component when we create it:

```
7_testing/50-angular-unit-test/shine/spec/javascript/CustomerSearchComponent.spec.js
describe("search", function() {
  var mockHttp = null;
  beforeEach(function() {
    mockHttp = td.object(["get"]);
    component = new CustomerSearchComponent(mockHttp);
  });
```

The object method on td creates an object that can respond to the methods given in the array. In our case, the code td.object(["get"]) means "create an object that has a get function." In a later test, you'll use more functions of Testdouble.js to specify the behavior of our mock object, but for now we just need it to exist.

Now, let's implement the first test that asserts that the keywords property gets set to our search string when we call search:

```
7_testing/50-angular-unit-test/shine/spec/javascript/CustomerSearchComponent.spec.js
it("sets the keywords to be 'pa'",function() {
  component.search("pa");
  expect(component.keywords).toBe("pa");
});
```

Next, we'll write a test that explicitly requires that the get method on http was not called. This is how we'll assert that a search for a string shorter than three characters doesn't hit the back end.

```
7_testing/50-angular-unit-test/shine/spec/javascript/CustomerSearchComponent.spec.js
it("does not make an HTTP call", function() {
  component.search("pa");
  td.verify(mockHttp.get(), { times: 0 });
});
```

This is using the verify function of Testdouble, which is usually used to check that a method *was* called. In our case, because we want to make sure it wasn't, we use { times: 0 }.

Running our tests, they should pass. This wasn't too bad, but things are about to get a bit complex as we move onto the next test, where we need to arrange for our mock HTTP object to return results.

Stubbing Complex Interactions to Test HTTP

Let's write the test for a successful search of the term "pat." You can set up our beforeEach in much the same way, except now you have to provide an implementation of get.

If you look at the contract of the get function in Angular's HTTP library, it accepts a URL and returns an observable (which I talked about in *Get Data from the Back End*, on page 81). You then call subscribe on that observable, passing it two functions: one for a successful result and one for an error. The success function is expecting the data from the back end, and it's going to call json() on that data to parse it. Whew!

First, we'll create a test double for the response passed to our success function. We'll create it using object, just as we did with http, but we'll use td.when to specify the behavior of the json function. (Note this is all new code)

```
7_testing/50-angular-unit-test/shine/spec/javascript/CustomerSearchComponent.spec.js
describe("A search for 'pat', three or more characters", function() {
  var mockHttp = null;
  var customers = [
    {
      id: 1,
      created_at: (new Date()).toString(),
      first_name: "Pat",
      last_name: "Jones",
      username: "pj",
      email: "pjones@somewhere.net"
    },
    {
      id: 2,
      created_at: (new Date()).toString(),
      first_name: "Pat",
      last_name: "Jones",
      username: "pj",
      email: "pjones@somewhere.net"
    },
  ];
  beforeEach(function() {
    var response = td.object(["json"]);
    td.when(response.json()).thenReturn({ customers: customers });
    mockHttp = td.object(["get"]);
    component = new CustomerSearchComponent(mockHttp);
```

We've declared customers outside beforeEach because we'll eventually assert that our component's customers property was assigned these customers. Next, we'll create a test double for our observable.

Creating a test double is trickier because you need to define the subscribe function as "calls our success callback." You can do this by using td.callback along with td.when. Because subscribe takes two callbacks, and we only want one called, we'll use td.matchers.isA(Function) as the second argument. This tells Testdouble.js to not call the second callback, but to fail the test if something *other* than a function is passed to subscribe's second parameter.

```
7_testing/50-angular-unit-test/shine/spec/javascript/CustomerSearchComponent.spec.js
beforeEach(function() {
  var response = td.object(["json"]);
  td.when(response.json()).thenReturn({ customers: customers });

  var observable = td.object(["subscribe"]);
  td.when(observable.subscribe(
    td.callback(response),
    td.matchers.isA(Function))).thenReturn();
```

Now when our production code calls subscribe, the test double called observable will first make sure that the two arguments passed to it are functions. If they are, it will then execute the first function, passing it response. It will not execute the second function, and simulates a successful response. This part is rather tricky to get your head around, but it's ultimately the easiest way to deal with callbacks in your test code and maintain isolation in your testing. Another way to read this might be "when we call subscribe on observable, call the callback passed as the first parameter with our mock response, and make sure the second parameter is also a function."

Last, we need to configure our mock HTTP object to return this mock observable when get is called:

```
7_testing/50-angular-unit-test/shine/spec/javascript/CustomerSearchComponent.spec.js
mockHttp = td.object(["get"]);

td.when(mockHttp.get("/customers.json?keywords=pat")).thenReturn(observable);

component = new CustomerSearchComponent(mockHttp);
```

With all that setup, we can now write our two tests (note this code appears below the beforeEach block where the code above was placed—consult the downloaded code to see the entire picture):

```
7_testing/50-angular-unit-test/shine/spec/javascript/CustomerSearchComponent.spec.js
describe("A successful search", function() {
  it("sets the keywords to be 'pat'",function() {
    component.search("pat");
```

```
➤          expect(component.keywords).toBe("pat");
         });
         it("sets the customers to the results of the HTTP call", function() {
➤          component.search("pat");
➤          expect(component.customers).toBe(customers);
         });
       });
```

Running the tests, we should see that they pass. We've now successfully mocked the HTTP calls and can test in complete isolation! Also note that you didn't have to do anything Angular-specific. This is an interesting side effect of the way Angular wants us to write code. *Our* code has no real ties to Angular, even though it uses some of Angular's classes. In the end, our code is just some JavaScript that you can execute.

Next, let's test the error case, which will create some complications around our use of window.

Testing the Error Case and Removing window

In *Get Data from the Back End*, on page 81, we decided to use window.alert as the means of letting the user know that an error had occurred. As you'll see, this is going to be a slight problem. To see the problem, let's get our test setup. We'll set it up much as we did the success case, but we'll arrange to have Testdouble.js call the error callback instead. The main difference in setup is how you configure the call to subscribe: you'll pass td.callback(response) as the *second* argument, to make sure the error callback is called when the test runs.

```
7_testing/50-angular-unit-test/shine/spec/javascript/CustomerSearchComponent.spec.js
     describe("A search that fails on the back-end", function() {
➤      beforeEach(function() {
➤        var response = "There was an error!";
➤        var observable = td.object(["subscribe"]);
➤
➤        td.when(observable.subscribe(
➤          td.matchers.isA(Function),
➤          td.callback(response))).thenReturn();
➤
➤        mockHttp = td.object(["get"]);
➤        td.when(mockHttp.get("/customers.json?keywords=pat")).thenReturn(observable);
➤
➤        component = new CustomerSearchComponent(mockHttp);
➤      });
       it("sets the keywords to be 'pat'",function() {
➤        component.search("pat");
➤        expect(component.keywords).toBe("pat");
       });
       it("leaves customers as null", function() {
```

```
    component.search("pat");
    expect(component.customers).toBe(null);
  });
  it("alerts the user with the response message",function() {
    // ???
  });
});
```

You can already see what the problem will be, since it's not clear how to test that window.alert was called with our error message. When you run rake karma, you can see that the error message we configured is getting printed out (as Karma's output shows whatever PhantomJS receives from a call to window.alert).

```
> bundle exec rake karma
«lots of output»
ALERT: 'There was an error!'
PhantomJS 2.1.1 (Mac OS X 0.0.0):
  Executed 10 of 10 SUCCESS (0.014 secs / 0.012 secs)
```

The test passes because we aren't asserting anything, but we need to figure out how to assert that the call to window.alert happened. We can do that by using Testdouble to replace the alert function on window with one that we can observe. The replace function from Testdouble will do just this:

```
7_testing/50-angular-unit-test/shine/spec/javascript/CustomerSearchComponent.spec.js
it("alerts the user with the response message",function() {
  td.replace(window,"alert");
  component.search("pat");
  td.verify(window.alert("There was an error!"));
});
```

We're using the more typical form of td.verify, and this code does more or less what it appears to. It will fail the test if window.alert was called with an argument *other* than "There was an error!"

This is obviously brittle. Our test has to much with a global variable in order to work. Angular 1 provided an abstraction for us—$window—but this is not available in later versions of Angular. You could create a *service class* that handles the error notification, and inject that the same way you did with Http. (you'll see this sort of thing in action in *Extracting Reusable Code into Services*, on page 269.) It would probably be a better user experience to stop using window.alert and design a real alerting component using Bootstrap.

We won't do that here, as you now know enough to both design such a component and—now—write a test for it. For the latter, you could check that CustomerSearchComponent exposed the right error message to its view, much like how we've been checking that customers has been set appropriately.

Now that you can successfully write unit tests using Jasmine (running them with Karma), and mock out Angular-provided classes easily with Testdouble.js, you have the tools you need to test your JavaScript code. Our mocking of Http was complex enough that you should be able to tackle any test you need.

Next: Level Up on Everything

You learned a ton in this chapter about testing our Rails application at every level of the stack. Now that you can test anything from database constraints to JavaScript functions to end-to-end user interactions, you're ready to move on to more complex features.

Now it's time to up our game on everything. Over the next several chapters, you'll build a complex customer detail view. This will be a great chance to learn how to design a dense UI with Bootstrap, wrangle multiple data sources with Angular, and optimize complex queries inside Postgres. But first, we need to turn our simple search screen into a *single-page app* by learning about Angular's router and navigation services.

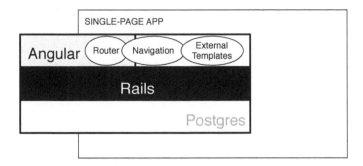

## CHAPTER 8

Create a Single-Page App Using Angular's Router

At this point, you're probably starting to feel confident. You experimented with some powerful features of Postgres, quickly made great-looking screens with Bootstrap, and created a dynamic user interface without a lot of code thanks to Angular. You also have rock-solid tests for every part of it. Now, it's time to level up.

In this chapter, we'll turn our simple customer search feature into a full-fledged *single-page app* using Angular's router and navigating users between pages—all within the browser. You'll learn how to put our view templates in separate files instead of string literals inside our JavaScript code, and see how to use test-driven development (TDD) to add features.

To illustrate all this, we'll start on a feature we'll build over the next few chapters. The feature is a detailed view of the customer's information, which includes more data than we saw on the result page and requires pulling in data from many different sources, all viewable on one screen, similar to what is shown in the figure on page 128.

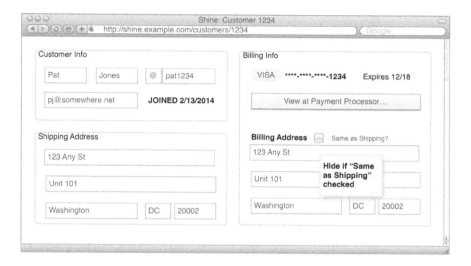

First, we'll turn our existing Angular app into a single-page app that allows navigating from the search results to the detailed view (which will just be bare-bones, initially), like what is shown in the next figure.

To make this happen, we'll set up Angular's router, making sure our Angular routes play well with Rails's routes. We'll then add a second component to represent the detailed view, and write code to navigate to it when the user clicks a new button that we'll add to the search results. This allows you to learn about one of Angular's component life-cycle methods, which we'll use to parse Angular's route. Finally, we'll use TDD to connect our new component to the back end in order to fetch customer details. This will give you an outline of how you can develop features using Angular and Rails, as well as serve as a second example of how to test this code.

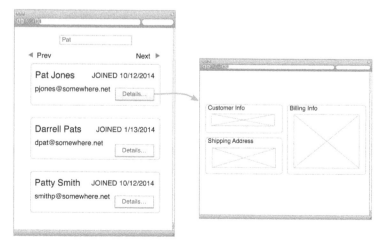

But first, let's extract our templates out of string literals and into HTML files, since this will make it much easier to manage our application in the face of multiple components.

Storing View Templates in HTML Files

Currently, the view templates are strings inside our JavaScript. This might be okay if we have a single small view, but as we create more components and have to manage more views, it will be increasingly difficult to keep them as strings. The trailing backslashes and general clunkiness of managing view code in JavaScript is something that's best to avoid.

Fortunately, Webpack makes this easy. With Angular 1, which was used in the previous edition of this book, you had to install a special Rails plugin to convert your templates into something the asset pipeline could serve up. Now, we need to bring in the HTML as a string and pass that string to the template: key when declaring our components. Doing this requires adding a special plugin called a *loader* to Webpack, and configuring TypeScript to trigger the loader. It makes sense when you see the code.

First, we'll install Webpack's html loader[1] with yarn:

```
> yarn add html-loader
```

Next, create the file config/webpack/loaders/html.js like so:

```
8_angular-routes/10-separate-templates/shine/config/webpack/loaders/html.js
module.exports = {
  test: /\.html$/,
  use: [{
    loader: 'html-loader',
    options: {
      minimize: true,
      removeAttributeQuotes: false,
      caseSensitive: true,
      customAttrSurround: [ [/#/, /(?:)/], [/\*/, /(?:)/], [/\[?\(?/, /(?:)/] ],
      customAttrAssign: [ /\)?\]?=/ ]
    }
  }]
}
```

This file tells Webpack what to do if we try to import a file that ends in .html. By default, Webpack will treat this as a JavaScript file and generate an error (since HTML is not JavaScript). The values for options are a set of esoteric configuration parameters that allow Angular's additions to HTML to work.

---

1. https://github.com/webpack-contrib/html-loader

Although we are writing pure JavaScript, we are doing it in .ts, which means they are run through the TypeScript compiler. Although Webpack is now configured to read HTML files, TypeScript isn't. We need to tell TypeScript that when it encouters an HTML file, to not touch it. We can do this by creating the file app/javascript/CustomerSearchComponent/html.d.ts, like so:

```
8_angular-routes/10-separate-templates/shine/app/javascript/CustomerSearchComponent/html.d.ts
declare module "*.html" {
  const content: string
  export default content
}
```

It's not important what this means and, sadly, is extremely difficult to derive or understand (this comes from the Webpacker setup instructions for Angular templates[2]). It's needed to make this all work.

With this in place, you can move all the HTML from app/javascript/CustomerSearch-Component/index.ts into app/javascript/CustomerSearchComponent/template.html (don't forget to remove all the trailing backslashes), and then bring it back in using import. This will create the variable template that you can pass to template: when setting up the component:

```
8_angular-routes/10-separate-templates/shine/app/javascript/CustomerSearchComponent/index.ts
import { Component } from "@angular/core";
import { Http      } from "@angular/http";
➤ import    template    from "./template.html";

var CustomerSearchComponent = Component({

  selector: "shine-customer-search",
➤  template: template
}).Class({
```

Note that for this use of import we are preceding the file with dot and a slash. This tells Webpack to locate the file in the current directory, and not in node_modules or app/javascript.

Because this didn't change any behavior, you can use our tests to make sure this change was good. If you run rake, you shouldn't see any test failures. Now that we've cleaned up our code, let's install and configure Angular's router so that we can detect when a user is navigating to a different URL and render a different view.

---

2. https://github.com/rails/webpacker#use-html-templates-with-typescript-and-angular

Configuring Angular's Router for User Navigation

Like Rails, Angular has a way to support navigation-by-URL. Because Angular's design ethos is based around flexibility, an Angular app isn't required to use the router, though in most cases you would, and you would set it up from the start. We didn't initially, just to keep our introduction to Angular as simple as possible and reduce the number of new concepts you had to absorb.

Now, we'll need to convert our existing Angular app to use the router.

Currently, our Angular app just renders the CustomerSearchComponent's view, since we're using its selector—shine-customer-search—in our Rails view. Instead, we're going to configure Angular's router, which allows us to specify which components are rendered for which URLs the user has navigated to.

To do this, make a top-level component for the entire application, whose view will contain markup that the router can hook into. To validate this is working, create a second component that renders a static view and see how changing URLs changes which component is being used. You'll also have to make a small change to our Rails routing configuration to make the URLs bookmarkable.

Create a Bare-Bones Second Component

Now that you know how to put our components and their templates into separate files, creating a shell for our second component is straightforward. First, create the directory app/javascript/CustomerDetailsComponent, which will hold the files for the component. Next, create a simple static view in app/javascript/CustomerDetailsComponent/template.html:

```
8_angular-routes/20-angular-router/shine/app/javascript/CustomerDetailsComponent/template.html
<h1>Customer Details!</h1>
```

We'll require this view in our component's definition, which we'll create in app/javascript/CustomerDetailsComponent/index.ts:

```
8_angular-routes/20-angular-router/shine/app/javascript/CustomerDetailsComponent/index.ts
import { Component } from "@angular/core";
import    template    from "./template.html";

var CustomerDetailsComponent = Component({
  selector: "shine-customer-details",
  template: template
}).Class({
  constructor: [
    function() { }
  ]
});
export { CustomerDetailsComponent };
```

Next, bring it into the customers pack in app/javascript/packs/customers.js:

```
8_angular-routes/20-angular-router/shine/app/javascript/packs/customers.js
import { Component, NgModule    } from "@angular/core";
import { BrowserModule          } from "@angular/platform-browser";
import { FormsModule            } from "@angular/forms";
import { platformBrowserDynamic } from "@angular/platform-browser-dynamic";
import { HttpModule             } from "@angular/http";
import { RouterModule           } from "@angular/router";

import { CustomerSearchComponent  } from "CustomerSearchComponent";
import { CustomerDetailsComponent } from "CustomerDetailsComponent";
```

Finally, pass it to NgModule (which you first learned about in *Validate the Angular Install Using The Demo Component*, on page 68):

```
var CustomerAppModule = NgModule({
  imports:      [
    BrowserModule,
    FormsModule,
    HttpModule ],
  declarations: [
    CustomerSearchComponent,
    CustomerDetailsComponent
  ],
  bootstrap:    [ CustomerSearchComponent ]
})
.Class({
  constructor: function() {}
});
```

We'll make more changes to this code before our system is working again, so if you try the application in this state, it might not work as expected. Hold on as we complete the setup of router. The next step is to bring the router into our code and configure it.

Install and Configure Angular's Router

I mentioned earlier that Angular apps aren't required to use the router, so it's not available by default. We can install it using yarn add:

```
> yarn add @angular/router # note that @-sign
```

We can now bring it in to app/javascript/packs/customers.js, where we are requiring the other Angular libraries:

```
8_angular-routes/20-angular-router/shine/app/javascript/packs/customers.js
import { Component, NgModule    } from "@angular/core";
import { BrowserModule          } from "@angular/platform-browser";
import { FormsModule            } from "@angular/forms";
import { platformBrowserDynamic } from "@angular/platform-browser-dynamic";
```

```
import { HttpModule              } from "@angular/http";
import { RouterModule            } from "@angular/router";
```

Note that we've brought back Component as we'll need that later. Now, we must configure the router. To do that, we'll pass an object describing our routes to the forRoot function of RouterModule, which we just imported.

```
8_angular-routes/20-angular-router/shine/app/javascript/packs/customers.js
var routing = RouterModule.forRoot(
[
  {
    path: "",
    component: CustomerSearchComponent
  },
  {
    path: ":id",
    component: CustomerDetailsComponent
  }
]);

var CustomerAppModule = NgModule({

  // rest of the code...
```

The paths are somewhat odd, in that they have no leading slashes, and one of them is just the empty string! These paths are considered relative to a base URL that we must specify using the base[3] element. This configuration means that a URL that is *just* the base URL will match the empty string path, and thus use our existing CustomerSearchComponent to handle the view. A URL with an identifier under the base element will match the second path (using a wildcard value similar to what Rails's router does) and use our newly created CustomerDetailsComponent to handle the view.

I'll talk about the base URL in a moment, but before that, let's finish configuring the router inside our Angular app.

Given the configuration we just saw, you'll need to pass it to NgModule:

```
var CustomerAppModule = NgModule({
  imports:        [
    BrowserModule,
    FormsModule,
    HttpModule,
    router
  ],
```

---

3. https://developer.mozilla.org/en-US/docs/Web/HTML/Element/base

```
declarations: [
  CustomerSearchComponent,
  CustomerDetailsComponent
],
bootstrap:      [ CustomerSearchComponent ]
})
.Class({
  constructor: function() {}
});
```

The mere presence of routing in the array given to imports is sufficient for Angular to know what to do and set up routing. Before you configure Rails and see this working, you need to create a top-level application component so that you have a place to tell the router where views should be rendered.

Wrap the App in a Top-Level Component

The way we've created our Angular app isn't common. Most Angular apps have several different components and tend to be designed with a single top-level component that wraps them all. Now that we have a second component (CustomerDetailsComponent), we should move to this design. It also makes the routing we are trying to achieve easier to set up.

Since this new component exists only to hold the other components, there's little value in placing it in app/javascript, so we can inline it into app/javascript/packs/customers.js. First we'll create the component using the selector shine-customers-app (which we'll place into the Rails view in a moment):

8_angular-routes/20-angular-router/shine/app/javascript/packs/customers.js
```
var AppComponent = Component({
  selector: "shine-customers-app",
  template: "<router-outlet></router-outlet>"
}).Class({
  constructor: [
    function() {}
  ]
});
```

Note that we've inlined the HTML as just using the element router-outlet. This element is special to Angular and tells it where to render components that are being changed due to routing changes. The reason we've inlined it is just for simplicity—we don't need any more markup in our top-level component.

Next, let's change our Rails view in app/views/customers/index.html.erb to use this new selector:

```
8_angular-routes/20-angular-router/shine/app/views/customers/index.html.erb
<section>
  <shine-customers-app></shine-customers-app>
</section>
<%= javascript_pack_tag "customers" %>
```

Last, we need to modify the call to NgModule to tell it about our new top-level component. This requires adding it to the declarations key and changing the bootstrap key from CustomerSearchComponent to our new AppComponent:g>

```
8_angular-routes/20-angular-router/shine/app/javascript/packs/customers.js
var CustomerAppModule = NgModule({
  imports:      [
    BrowserModule,
    FormsModule,
    HttpModule,
    routing
  ],
  declarations: [
    CustomerSearchComponent,
    CustomerDetailsComponent,
    AppComponent
  ],
  bootstrap: [ AppComponent ]
})
.Class({
  constructor: function() {}
});
```

This completes the Angular setup, but you still need to set the base element to the right value, as well as do a bit more Rails configuration.

Configure Rails to Work with Angular's Router

Angular makes no prescription about what the server side should look like—that lack of direction is one of the main reasons for writing this book. The problem with being server-agnostic is we now have to make some complex decisions about how Rails's routing and Angular's routing will interact. We can solve this problem by judiciously choosing what our base URL should be.

Suppose we choose the fairly obvious base URL of /customers. That's the URL we're using now to have Rails render the Angular app's initial view. This means that, in our current configuration, if the user navigates to /customers/42, we'd expect that to render the CustomerDetailsComponent. Later in this chapter, we'll add the show method to CustomersController so that our Angular app can fetch a single customer's information. The idiomatic Rails configuration for that endpoint would be the URL /customers/:id, which clashes with our Angular configuration *assuming the base URL is /customers*.

It's possible to make that URL work for both our Ajax requests and for our Angular app, but it's pretty darn confusing. In Angular 1, the part of the path owned by Angular came after an anchor in the URL, so our Angular app's detail view would be available via /customers#/42, which has a *Rails route* of /customers. New versions of Angular don't do this by default, so we need a convention where it's obvious what part of the URL is handled by Rails and what part is handled by Angular. In a sense, we need to re-create the delimiter that the octothorpe provided in Angular 1.

This is confusing. It has confused every developer I work with, and has confused many readers of the first edition. In an effort to make what's going on as explicit as possible, let's decide that our base URL is going to be /customers/ng. That means that /customers/ng will show our existing customer search feature, and /customers/ng/42 will show the new CustomerDetailsComponent. It's slightly icky, but it has the virtue of being more explicit.

To make this happen, you'll need to implement the ng method in CustomersController, modify index to redirect to it, and modify our application layout to set the base URL.

Let's change config/routes.rb to account for this new setup. Note that you need two routes to make this work: one for just /customers/ng and a second that *globs* the remaining route. This is so *any* URL that starts with /customers/ng/ will be handled by our new ng method, which makes all of the URLs our Angular app will create bookmarkable.

```
8_angular-routes/20-angular-router/shine/config/routes.rb
Rails.application.routes.draw do
  devise_for :users
  root to: "dashboard#index"
  # These supercede other /customers routes, so must
  # come before resource :customers
  get "customers/ng",               to: "customers#ng"
  get "customers/ng/*angular_route", to: "customers#ng"
  resources :customers, only: [ :index ]
end
```

If you haven't seen route-globbing in Rails before, the string after the asterisk can be anything, and is used to populate params in our controller. In this case, we could access params[:angular_route] to get the Angular-owned part of the route server-side. We won't need this, but using a descriptive name makes it clear to other developers what's going on.

Also note the ordering of our routes. In Rails, the routes are matched in the order listed in config/routes.rb. We want the route /customers/ng to have priority over a route like /customers/42, which we'll add later in this chapter to provide a way to access customer data via Ajax.

Next, let's implement the ng method in CustomersController. Note that we're setting the base URL as an ivar. (I'll explain that in a moment.)

8_angular-routes/20-angular-router/shine/app/controllers/customers_controller.rb

```ruby
class CustomersController < ApplicationController

  PAGE_SIZE = 10

➤  def ng
➤    @base_url = "/customers/ng"
➤    render :index
➤  end
```

We're also rendering the existing index view so we don't have to copy any markup.

Finally, you're ready to set the base URL in our application layout. You don't want to hard-code it as /customers/ng. It's possible (and a good architectural pattern) for our Rails application to host many small, single-purpose Angular apps. This design is a great way to scale an application's codebase, and you want to allow for that as Shine grows. So, we'll do something simple, which is to check if the ivar @base_url has been set by the controller and, if it has, use it to set the base element in our head:

8_angular-routes/20-angular-router/shine/app/views/layouts/application.html.erb

```erb
<!DOCTYPE html>
<html>
  <head>
    <title>Shine</title>
    <%= csrf_meta_tags %>

    <%= stylesheet_link_tag    'application', media: 'all' %>
    <%= javascript_include_tag 'application' %>
    <%= javascript_pack_tag 'application' %>
    <%= stylesheet_pack_tag "application" %>
➤    <% if @base_url %>
➤      <base href="<%= @base_url %>">
➤    <% end %>
  </head>
```

You could create a helper to dynamically derive this and avoid the ivar, but this is a case where a few simple lines of explicit code are better than a highly complex dynamic solution.

You need to do one last thing, which is to redirect from /customers to /customers/ng. You should do this only when a browser requests that URL, which you can easily do inside the respond_to block in the index method:

8_angular-routes/20-angular-router/shine/app/controllers/customers_controller.rb
```ruby
def index

  # method as it was before...

  respond_to do |format|
    format.html {
      redirect_to customers_ng_path
    }
    format.json {
      render json: { customers: @customers }
    }
  end
end
```

Note the use of customers_ng_path, which was provided by Rails due to our routing configuration. Now, any existing links to /customers will redirect to /customers/ng, which should render our existing Angular app.

After all this, you can restart Rails, navigate to http://localhost:5000/customers, see that we're redirected to http://localhost:5000/customers/ng, and see our existing customer search feature. You can *also* enter http://localhost:5000/customers/ng/42 into our browser and see our bare-bones customer details page:

> ## Customer Details!

You can also verify that things are working by running our tests. Because you haven't (yet) changed how our app functions, our existing tests should still pass. With the router configured, and our new component created, it's now time to add actual navigation between components.

Navigating the User Interface Client-Side

With the router and our routes configured, we need to implement the navigation. We want to be able to do two things with what we've set up. First, we need to add a button to each search result that, when clicked, navigates from /customers/ng to /customers/ng/«customer id». Second, we need to extract that customer ID from the URL so we know which customer's details we want to view.

Add Navigation to the Detail View

In *Respond to Click Events*, on page 74, you saw how to respond to click events. What we want to do here is exactly the same thing. First, let's add a button to each search result that the user will use to view a single customer's details. We'll add it to the bottom right of our search result using Bootstrap's pull-right class:

```
8_angular-routes/30-client-side-navigation/shin ... javascript/CustomerSearchComponent/template.html
<ol class="list-group">
  <li *ngFor="let customer of customers"
    class="list-group-item clearfix">
    <h3 class="pull-right">
      <small class="text-uppercase">Joined</small>
      {{customer.created_at}}
    </h3>
    <h2 class="h3">
      {{customer.first_name}} {{customer.last_name}}
      <small>{{customer.username}}</small>
    </h2>
    <div class="pull-right">
      <button class="btn btn-small btn-primary"
              on-click="viewDetails(customer)">
        View Details...
      </button>
    </div>
    <h4>{{customer.email}}</h4>
  </li>
</ol>
```

When the page is reloaded, you should see the button, nicely located inside each search results, as shown in the following screen.

Patricia Hettinger baylee99
vita_kilback99@hintz.co

JOINED **2017-05-28T17:33:29.006Z**

View Details...

The on-click attribute we used is assuming the existence of a function called viewDetails in our component, so let's add that next.

We want to navigate the user to /customers/ng/«customer.id» inside viewDetails. You'll recall that Rails owns the route /customers/ng, so we need to tell Angular's router to route to customer.id. That will trigger the second configured route (the one with the path ":id") and show CustomerDetailsComponent. To do this, we need access to a Router,[4] which we can import:

First, we need to require that inside CustomerSearchComponent:

```
8_angular-routes/30-client-side-navigation/shine/app/javascript/CustomerSearchComponent/index.ts
import { Component } from "@angular/core";
import { Http     } from "@angular/http";
import { Router   } from "@angular/router";
import   template    from "./template.html";
```

---

4. https://angular.io/docs/ts/latest/api/router/index/Router-class.html

We next need to tell Angular to provide an instance of the router to our component by adding it to the special constructor object:

```
8_angular-routes/30-client-side-navigation/shine/app/javascript/CustomerSearchComponent/index.ts
}).Class({
  constructor: [
    Http,
➤   Router,
➤   function(http,router) {
      this.customers = null;
      this.http      = http;
      this.keywords  = "";
➤     this.router    = router;
    }
  ],
```

Now, we can implement viewDetails. To do this, call the navigate method and pass it an array of the parts of the URL we want to send the user to. It uses an array so that we don't have build up a string, though in our case, we only have one part of our URL—the customer's ID.

```
8_angular-routes/30-client-side-navigation/shine/app/javascript/CustomerSearchComponent/index.ts
➤ viewDetails: function(customer) {
➤   this.router.navigate(["/",customer.id]);
➤ },
  search: function($event) {
```

Now, when you reload the page, perform a search, and click on the new "View Details" button, you're taken to CustomerDetailsComponent. You'll notice the URL contains the ID of the customer you clicked on, and if you look at the Rails logs, you'll see that we did *not* hit the server. The navigation was all performed client-side.

Let's build out the detail view just a little bit so we can see how to extract that ID from the URL. We'll use that ID to fetch the details for that customer from the server via Ajax in the final section of this chapter.

Extract Details from the Route

In a Rails application, every controller has access to the params hash that contains, among other things, the parameters extracted from the route. For example, if your route is /customers/42, you'll likely use params[:id] to get the 42 from that route. With Angular, it's slightly more complicated. This is partly due to the asynchronous nature of JavaScript, but also due to Angular's overall design philosophy of explicit configuration over implicit behavior through convention.

To get access to the route parameters, you need to ask Angular for an instance of the ActivatedRoute[5] for the route we've navigated the user to. An ActivatedRoute has a method params, which returns an Observable. That observable will provide the routing parameters to us. You'll recall observables from *Get Data from the Back End*, on page 81 when we integrated our Angular app with our Rails back end.

For now, we'll just extract the customer ID from the route and display that in the view to prove that everything's hooked up properly. This means we have to figure out where we can access the ActivatedRoute. It might seem intuitive that the constructor would be the place to examine the ActivatedRoute, but the constructor is only called once. You need a method that's called every time the component is about to be displayed. In Angular, that method is ngOnInit, which is part of the OnInit interface. Interfaces are a concept heavily used in TypeScript to describe "hook" methods we can implement to get certain behaviors. Because ES5 has no concept of interfaces, all you have to do is provide an implementation of ngOnInit and Angular will call it (this is part of many *life-cycle hooks*[6] Angular provides).

Let's see what this looks like. First, require Angular's router:

```
8_angular-routes/30-client-side-navigation/shine/app/javascript/CustomerDetailsComponent/index.ts
import { Component } from "@angular/core";
➤  import { ActivatedRoute } from "@angular/router";
import    template    from "./template.html";
```

Next, tell Angular that we want the ActivatedRoute given to us. We do that by adding it to the special constructor array:

```
8_angular-routes/30-client-side-navigation/shine/app/javascript/CustomerDetailsComponent/index.ts
var CustomerDetailsComponent = Component({
  selector: "shine-customer-details",
  template: template
}).Class({
  constructor: [
➤    ActivatedRoute,
➤    function(activatedRoute) {
➤      this.activatedRoute = activatedRoute;
➤      this.id            = null;
➤    }
  ],
```

Note that we've also initialized id to null. This is the property we'll set from the route and that we'll show in the view.

---

5.   https://angular.io/docs/ts/latest/api/router/index/ActivatedRoute-interface.html
6.   https://angular.io/docs/ts/latest/guide/lifecycle-hooks.html

To set it, implement ngOnInit. This is less straightforward than you'd think because we have to deal with the observable. As before, use subscribe to configure the callback that should be given the results of the observable. In this case, it's an object called params. Also, note that you have to use the self trick you saw in *Get Data from the Back End*, on page 81 to ultimately set the id property to the value from the route.

8_angular-routes/30-client-side-navigation/shine/app/javascript/CustomerDetailsComponent/index.ts

```
    ],
➤   ngOnInit: function() {
➤     var self = this;
➤     self.activatedRoute.params.subscribe(function(params) {
➤       var id = +params['id'];
➤       self.id = id;
➤     });
➤   },
    });
export { CustomerDetailsComponent };
```

Finally, let's modify app/javascript/CustomerDetailsComponent/template.html to show the customer ID we've extracted from the route:

8_angular-routes/30-client-side-navigation/shin … avascript/CustomerDetailsComponent/template.html

```
<section class="customer-details">
  <h1>Customer Details {{id}}</h1>
</section>
```

I'll explain the reasoning for the section tag in a moment. With all this done, you should be able to reload the customer search page, perform a search, click the "View Details" button, and see our customer details page showing that customer's ID:

> ## Customer Details 42

We're almost done. We'd now like to use that ID to query the back end and get the customer's details so that we can show them in our new component. We also want this new feature covered by tests. Let's take this opportunity to use TDD to add this final feature, so we can see what that workflow is like with all the new tools and libraries we've learned.

Implementing Back-End Integration Using TDD

You already know how to fetch the customer's details from the server—you'd do it just the way you did in *Get Data from the Back End*, on page 81. You've also seen how to write acceptance and unit tests for a feature like this, but another example could really help cement your understanding of these complex concepts. It's also worth seeing how a TDD-based flow could work, for those of you who prefer test-driven development. (If you aren't familiar with TDD, *Test Driven Development [Bec10]* is a great place to get started.)

In this section, we'll create an acceptance test that works with the client-side navigation we just implemented. Then we'll create a unit test for ngOnInit that confirms that it's calling the back end. When we write code in our Angular component to get that to pass, our acceptance test will pass as well. This should give you a basic understanding of how to use TDD to build additional features.

Acceptance Test for Navigation to the Details View

In *Running Headless Acceptance Tests in PhantomJS*, on page 99, you learned about writing acceptance tests using Capybara and PhantomJS. spec/features/customer_search_spec.rb is the result of our efforts. Here we'll augment the test named "Search by Email" to navigate to one customer's detail view.

After the existing code for this test, we'll want to find the first button labeled "View Details," click it, wait for the component to re-render, and fetch the customer details. Then, we'll make some expectations about what content we expect to see on the details page. You already have all the tools in your toolbox to do this, so let's see the code.

```
8_angular-routes/40-backend/shine/spec/features/customer_search_spec.rb
require 'rails_helper'

feature "Customer Search" do

  # existing setup helper methods, and tests...

  scenario "Search by Email" do
    visit "/customers"

    # Login to get access to /customers
    fill_in "Email",    with: email
    fill_in "Password", with: password
    click_button "Log in"

    within "section.search-form" do
      fill_in "keywords", with: "pat123@somewhere.net"
    end
    within "section.search-results" do
      expect(page).to have_content("Results")
      expect(page.all("ol li.list-group-item").count).to eq(4)

      list_group_items = page.all("ol li.list-group-item")

      expect(list_group_items[0]).to have_content("Pat")
      expect(list_group_items[0]).to have_content("Jones")
      expect(list_group_items[1]).to have_content("Patricia")
```

```
        expect(list_group_items[1]).to have_content("Dobbs")
        expect(list_group_items[3]).to have_content("I.T.")
        expect(list_group_items[3]).to have_content("Pat")
      end
➤     click_on "View Details...", match: :first
➤
➤     customer = Customer.find_by!(email: "pat123@somewhere.net")
➤     within "section.customer-details" do
➤       expect(page).to have_content(customer.id)
➤       expect(page).to have_content(customer.first_name)
➤       expect(page).to have_content(customer.last_name)
➤       expect(page).to have_content(customer.email)
➤       expect(page).to have_content(customer.username)
➤     end
    end
  end
```

When using click_on, Capybara throws an exception if there is more than one match. In our case, that will definitely be true, so we use match: :first to tell Capybara to click on the first button it finds. Because we did an email-based search, you know that the first result is the customer with the email pat123@somewhere.net, so after we click the button, we'll find that customer in our database.

To wait for the page to reload, we'll use within as we did before. This is why we used a section element earlier—it's something we can configure to only appear once we have our results. Finally, we'll assert that the customer's various bits of data are somewhere on the screen.

Running this, it will fail, but this is expected since we're doing TDD.

```
> bin/rails spec SPEC=spec/features/customer_search_spec.rb
```

《Irrelevant output》

```
Failures:

  1) Customer Search Search by Email
     Failure/Error: expect(page).to have_content(customer.first_name)
       expected to find text "Pat" in "Customer Details 5"
     # ./spec/features/customer_search_spec.rb:115:in `block (3 leve…
     # ./spec/features/customer_search_spec.rb:113:in `block (2 leve…

Top 2 slowest examples (5.29 seconds, 97.7% of total time):
  Customer Search Search by Email
    2.74 seconds ./spec/features/customer_search_spec.rb:85
  Customer Search Search by Name
    2.55 seconds ./spec/features/customer_search_spec.rb:59

Finished in 5.41 seconds (files took 2.57 seconds to load)
2 examples, 1 failure
```

```
Failed examples:

rspec ./spec/features/customer_search_spec.rb:85 # Customer Search S…
```

When this passes, we'll know we've completed our task. Let's next write a unit test for ngOnInit, since that's doing all the hard work to make this feature happen.

Unit Test for ngOnInit

You should already know how to write this test, but there's a few gotchas that are hard to track down, related to the mocking you'll need to do. But first, we'll create spec/javascript/CustomerDetailsComponent.spec.js in a similar fashion to our existing unit test in spec/javascript/CustomerSearchComponent.spec.js:

```
import "./SpecHelper";
import { CustomerDetailsComponent } from "CustomerDetailsComponent";
import td from "testdouble/dist/testdouble";

var component = null;

describe("CustomerDetailsComponentComponent", function() {
  describe("initial state", function() {
    beforeEach(function() {
      component = new CustomerDetailsComponent();
    });
    it("sets customer to null", function() {
      expect(component.customer).toBe(null);
    });
  });

  describe("ngOnInit", function() {

    // ...

  });
});
```

This is the same boilerplate you've seen before, plus a basic test of our constructor (namely, that it sets its customer property to null). Next, let's create the shell of our test for ngOnInit. The contract of ngOnInit is to set the property customer to an object it receives from the back end. Let's assume two helper functions exist called createMockHttp and createMockRoute, which will provide the test doubles we can provide to CustomerDetailsComponent's constructor.

The basics of the test look like so:

```
8_angular-routes/40-backend/shine/spec/javascript/CustomerDetailsComponent.spec.js
describe("ngOnInit", function() {

  // ...

  var customer = {
```

```
  id: 1,
  created_at: (new Date()).toString(),
  first_name: "Pat",
  last_name: "Jones",
  username: "pj",
  email: "pjones@somewhere.net"
}

// more setup to come...

beforeEach(function() {
  var route = createMockRoute(customer.id);
  var http  = createMockHttp(customer);

  component = new CustomerDetailsComponent(route,http);
});

it("fetches the customer from the back-end", function() {
  component.ngOnInit();
  expect(component.customer).toBe(customer);
});
});
```

The implementation of createMockHttp will look more or less the same as our mocking setup in spec/javascript/CustomerSearchComponent.spec.js:

8_angular-routes/40-backend/shine/spec/javascript/CustomerDetailsComponent.spec.js
```
var createMockHttp = function(customer) {
  var response = td.object(["json"]);
  td.when(response.json()).thenReturn({ customer: customer });

  var observable = td.object(["subscribe"]);
  td.when(observable.subscribe(
    td.callback(response),
    td.matchers.isA(Function))).thenReturn();

  var mockHttp = td.object(["get"]);

  td.when(
    mockHttp.get("/customers/" + customer.id + ".json")
  ).thenReturn(observable);

  return mockHttp;
}
```

You could certainly generalize this and extract so both tests could use it, but I'll leave that as an exercise for you to do on your own.

Finally, we need to implement createMockRoute. Our code accesses the params key on the ActivatedRoute, and is expecting the value to be an observable. So, createMockRoute will return a simple object with a params key that maps to a test double observable that we can set up in a similar fashion to how we set it up for mocking Http.

Ultimately, we want our callback to subscribe to be given an object that maps id to the customer's ID.

8_angular-routes/40-backend/shine/spec/javascript/CustomerDetailsComponent.spec.js
```
var createMockRoute = function(id) {
  var observable  = td.object(["subscribe"]);
  var routeParams = { "id" : id };
  var mockActivatedRoute = { "params": observable };

  td.when(observable.subscribe(
    td.callback(routeParams),
    td.matchers.isA(Function)
  )).thenReturn();

  return mockActivatedRoute;
}
```

When you run the tests, you should see a failure, which, again, is expected, since we haven't written the code yet:

```
> bin/rails karma
```

≪Lots of output≫

```
Phantom.JS 2.1.1 (Mac OS X 0.0.0) CustomerDetailsComponentComponent ini…
        Expected undefined to be null.
        ZoneAwareError@CustomerDetailsComponent.spec.js:29210:28
        CustomerDetailsComponent.spec.js:55488:38
        loaded@http://localhost:9876/context.js:151:17
PhantomJS 2.1.1 (Mac OS X 0.0.0) CustomerDetailsComponentComponent ngO…
        Expected undefined to be Object({ id: 1, created_at: 'Wed Mar 29 201…
        ZoneAwareError@CustomerDetailsComponent.spec.js:29210:28
        CustomerDetailsComponent.spec.js:55548:38
        loaded@http://localhost:9876/context.js:151:17
ALERT: 'There was an error!'
ALERT: 'There was an error!'
PhantomJS 2.1.1 (Mac OS X 0.0.0): Executed 12 of 12 (2 FAILED) (0.011 s…
```

≪Huge stack trace≫

Your output might not be exact, but it *is* important that your failures are the right ones. You want your test to fail at your test expectations. For the first test, we want to see a failure because customer *hasn't* been set to null. For the second test, we want it to fail because customer hasn't been set to the test customer we arranged Http.get to return.

Now that we've specified both the behavior of CustomerDetailsComponent as well as the behavior of Shine as a whole, let's write the code to finish our feature and make these tests pass.

Make Our Tests Pass by Implementing the Back-End Integration

We'll start with CustomerDetailsComponent. Let's tackle the easy issue first and make our constructor test pass. We'll set customer to null as expected by the test:

```
var CustomerDetailsComponent = Component({
  selector: "shine-customer-details",
  template: template
}).Class({
  constructor: [
    ActivatedRoute,
    function(activatedRoute) {
      this.activatedRoute = activatedRoute;
      this.id            = null;
      this.customer      = null;
    }
  ],
```

If you rerun the tests, you should see that the first one is now passing.

Next, we'll change ngOnInit to perform the HTTP request to get the customer's details. First, we'll need to require http and inject an instance of Http into our component:

```
8_angular-routes/40-backend/shine/app/javascript/CustomerDetailsComponent/index.ts
import { Component }       from "@angular/core";
import { ActivatedRoute } from "@angular/router";
import { Http }           from "@angular/http";
import    template         from "./template.html";

var CustomerDetailsComponent = Component({
  selector: "shine-customer-details",
  template: template
}).Class({
  constructor: [
    ActivatedRoute,
    Http,
    function(activatedRoute,http) {
      this.activatedRoute = activatedRoute;
      this.http          = http;
      this.id            = null;
      this.customer      = null;
    }
  ],
```

Now, we can use http to make our request of the server. This will look similar to how you fetched search results in *Get Data from the Back End*, on page 81, but we'll put this code inside the callback related to the route parameters. Because callbacks within callbacks are quite messy, let's pull everything into local functions. We'll start by holding a reference to this in self (which should be there already), and then defining a generic error handling function to pass in as our error handler:

8_angular-routes/40-backend/shine/app/javascript/CustomerDetailsComponent/index.ts

```
ngOnInit: function() {
  var self = this;
➤  var observableFailed = function(response) {
➤    alert(response);
➤  }

  // more to come...

},
```

Next, we'll define customerGetSuccess as the callback that will receive the response from the back end, and routeSuccess as the callback that will be called with the route parameters:

8_angular-routes/40-backend/shine/app/javascript/CustomerDetailsComponent/index.ts

```
➤ var customerGetSucces = function(response) {
➤   self.customer = response.json().customer;
➤ }
➤ var routeSuccess = function(params) {
➤   self.http.get(
➤     "/customers/" + params["id"] + ".json"
➤   ).subscribe(
➤     customerGetSucces,
➤     observableFailed
➤   );
➤ }
```

Finally, we'll make our call to activatedRoute.params.subscribe:

```
self.activatedRoute.params.subscribe(routeSuccess);
```

Running our JavaScript tests will *still* show a failure, however. It's as if our mock observable callback isn't being called. If you were to pepper your code with calls to console.log or debug into your code, you'd see it's true—our callback isn't being called.

If you look closely at our test, we're telling Testdouble.js that subscribe is expecting two arguments: both functions. If you look at our actual code, we're only passing one argument to subscribe. Testdouble.js notices this and assumes we don't want *this* call to subscribe mocked. Oops!

I'm pointing this out as it's a subtle failure on our part, and hard to track down (it took me over an hour to figure this out when I was first writing this example). It's fixed by passing our observableFailed function as the second argument:

8_angular-routes/40-backend/shine/app/javascript/CustomerDetailsComponent/index.ts

```
➤ self.activatedRoute.params.subscribe(routeSuccess,observableFailed);
```

The complete ngOnInit function now looks like so:

8_angular-routes/40-backend/shine/app/javascript/CustomerDetailsComponent/index.ts
```
ngOnInit: function() {
  var self = this;
➤ var observableFailed = function(response) {
➤   alert(response);
➤ }

➤ var customerGetSucces = function(response) {
➤   self.customer = response.json().customer;
➤ }
➤ var routeSuccess = function(params) {
➤   self.http.get(
➤     "/customers/" + params["id"] + ".json"
➤   ).subscribe(
➤     customerGetSucces,
➤     observableFailed
➤   );
➤ }
➤ self.activatedRoute.params.subscribe(routeSuccess,observableFailed);
},
```

And now, our JavaScript tests should pass:

```
> bin/rails karma
```

«Lots of output»

```
PhantomJS 2.1.1 (Mac OS X 0.0.0):
  Executed 12 of 12 SUCCESS (0.008 secs / 0.023 secs)
```

If you rerun the acceptance test, it's still failing, but in a different way:

```
> bin/rails spec SPEC=spec/features/customer_search_spec.rb
```

```
Randomized with seed 42474
```

```
Customer Search
http://localhost:3808/webpack-dev-server/
webpack result is served from //localhost:3808/webpack/
content is served from /Users/davec/Projects/rails-book/shine
Angular is running in the development mode. Call enablePro…
  Search by Email (FAILED - 1)
Angular is running in the development mode. Call enablePro…
  Search by Name
Killing webpack-dev-server
```

```
Failures:

  1) Customer Search Search by Email
 Failure/Error: raise ActionController::RoutingError,
  "No route matches [#{env['REQUEST_METHOD']}] #{env['PATH_INFO'].inspect}"

     ActionController::RoutingError:
       No route matches [GET] "/customers/5.json"
```

≪giant stack trace≫

Failed examples:

```
rspec ./spec/features/customer_search_spec.rb:71
```

Because our code is now getting far enough to hit Rails, Rails is returning a 404, since there is no endpoint yet to find a customer. You can add it with a few lines of code.

First, add :show as an allowed action for our customers resource in config/routes.rb:

```
8_angular-routes/40-backend/shine/config/routes.rb
Rails.application.routes.draw do
  devise_for :users
  root to: "dashboard#index"
  # These supercede other /customers routes, so must
  # come before resource :customers
  get "customers/ng",                 to: "customers#ng"
  get "customers/ng/*angular_route", to: "customers#ng"
➤ resources :customers, only: [ :index, :show ]
➤   #                                     ^^^^^
end
```

Next, add a few lines of code to CustomersController to implement show and return the customer being requested:

```
8_angular-routes/40-backend/shine/app/controllers/customers_controller.rb
class CustomersController < ApplicationController

  # Existing controller code...

➤ def show
➤   customer = Customer.find(params[:id])
➤   respond_to do |format|
➤     format.json { render json: { customer: customer } }
➤   end
➤ end
end
```

If you rerun the tests now, they still fail, but we get a new failure about missing content:

```
> bin/rails spec SPEC=spec/features/customer_search_spec.rb
```

≪output≫

```
Failures:

  1) Customer Search Search by Email
     Failure/Error: expect(page).to have_content(customer.id)
       expected to find text "5" in "Customer Details"
```

≪stack trace≫

Failed examples:

```
rspec ./spec/features/customer_search_spec.rb:71 # Customer Search Search by Email
```

To fix this, we'll create a simple view that shows the content we're expecting in app/javascript/CustomerDetailsComponent/template.html:

```
8_angular-routes/40-backend/shine/app/javascript/CustomerDetailsComponent/template.html
<section class="customer-details" *ngIf="customer">
  <h1>Customer {{customer.id}}</h1>
  <h2>{{customer.first_name}} {{customer.last_name}}</h2>
  <h3>{{customer.email}}</h3>
  <h4>{{customer.username}}</h4>
  <h5>
    <small class="text-uppercase">Joined</small>
    {{customer.created_at}}
  </h5>
</section>
```

Note the use of *ngIf on customer. This is how our acceptance test can successfully wait for the page to be rendered. Angular won't even show the section tag until customer has a value, so the within we're using will wait for it to appear. This prevents you from having flaky tests. We've also put the content in the appropriate h tags based on its importance. Now when we run our acceptance test, it passes!

```
> bin/rails spec SPEC=spec/features/customer_search_spec.rb

Randomized with seed 11944

Customer Search
http://localhost:3808/webpack-dev-server/
webpack result is served from //localhost:3808/webpack/
content is served from /Users/davec/Projects/rails-book/shine
  Search by Name
  Search by Email
Killing webpack-dev-server

Finished in 6.81 seconds (files took 1.89 seconds to load)
2 examples, 0 failures

Randomized with seed 11944
```

More important, when you try it in the browser, everything works great, as shown in the following screen.

Customer 6

Patricia Boehm

beryl_weinat99@wolf.io

celestine_jacobson99

JOINED 2017-05-28T22:24:36.891Z

We've now turned our simple search into a small single-page application using Angular. You learned how to configure Angular's routing as well as a better way to manage your HTML templates. You also got a realistic view of how you can use TDD to drive out our features.

Next: Design Using Grids

The power we've just gained in using Angular is great, but our customer details view isn't that useful. It's now time to focus again on Bootstrap and use its *grid* in order to design a better details view. Grid-based design, and Bootstrap's implementation of it, will unlock your inner web designer and give you the ability to mock up, design, and implement a complex user interface without writing any CSS.

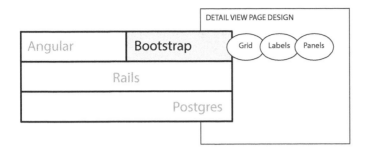

## CHAPTER 9

Design Great UIs with
Bootstrap's Grid and Components

At the start of Chapter 8, *Create a Single-Page App*, on page 127, you saw a mock-up of the customer detail view. We're going to build this page now to learn about the true power of Bootstrap—its grid. We'll also examine some of Bootstrap's many components, which will allow us to create a polished and visually appealing user interface.

We'll tackle this topic in three parts. First, I provide some background on grid-based design. This will help you understand why Bootstrap is based on a grid, and how you can break down any UI into grids to make your work easier. Next, you'll lay out the customer detail screen I hinted at in the previous chapter, using Bootstrap's grid to make it easy. Finally, you'll use various Bootstrap components, such as panels and labels, to polish up our UI. By the end of the chapter you'll have a solid foundation in building user interfaces with Bootstrap, and even a bit of confidence in designing them yourself. You'll still be a far cry from being a "real" web designer, but you'll be able to do common, simple tasks on your own.

You saw the mock-up in the previous chapter, but here it is again, in a slightly expanded form, so you know where we're headed:

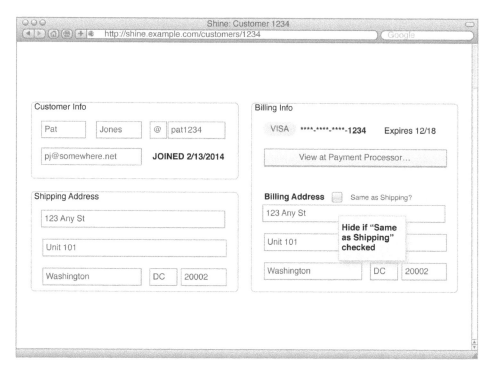

Now, let's learn about the grid and how it helps create user interfaces.

The Grid: The Cornerstone of a Web Design

I don't know about you, but looking at a complex layout like the one we're going to build gives me a bit of anxiety. It's not just that CSS can be difficult to use, but it's also not immediately clear how to wrangle all the parts of this design.

Like functional decomposition in programming, a *grid* is how you can break down a user interface into smaller parts. You can focus on each part of the design, and rely on the grid to keep everything looking visually cohesive.

A grid is more or less what it sounds like—a means of aligning elements along a fixed horizontal and/or vertical axis. You might not have realized it, but you've been using a grid already. By just using Bootstrap's default styles and form classes, the forms we created in Chapter 2, *Create a Great-Looking Login with Bootstrap and Devise*, on page 15 (as well as the search results from Chapter 5, *Create Clean Search Results*, on page 55) use a *horizontal grid*. This means that each row of information is spaced in a particular way to make the text and other elements pleasing and orderly.

For the view here, we need a vertical grid, which allows us to place content into side-by-side columns. This is how we'll achieve most of the layout we want. Bootstrap provides a set of CSS classes that allow us to create a grid. Under the covers, it uses CSS floats, which can get messy quickly, but Bootstrap's grid abstracts that away.

Bootstrap's grid has 12 columns. You can combine columns in any way you like to make larger columns, without disrupting the flow and spacing of the grid. For example, you could have a two-column layout where the first column is 25% of the entire width, leaving the remaining 75% for the second column, or you could have three columns of equal size, each taking 33% of the available width.

If you think about your design in terms of rows and columns, you can start to see the grids pop out of our design. Take a look at the following figure.

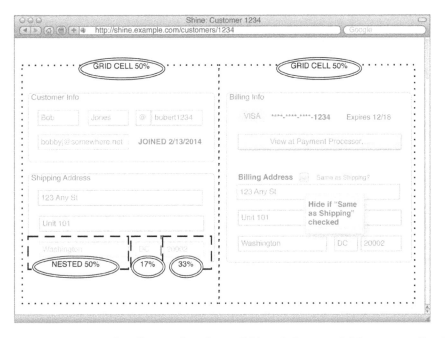

You can see two grid cells, each taking 50% of the available space, for the main columns of our design, but you can also see a grid nested in each form. The city/state/zip part of the shipping address could be thought of as a grid where the city takes 50% (six grid cells), the state takes 17% (or two grid cells), and the zip code takes the remaining 33% (or four grid cells).

What this means is that, if we have sufficiently generic CSS classes that allow us to place content into grid cells, and to place those cells into rows, and to nest grids within each other, all with proper padding, spacing, and margins, we can break up any design into a series of grids.

This is exactly what Bootstrap's grid system will do.

Using Bootstrap's Grid

Bootstrap's grid is quite powerful, especially if you've never used one before. In this section, we'll build the layout for our view using Bootstrap's grid. As we saw in the previous section, our layout starts with two equal-sized grid cells: one that holds the customer information and shipping address, and the other that holds the billing information.

First, we'll create these cells, which will demonstrate the various CSS classes needed to enable Bootstrap's grid. Then, we'll see how the grid can nest within itself to lay out the customer information and shipping address as a grid-within-a-grid.

Lay Out the Two Main Columns

The most obvious grid in our design is one that holds the two main columns, each taking half the available space. To do this, we'll create two nested div tags inside a parent div, giving each the appropriate CSS class—provided by Bootstrap—to lay it all out in a grid (see on page 159 for some details on why we're using divs).

The outer div has the class row, which tells Bootstrap we're going to place columns inside it. The divs inside the row have class col-md-*X*, where *X* is the number of columns, out of 12, that this particular column should take up. Because we want two equal-sized columns, we want each of *our* columns to take up six of Bootstrap's. Thus, each div will get the class col-md-6 (see Chapter 13, *Dig Deeper*, on page 249 for what the -md- means).

We can add this markup to app/javascript/CustomerDetailsComponent/template.html, replacing the bare-bones markup we had there from the last section.

```html
<section class="customer-details" *ngIf="customer">
<form><div class="row">
  <div class="col-md-6">
    <h1>Customer</h1>
  </div>
  <div class="col-md-6">
    <h1>Billing Info</h1>
  </div>
</div></form>
</section>
```

Why Do We Sometimes Use div and Sometimes Not?

Before HTML5, there weren't a lot of standard elements you could use to describe your content. As a result, the div element came into favor as the way to organize content, particularly for targeting by CSS styling. With the advent of HTML5, more meaningful elements are available, such as article, section, header, and footer.

Because of this, the W3C recommends that div be used only as a last resort,[a] when no other elements are available.

What this means is that you want to use the right tags when describing your content, regardless of the visualization you are going for. You can then use div tags to achieve the layouts you want. Because div is semantically meaningless, it allows anyone reading your view templates to see clearly what parts of the view are for styling and layout and what parts are for organizing the content.

So, the general rule of thumb is to use divs in cases where you need an element to style against, and *not* as a way to describe content.

---

a.   http://www.w3.org/TR/html5/grouping-content.html#the-div-element

If you bring this up in your browser, you'll see that our two headings are shown side by side:

Customer	Billing Info

Now, let's tackle the content *inside* these columns. As we saw earlier, we can think of each section of our page as having a nested grid inside this one. Bootstrap's grid works exactly this way.

Build Forms Using a Grid-Within-a-Grid

Bootstrap's grid is not a fixed width, so whenever you write <div class="row">, Bootstrap will divide up the grid in that row based on the available space. This is a powerful feature of the grid system. Much like how we decompose complex objects into smaller ones to make our code easier to understand, we can decompose larger views into smaller ones using the grid.

By thinking of each page's component as a grid, we can design that component without worrying about where it is on the page. Bootstrap's grid components will make sure it works.

Let's style the customer information section using the grid. We can see from our mock-up that we have three rows, and the first row has three columns. Since the second and third rows just have one column that takes up the entire row, we don't need to use the grid markup for them. So, we just need to create a grid for the first row.

We'll be using the form classes we saw in Chapter 2, *Create a Great-Looking Login with Bootstrap and Devise*, on page 15, so hopefully this will look familiar. The first name, last name, and username are all about the same size data-wise, so we can create three equal-sized columns for them. Because Bootstrap's grid is 12 columns, we want each of our columns to take up four of Bootstrap's columns, so we'll use the class col-md-4 on each div.

```
<section class="customer-details" *ngIf="customer">
<form><div class="row">
  <div class="col-md-6">
    <h1>Customer</h1>
    <div class="row">
      <div class="col-md-4">
        <div class="form-group">
          <label class="sr-only" for="first-name">First Name</label>
          <input type="text" class="form-control"
                 name="first-name" value="Bob">
        </div>
      </div>
      <div class="col-md-4">
        <div class="form-group">
          <label class="sr-only" for="last-name">Last Name</label>
          <input type="text" class="form-control"
                 name="last-name" value="Jones">
        </div>
      </div>
      <div class="col-md-4">
        <div class="form-group">
          <label class="sr-only" for="username">Username</label>
          <input type="text" class="form-control"
                 name="username" value="bobert123">
        </div>
      </div>
    </div>
    <div class="form-group">
      <label class="sr-only" for="email">Email</label>
      <input type="text" class="form-control"
             name="email" value="bobbyj@somewhere.net">
    </div>
    <label for="joined">Joined</label> 12/13/2014
    <h2>Shipping Address</h2>
```

Note that we used form-group on a different element as col-md-4. This isn't technically required but is commonly done to separate concerns. Generally, you want classes used for your grid to be separate from classes used for styling so that you can be sure your grid doesn't get messed up by styling classes.

Also, we can add more styling later without worrying about how the grid will affect it. Take a look at what we've done in our browser (see the following figure), and you can see that it looks pretty good!

Customer	Billing Info

Pat   Jones   pat123

pattyj@somewhere.net

Joined 12/13/2014

Shipping Address

Up to now, we've created grid cells that are all the same size. Let's lay out the shipping address part of our page, which requires that some of the grid cells be larger than others.

Use Grid Cells of Different Sizes

The main columns of our view, as well as the user information, all used grid cells of the same size. That won't work for the address views, since the city, state, and zip code are all different sizes. It also won't work for the credit card information view, because the card number and type can be quite long, but we still need room for the button that will (eventually) take the user to the payment processor's page for the customer's card.

In this section, we'll style both of these views using different grid sizes. The result will be a cohesive, well-laid-out page, even though the grid cells aren't the same size.

First, we'll start with the addresses.

Laying Out the Addresses

In a typical U.S. address, the state code is short—two characters—and the zip code is typically five or nine characters. So, let's make a column for the city—which is usually longer—that takes up half the available space. In the remaining half, we'll give the zip code two-thirds of the remaining space, leaving the last third for the state code.

That works out to six columns for the city, two for the state code (since 6 ÷ 3 is 2), and the remaining four for the zip code (the two street address lines can use up an entire row each, so we don't need the grid markup for them).

```
<h2>Shipping Address</h2>
<div class="form-group">
  <label class="sr-only" for="street-address">
    Street Address
```

```
    </label>
    <input type="text" class="form-control"
           name="street-address" value="123 Any St">
  </div>
  <div class="form-group">
    <label class="sr-only" for="street-address-extra">
      Street Address Extra
    </label>
    <input type="text" class="form-control"
           name="street-address-extra" value="Unit 101">
  </div>
➤ <div class="row">
➤   <div class="col-md-6">
      <div class="form-group">
        <label class="sr-only" for="city">City</label>
        <input type="text" class="form-control"
               name="city" value="Washington">
      </div>
    </div>
➤   <div class="col-md-2">
      <div class="form-group">
        <label class="sr-only" for="state">State</label>
        <input type="text" class="form-control"
               name="state" value="DC">
      </div>
    </div>
➤   <div class="col-md-4">
      <div class="form-group">
        <label class="sr-only" for="zip">Zip</label>
        <input type="text" class="form-control"
               name="zip" value="20001">
      </div>
    </div>
  </div>
```

You can repeat this markup for the billing address, which just leaves us the credit card information section to style.

Laying Out the Credit Card Info

The credit card area has two distinct parts: the card information itself, and the button that will link the user to the payment processor's page for that card. We'll give the card information seven of the twelve columns, and use the remaining five for the button (these values might seem somewhat magic, and they were arrived at experimentally—feel free to change them and see how it affects the layout, making sure everything in the row adds up to 12).

```
<div class="col-md-6">
  <h2>Billing Info</h2>
➤ <div class="row">
```

```
➤    <div class="col-md-7">
       <p>
         ****-****-****-1234
         VISA
       </p>
       <p>
         <label>Expires:</label> 04/19
       </p>
     </div>
➤    <div class="col-md-5 text-right">
       <button class="btn btn-lg btn-default">
         View Details…
       </button>
     </div>
   </div>
 </div>
 <h3>Billing Address <input type="checkbox"> Same as shipping?  </h3>
   <!-- Same markup as used for the shipping address -->
```

Note that we've used the helper class text-right on the button so that it aligns to the right side of the grid, and thus stands apart from the card info. Previously, we used pull-right to achieve this in our search results. Thinking back now, you might have more success using a grid for each result, rather than using floats. Fortunately, it's easy enough to try on your own!

Now that we've placed everything in a grid, you can see in the following figure that the page is really starting to come together.

Bootstrap's grid is probably its single most useful feature. Before I knew about grids as design tools, and before I'd used one like Bootstrap's for creating them in CSS, a design like this would've taken me a long time to create. Depending on the time pressure I was under, I might've opted for a different, less optimal design that was easier to build, simply because my ability to create the right view was hampered by my lack of knowledge and lack of tools.

Now that the layout is solid, let's go through our view and polish up a few of the rough edges.

Adding Polish with Bootstrap Components

Our view looks pretty good—certainly better than what we might achieve in the same amount of time without Bootstrap—but it could be better. For example, the header text is a bit too large, no clear distinction exists between the three sections of the view, and the credit card information is a bit jumbled, since all the text uses the same size and weight font.

We'd like to distinguish parts of the view to make it easier for the user to visually navigate. If you look through Bootstrap's documentation, you can get some inspiration as to how we can do this. The trick with complex forms is to allow users to navigate all the data with their eyes. We can get a long way with the *panel* component, which is a box surrounding our content along with a header and footer.

Use Panels

A panel looks like so:

It can be created with Bootstrap with markup like this:

```
<article class="panel panel-primary">
<header class="panel-heading">
  <h1>Panel Header</h1>
</header>
<section class="panel-body">
  Body of the panel
</section>
<footer class="panel-footer">
  Panel Footer
</footer>
</article>
```

Let's put each of the three sections of our screen inside its own panel. Panels can be given different styles, so let's make the customer information panel styled differently from the other two so it stands out more clearly. Each panel requires two classes: panel and then a second one that determines its style.

We'll use panel-primary for the customer info, which will use an inverse color scheme for the header, and panel-default for the other two. Finally, we'll move the *joined* field inside the customer panel's footer. As we'll see, this value won't be editable by the user, so moving it to the footer will reinforce this fact.

As shown in the following screen, the result looks pretty nice.

Customer

| Pat | Jones | @ | pat123 |

pattyj@somewhere.net

Joined 12/13/2014

Shipping Address

123 Any St

Unit 101

| Washington | DC | 20001 |

Billing Info

****-****-****-1234 VISA   View Details...
Expires: 04/19

Billing Address ⌐ Same as shipping?

123 Any St

Unit 101

| Washington | DC | 20001 |

Next, let's improve the credit card information section. If we could have the card type more distinct from the card number and expiration, that would help users quickly distinguish this information. We can do that using *labels*.

Highlight Information with Labels

A *label* is a Bootstrap component that renders text inside a colored box with an inverse color scheme (not to be confused with the HTML element label, which is used to label fields in a form). In lieu of finding and downloading images for each credit card type, we can put the credit card type inside a label, and it'll stand out.

Labels, like panels, take two classes: a label class, and a decorative one that controls the color. We'll use label-success, which will create a green label.

```
<div class="col-md-7">
<p>
  ****-****-****-1234
➤  <span class="label label-success">VISA</span>
</p>
<p>
  <label>Expires:</label> 04/19
</p>
</div>
```

With just this markup, the credit card type stands out pretty well:

Last, we'll make a few adjustments to the typography—the headers are a bit too large.

Use h Classes to Tame Typography

The headers in our view are all a bit too large, and although our markup is semantically correct, some subheadings are larger than others. Further, the masked credit card number is a bit too small.

You can use the h classes provided by Bootstrap to manage the size of our headings (it may seem strange, but these classes allow us to keep the semantically correct element without inheriting their visual size). You can also use them on the p tag surrounding the credit card number to make it stand out a bit.

You'll see the entire markup in a moment, but here's an example of what I'm talking about:

```
<article class="panel panel-default">
<header class="panel-heading">
   <h2 class="h4">
      Billing Info
   </h2>
</header>
<!-- ... -->
         <p class="h4">
         ****-****-****-1234
         <span class="label label-success">VISA</span>
         </p>
```

This sort of thing is more art than science, so the values I've chosen here represent what looks right to me. The great thing about Bootstrap is that it's easy to play around with this stuff, and whatever you do will end up looking pretty decent, thanks to the horizontal grid that underlies all of the type.

One last bit of polish I'd like to add is to distinguish the username from the first and last names in the Customer Information section. As you'll notice on our mock-up, the username was preceded with an @ symbol. Bootstrap makes this easy using *form add-ons*.

Form Add-Ons

Often, a symbol prepended (or appended) to a value can give it enough context for users to understand what it means, without using a label. This can be handy on dense pages like our customer detail view. Because the first row of the customer information section is just three equal-sized strings, it might not be clear what they mean.

If we prepend the username with @ (similar to what Twitter does for mentioning someone in a tweet), that can be enough context for users to know that the third field is the username, and the first two are the first and last names, respectively.

Bootstrap provides the class input-group-addon that will do this in a pleasing way. We just surround the form element with an input-group and create an inner div with the class input-group-addon that contains the text we'd like prepended (you can place that div after the element to append it instead).

```
<div class="input-group">
  <div class="input-group-addon">@</div>
  <input type="text" class="form-control"
         name="username" value="bobert123">
</div>
```

With all of these tweaks in place, the rendered form looks polished and professional (as shown in the screen that follows), embodying the spirit of the mock-up.

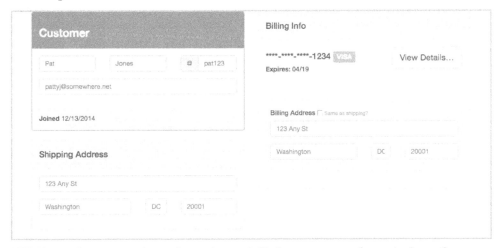

HTML markup is quite verbose (especially because you have to heavily wrap it to fit the margins in this book), so you've only seen bits and pieces. The entire screen's markup can be seen in Appendix 1, *Full Listing of Customer Detail Page HTML*, on page 279, although it will be easier to examine it by downloading the sample code.[1]

Note that you *still* haven't written any CSS. We were able to create a highly complex form that displays a lot of data in a clean and easy-to-read way, using just a few simple classes, coupled with Bootstrap's grid system.

---

1. https://pragprog.com/titles/dcbang2/source_code

In this chapter, you saw several new features of Bootstrap, notably its grid system, but also some UI components that allowed us to polish our UI quickly and easily. What you should take away from this is what I mentioned at the start of the section: these are tools that allow you to design and build in the browser.

This eliminates much of the friction in getting started on a new user interface. Armed with just Bootstrap, you can create complex interfaces quickly, and iterate on them as you find the most optimal design.

Next: Populating the View Easily and Efficiently

This chapter focused on the top of the stack: the view. You learned how to configure our Angular app to allow for routing to different views, backed by different controllers. You saw how easy it is to design a complex UI for our customer detail view.

In the next chapter, you'll learn how to bring the actual data into the UI we've created. We'll use a feature of Postgres called *materialized views* to make querying the data from Rails quite easy. You'll also see how Angular's asynchronous nature allows us to easily implement our UI using data from our database as well as from our third-party payment processor's system.

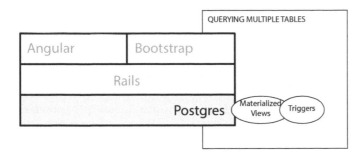

CHAPTER 10

Cache Complex Queries
Using Materialized Views

When you need to query data stored in several tables, there is a trade-off. Either you keep the code simple by using Active Record—which makes several queries to the database—or you make the code more complex by using a single, efficient query specific to your needs. Performance is an issue in both cases because you're pulling back a lot of data. Postgres solves this dilemma with its *materialized views* feature, which provides clean code, accesses data with a single query, and exhibits high performance.

In this chapter, we'll continue to build on our running example where we display a customer's details. To do this, we need to fetch data from five different tables. You'll see how the idiomatic *Rails Way*, using Active Record, actually results in our having to make seven queries to the database. In contrast, a single, more direct query results in convoluted code but with potentially better performance.

We'll then create a materialized view of our single query. A materialized view is part view and part table. Like a view, it's backed by a query that is the source of its data. Like a table, the data is stored on disk. The materialized view provides a way to update the data on disk by rerunning the backing query. This means you get to use Active Record in our Rails code in an idiomatic way but still get extremely high performance: the best of both worlds! You'll also see how we can use *database triggers* to automatically keep the view up-to-date.

First, let's look at the performance characteristics of the two approaches—Active Record versus using a single, more complex query—by learning about the tables we need to access.

Understanding the Performance Impact of Complex Data

In Chapter 9, *Design Great UIs with*, on page 155, you built the user interface for the data we'll be querying here. In addition to the data you've already seen in the CUSTOMERS table, we need to display the customer's billing address, shipping address, and credit card information. The credit card information is stored elsewhere (we'll deal with that in the next chapter), so we're just querying the customer's billing and shipping addresses for now.

You've already seen the CUSTOMERS table, and you know it doesn't include either of these pieces of data. As you'll recall from Chapter 4, *Perform Fast Queries with*, on page 37, our hypothetical company has tables in a shared database, which Shine can access. In this case, we'll assume that the tables we need to access billing and shipping addresses are also available to us via the shared database.

Let's look at how well both Active Record and a single query perform when accessing all of these tables together. We start with the structure so we know what we're dealing with.

The Tables We'll Query

The diagram on page 171 shows the tables we'll be accessing and their relationships to one another.

In our hypothetical system, all addresses are stored in the table ADDRESSES. This table contains fields you'd expect in a U.S.-style address, except for the postal codes for U.S. states. The states are stored in STATES, and ADDRESSES references that table via the column state_id (marked "1" on the diagram).

Because all addresses are stored in ADDRESSES, we need to know which of those are for billing and which are for shipping. To determine that, we have two join tables called CUSTOMERS_BILLING_ADDRESSES and CUSTOMERS_SHIPPING_ADDRESSES.

In the diagram, you can see that the relationship marked "2" references a customer via customer_id, while the relationship marked "3" references an address via address_id. This is how you join the two tables together.

CUSTOMERS_SHIPPING_ADDRESSES uses a similar structure, with the relationships marked "4" and "5." You'll notice, however, that there's a column called primary. This is because, in our hypothetical system, a customer may have more than

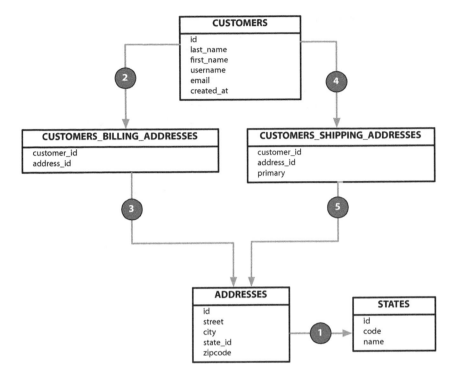

one shipping address. primary denotes their primary shipping address, and this is the one we'll display in Shine.

Just as we did with CUSTOMERS in *Set Up the New Table and Data*, on page 38, we'll set up these new tables for our local development. In the real world, these would already exist, but we have to create them manually here in order to follow this example.

Let's do that and then populate these tables with sample data. First, create an empty migration via rails g migration add_addresses. Next, fill in that file like so:

```
10_materialized-views/10-data-model/shine/db/migrate/20161006115532_add_addresses.rb
class AddAddresses < ActiveRecord::Migration[5.0]
  def change
    create_table :states do |t|
      t.string     :code, size: 2, null: false
      t.string     :name,         null: false
    end
    create_table :addresses do |t|
      t.string     :street,    null: false
      t.string     :city,      null: false
      t.references :state,     null: false
      t.string     :zipcode,   null: false
    end
```

```
  create_table :customers_billing_addresses do |t|
    t.references :customer,      null: false
    t.references :address,       null: false
  end
  create_table :customers_shipping_addresses do |t|
    t.references :customer,      null: false
    t.references :address,       null: false
    t.boolean    :primary,       null: false, default: false
  end
 end
end
```

Finally, run bin/rails db:migrate to create the tables. Although we won't ultimately be using the Active Record models for these tables, let's create them anyway, as it'll make it easier to poke around in the Rails console to evaluate their performance. It will also make it easier to populate some seed data.

To do this, you'll need to create the files state.rb, address.rb, customers_billing_address.rb, and customers_shipping_address.rb in app/models like so:

10_materialized-views/10-data-model/shine/app/models/address.rb
```
class Address < ActiveRecord::Base
  belongs_to :state
end
```

10_materialized-views/10-data-model/shine/app/models/state.rb
```
class State < ActiveRecord::Base
  has_many :addresses
end
```

10_materialized-views/10-data-model/shine/app/models/customers_billing_address.rb
```
class CustomersBillingAddress < ActiveRecord::Base
  belongs_to :address
  belongs_to :customer
end
```

10_materialized-views/10-data-model/shine/app/models/customers_shipping_address.rb
```
class CustomersShippingAddress < ActiveRecord::Base
  belongs_to :address
  belongs_to :customer
end
```

You'll also need to modify app/models/customer.rb to add the Active Record relationships:

10_materialized-views/10-data-model/shine/app/models/customer.rb
```
class Customer < ApplicationRecord
➤  has_many :customers_shipping_address
➤
➤  # Helper to get just the primary shipping address
➤  def primary_shipping_address
```

```
➤       self.customers_shipping_address.find_by(primary: true).address
➤     end
➤     has_one :customers_billing_address
➤     has_one :billing_address, through: :customers_billing_address,
➤                               source: :address
    end
```

If you haven't used some of these features of Active Record (namely has_one :through), the Rails Guide on Active Record associations[1] is a great resource to see what you can do with mapping your database tables to models.

With our database tables and models set up, we'll need some data in the tables in order to examine the performance of our database. The code to do this is quite lengthy, so I recommend you copy db/seeds.rb from 10_materialized-views/10-data-model/shine from the book's webpage.[2] For your reference, the code is also listed in Appendix 2, *Creating Customer Address Seed Data*, on page 283.

Once you have this file in your project, run bin/rails db:seed to populate the data. It will take a long time, but it's worth it. This much data will stress our local database and demonstrate the power of materialized views to fetch data more quickly.

There are two main ways to access this data: you can use the Active Record relationships we've modeled and navigate them in our Ruby code, or you can pull the data back with one big query. Let's examine the performance of each of these approaches.

Performance Using Active Record

We aren't going to use Active Record relationships to access our data in the end, but this is how it might look to send back a JSON blob of the customer's data and relevant addresses:

```
def show
  customer = Customer.find(params[:id])
  respond_to do |format|
    format.json do
      render json: {
                customer: customer,
          shipping_address: customer.shipping_address,
           billing_address: customer.billing_address,
      }
    end
  end
end
```

---

1. http://guides.rubyonrails.org/association_basics.html
2. https://pragprog.com/titles/dcbang2/source_code

This code is going to run seven queries: one to pull back data from CUSTOMERS, one to query CUSTOMERS_BILLING_ADDRESSES, followed by a query to ADDRESSES and STATES. It will then query CUSTOMERS_SHIPPING_ADDRESSES, followed by second queries to ADDRESSES and STATES. Let's use EXPLAIN ANALYZE to see how well these will perform.

Remember to use bin/rails dbconsole to get access to the Postgres console.

```
sql> EXPLAIN ANALYZE SELECT * FROM customers WHERE id = 2000;
QUERY PLAN
----------------------------------------------------------------------
Index Scan using customers_pkey on customers
  (cost=0.42..8.44 rows=1 width=79)
  (actual time=1.575..1.576 rows=1 loops=1)
   Index Cond: (id = 2000)
 Planning time: 0.515 ms
 Execution time: 1.590 ms

sql> EXPLAIN ANALYZE SELECT * FROM customers_billing_addresses
                WHERE customer_id = 2000;
QUERY PLAN
----------------------------------------------------------------------
Index Scan using index_customers_billing_addresses_on_customer_id on
  customers_billing_addresses
  (cost=0.42..8.44 rows=1 width=12)
  (actual time=0.291..0.292 rows=1 loops=1)
   Index Cond: (customer_id = 2000)
 Planning time: 1.744 ms
 Execution time: 0.307 ms

sql> EXPLAIN ANALYZE SELECT * FROM customers_shipping_addresses
                WHERE customer_id = 2000;
QUERY PLAN
----------------------------------------------------------------------
Index Scan using index_customers_shipping_addresses_on_customer_id on
  customers_shipping_addresses
  (cost=0.42..8.48 rows=3 width=13)
  (actual time=0.341..0.343 rows=4 loops=1)
   Index Cond: (customer_id = 2000)
 Planning time: 1.908 ms
 Execution time: 0.357 ms

sql> EXPLAIN ANALYZE SELECT * FROM addresses WHERE id = 2000;
QUERY PLAN
----------------------------------------------------------------------
Index Scan using addresses_pkey on addresses
  (cost=0.43..8.45 rows=1 width=47)
  (actual time=0.101..0.102 rows=1 loops=1)
   Index Cond: (id = 2000)
 Planning time: 0.087 ms
 Execution time: 0.121 ms
```

```
sql> EXPLAIN ANALYZE select * FROM states WHERE id = 5;
QUERY PLAN
------------------------------------------------------------------
 Seq Scan on states
  (cost=0.00..1.64 rows=1 width=16)
  (actual time=0.015..0.018 rows=1 loops=1)
   Filter: (id = 5)
   Rows Removed by Filter: 50
 Planning time: 0.131 ms
 Execution time: 0.034 ms
```

All of these queries perform well, which isn't surprising since they are all querying against the primary key of the tables in question. We can see this by the information Index Scan in the query plan (though, interestingly, the queries against STATES use a full table scan—Seq Scan—presumably because this table is so small, it's faster than using the primary key's index). If we assume the timing reported by our query plans is a reasonable average, this means the total of these seven queries is about 5 milliseconds.

The query time isn't the only time it takes to access this data, however. Each request requires network time, as does each response. This is commonly called the *network round-trip*.

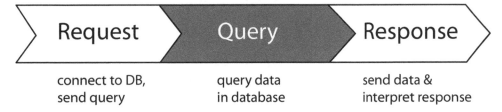

All of these queries perform well, which isn't surprising

We're running seven queries: that's seven network round-trips. A slow network can have a significant impact on our overall response time.

If we could get the data in a single query, our performance would be less tied to the network's performance, and our system would be more predictable (and possibly faster, if our network is habitually slow). Let's craft that query and see how it performs.

Performance Using SQL

To get this data using one query, we'll need to do a lot of joins. Let's build up the query first, and then see how it performs.

Crafting the Query

If you are comfortable with database joins, you can skip this section, but I've found that joins across many tables (especially when you need to join the same table twice, as we will for ADDRESSES) can be tricky, so it might help to see the query built piece by piece.

First, you need to itemize the fields you want back. In our case, we want all the fields from CUSTOMERS that we've been using, all the fields in ADDRESSES for both the billing and the shipping address, and the state codes from STATES for the same. The SELECT part of our query looks like this:

10_materialized-views/10-data-model/shine/db/customer_detail_view.sql
```
SELECT
    customers.id            AS customer_id,
    customers.first_name    AS first_name,
    customers.last_name     AS last_name,
    customers.email         AS email,
    customers.username      AS username,
    customers.created_at    AS joined_at,
    billing_address.id      AS billing_address_id,
    billing_address.street  AS billing_street,
    billing_address.city    AS billing_city,
    billing_state.code      AS billing_state,
    billing_address.zipcode AS billing_zipcode,
    shipping_address.id     AS shipping_address_id,
    shipping_address.street AS shipping_street,
    shipping_address.city   AS shipping_city,
    shipping_state.code     AS shipping_state,
    shipping_address.zipcode AS shipping_zipcode
FROM
    customers
```

Note a few things here. Because all addresses are stored in ADDRESSES, you'll need to join against that table twice (as you'll see). That means you need to know which join you're referencing—the join that brings in the shipping address, or the join that brings in the billing address. To know *that*, you'll be aliasing[3] the ADDRESSES tables in each join to shipping_address and billing_address so you know what you're referring to.

Now that you know the data you're bringing back, you need to add the necessary joins to get it. First, we'll join CUSTOMERS against CUSTOMERS_BILLING_ADDRESSES, because that's how we'll eventually get to the actual address.

10_materialized-views/10-data-model/shine/db/customer_detail_view.sql
```
JOIN customers_billing_addresses  ON
  customers.id = customers_billing_addresses.customer_id
```

Next, we'll join CUSTOMERS_BILLING_ADDRESSES to ADDRESSES. Note that this is where you alias ADDRESSES to billing_address.

---

3.   https://en.wikipedia.org/wiki/Alias_(SQL)

10_materialized-views/10-data-model/shine/db/customer_detail_view.sql
```
JOIN addresses billing_address        ON
  billing_address.id = customers_billing_addresses.address_id
```

Then, we'll need to join ADDRESSES to STATES so you can get the state code.

10_materialized-views/10-data-model/shine/db/customer_detail_view.sql
```
JOIN states billing_state             ON
  billing_address.state_id = billing_state.id
```

Note again that we've had to alias STATES to billing_state.

Finally, we'll repeat this structure for CUSTOMERS_SHIPPING_ADDRESSES, with the addition of restricting by primary in our join.

10_materialized-views/10-data-model/shine/db/customer_detail_view.sql
```
JOIN customers_shipping_addresses ON
  customers.id = customers_shipping_addresses.customer_id
  AND customers_shipping_addresses.primary = true
JOIN addresses shipping_address       ON
  shipping_address.id = customers_shipping_addresses.address_id
JOIN states shipping_state            ON
  shipping_address.state_id = shipping_state.id
```

With our query constructed, let's see how it fares.

Query Performance

You can use EXPLAIN ANALYZE on our query to see what sort of performance we might expect.

```
sql> EXPLAIN ANALYZE SELECT
  customers.id              AS customer_id,
  customers.first_name      AS first_name,
  customers.last_name       AS last_name,
  customers.email           AS email,me,
  customers.username        AS username,
  customers.created_at      AS joined_at,dress_id,
  billing_address.id        AS billing_address_id,
  billing_address.street    AS billing_street,
  billing_address.city      AS billing_city,
  billing_state.code        AS billing_state,
  billing_address.zipcode   AS billing_zipcode,_id,
  shipping_address.id       AS shipping_address_id,
  shipping_address.street   AS shipping_street,
  shipping_address.city     AS shipping_city,
  shipping_state.code       AS shipping_state,
  shipping_address.zipcode  AS shipping_zipcode
FROM
  customers

«remainder of the query»
```

```
WHERE
  customers.id = 2000
;
QUERY PLAN
-------------------------------------------------------------------
 Nested Loop  (cost=1.12..169.81 rows=1 width=157)
              (actual time=0.028..0.028 rows=0 loops=1)
   ->  Nested Loop  (cost=0.98..169.64 rows=1 width=158)
                    (actual time=0.027..0.027 rows=0 loops=1)
«Tons of query plan details omitted»

 Planning time: 24.776 ms
 Execution time: 1.399 ms
```

The planning time is a bit longer, but if you assume this is reasonably representative, at least as compared to the individual queries, it should take less than around 26 milliseconds. This is still pretty fast, but it's certainly slower than all seven queries combined. But this query incurs only one network round-trip. If we assume the network round-trip is 1 millisecond, that means this query will take 27 milliseconds, and our seven queries will take 12 milliseconds.

To me, this means that if there are *other* benefits to the single-query approach, it won't be at the cost of much performance and, if you were experiencing performance issues, reducing these seven queries down to one is an avenue worth pursuing. Let's try to use this in Rails and see what it's like.

A Word on Optimizations

You should absolutely avoid optimizing your system like this until you know that what you are optimizing is actually a problem, based on your observations. The use of EXPLAIN ANALYZE is helpful in explaining poor performance, not in identifying it.

This chapter is about teaching you a technique to deal with poor performance, and is not something you should use by default every time you need to query more than one table. Always measure your system's performance before optimizing it.

Using This Query in Rails

It will be difficult, if not impossible, to use Active Record's API to produce this query. In these cases, it's easier to just use a string of SQL and execute the query. You can do that by using the method execute on the underlying connection object available via the connection method on ActiveRecord::Base.

```
class CustomerDetail
  QUERY = %{
    «The big query from before»
  }

  def self.find(customer_id)
    ActiveRecord::Base.connection.execute(
      QUERY + " WHERE customers.id = #{customer_id}"
    ).first
  end
end
```

This code is not ideal, and we'd like to avoid having code like this in our application. First, it contains a SQL injection vulnerability, since we are constructing SQL without escaping the value of customer_id. You can work around this using Postgres's API directly, which would make the code even more difficult to understand. Second, this code doesn't return a nice object, but instead returns a hash that you must reach into in order to access the data.

It's not the worst code in the world, but it's not idiomatic Rails. This code, along with any code that calls it, will stick out like a sore thumb, confusing everyone who looks at it.

It may seem like a minor thing, but this sort of unnecessary complexity can make a codebase hard to read, understand, and manage. Sometimes, you have to live with code like this, but it's always worth trying to find a better way. Even if the Active Record version of the code executed more queries, and incurred a higher penalty for network round-trips, it looked like idiomatic Rails code.

You've now seen that the default *Rails Way* of modeling our access to this data will result in seven queries each time, and that those queries perform reasonably well, but incur a penalty in network round-trips. You've also seen that a large single query using joins *might* perform better but results in ugly, hard-to-maintain code.

Now, let's take a look at the third alternative: materialized views.

Using Materialized Views for Better Performance

Materialized views are a special form of *database view* that performs much better than a normal view. If you aren't familiar with views, they are a table-like construct that abstracts away a complex query. For example, you could create a view named ADDRESSES_WITH_STATES that abstracts away the need to join ADDRESSES and STATES together, like so:

```
CREATE VIEW addresses_with_states AS
  SELECT
    addresses.id,
    addresses.street,
    addresses.city,
    states.code AS state,
    addresses.zipcode
  FROM
    addresses
  JOIN states ON states.id = addresses.state_id;
```

Now, we can treat ADDRESSES_WITH_STATES just like a normal table for querying:

```
sql> select * from addresses_with_states where id = 12;
-[ RECORD 1 ]----------------
id      | 12
street  | 11828 Kuhn Turnpike
city    | Willmsmouth
state   | WA
zipcode | 46419-7547
```

We can *also* treat this like a regular table for mapping with Active Record:

```
class AddressesWithState < ActiveRecord::Base
end

AddressesWithState.find(12).state
# => WA
```

But a view is just a place to store the query. It would make our Rails code better-looking but would still not necessarily outperform the seven simpler queries—we'd still be running the complex join underneath.

If this join were the source of a performance problems, most relational databases wouldn't be able to help us solve it. We'd need to set up some sort of caching solution, like Memcached[4] or Elasticsearch.[5] We'd run our expensive query offline and populate our cache with the data, then query that data from the secondary cache at runtime.

Postgres provides this exact feature via *materialized views*. A materialized view is basically a table with the actual data from the underlying query. In effect, Postgres does what these alternative caching solutions do—stores the results of the query in another table that can be quickly searched.

The advantage is that, just like with a normal view, you can access the materialized view as if it were a regular table using Active Record, meaning

---

4. http://memcached.org
5. https://www.elastic.co

our Rails code will still be idiomatic. But, because the materialized view isn't doing the expensive query each time, you can fetch the data quickly (though this does come at a cost of increased disk space, because the data for the materialized view is stored on disk).

To create a materialized view, use CREATE MATERIALIZED VIEW instead of CREATE VIEW. Let's do that now by creating a new migration.

```
$ bin/rails g migration create-customer-details-materialized-view
invoke active_record
create db/migrate/20161007115613_create_customer_details_materialized_view.rb
```

Now, use execute in our migration to create the materialized view using the large and complex query we were using before. Since a materialized view creates a table under the covers, we're also going to create an index on customer_id, because that's the field we'll be using to query the materialized view (it will also allow us to keep the view up-to-date, as you'll see later).

10_materialized-views/10-data-model/shine/db/mi ... 613_create_customer_details_materialized_view.rb
```
class CreateCustomerDetailsMaterializedView < ActiveRecord::Migration[5.0]
def up
  execute %{
    CREATE MATERIALIZED VIEW customer_details AS
    SELECT
      customers.id              AS customer_id,
      customers.first_name      AS first_name,
      customers.last_name       AS last_name,
      customers.email           AS email,
      customers.username        AS username,
      customers.created_at      AS joined_at,
      billing_address.id        AS billing_address_id,
      billing_address.street    AS billing_street,
      billing_address.city      AS billing_city,
      billing_state.code        AS billing_state,
      billing_address.zipcode   AS billing_zipcode,
      shipping_address.id       AS shipping_address_id,
      shipping_address.street   AS shipping_street,
      shipping_address.city     AS shipping_city,
      shipping_state.code       AS shipping_state,
      shipping_address.zipcode  AS shipping_zipcode
    FROM
      customers
    JOIN customers_billing_addresses  ON
      customers.id = customers_billing_addresses.customer_id
    JOIN addresses billing_address     ON
      billing_address.id = customers_billing_addresses.address_id
    JOIN states billing_state          ON
      billing_address.state_id = billing_state.id
    JOIN customers_shipping_addresses ON
```

```
      customers.id = customers_shipping_addresses.customer_id AND
      customers_shipping_addresses.primary = true
    JOIN addresses shipping_address    ON
      shipping_address.id = customers_shipping_addresses.address_id
    JOIN states shipping_state         ON
      shipping_address.state_id = shipping_state.id
    }
    execute %{
      CREATE UNIQUE INDEX
        customer_details_customer_id
      ON
        customer_details(customer_id)
    }
  end

  def down
    execute "DROP MATERIALIZED VIEW customer_details"
  end
end
```

Next, run the migration with rails db:migrate. It will take a while, because it's
basically running this query for every row of all these tables. When it's done,
you'll be able to query this data quickly.

Let's do an EXPLAIN ANALYZE on our new materialized view:

```
sql> EXPLAIN ANALYZE
    SELECT * FROM customer_details WHERE customer_id = 2000;
QUERY PLAN
--------------------------------------------------------------------------
Index Scan using customer_details_customer_id on customer_details
  (cost=0.42..8.44 rows=1 width=163)
  (actual time=0.011..0.011 rows=1 loops=1)
   Index Cond: (customer_id = 2000)
 Planning time: 0.057 ms
 Execution time: 0.035 ms
```

This is pretty darn good! We're pulling back all of the data we need in under
one tenth of a millisecond. That is far faster than *both* the canonical Rails
Way using Active Record *and* our complex query.

We can now create a CustomerDetail class and query it just as we would any
other Active Record object, keeping our code clean and idiomatic, but it will
be blazingly fast.

10_materialized-views/10-data-model/shine/app/models/customer_detail.rb
```
class CustomerDetail < ApplicationRecord
  self.primary_key = 'customer_id'
end
```

As our materialized view doesn't have a field named id, we need to use prima-ry_key= to tell Active Record to use customer_id. With this in place, our controller looks like a regular Rails controller.

10_materialized-views/10-data-model/shine/app/controllers/customers_controller.rb
```ruby
class CustomersController < ApplicationController

  # Existing controller code...

  def show
➤   customer_detail = CustomerDetail.find(params[:id])
    respond_to do |format|
➤     format.json { render json: { customer: customer_detail } }
    end
  end
end
```

It seems we've addressed our performance problem by creating a fast way to get our data, but without having to write complex code that looks out-of-place or is hard to understand and maintain. Let's see what happens when we insert a new customer into our database:

```sql
sql> insert into customers(
    first_name,last_name,email,username,created_at,updated_at)
  values (
    'Dave','Copeland','dave@dave.dave','davetron5000',now(),now());
INSERT 0 1
> select id from customers where username = 'davetron5000';
  id   |
--------+
 388399 |
(1 row)

> insert into customers_billing_addresses(
    customer_id,address_id)
  values (388399,1);
INSERT 0 1
> insert into customers_shipping_addresses(
    customer_id,address_id,"primary")
  values (388399,1,true);
INSERT 0 1
```

Now, let's query our materialized view for this new customer:

```sql
sql> select * from customer_details where customer_id = 388399;
(No rows)
```

Oops. It looks like something's wrong. This is due to how materialized views are implemented by Postgres. Like any caching solution, the cache (in our case, the materialized view) must be updated when data changes. This is the trade-off of a cache and is why it's able to be fast.

In the next section, you'll see how to set up our database to keep the materialized view updated.

Keeping Materialized Views Updated

The reason our materialized view is so much faster than the regular view is because it essentially caches the results of the backing query into a real table. The trade-off is that the contents of the table could lag behind what's in the tables that the backing query queries.

Postgres provides a way to refresh the view via REFRESH MATERIALIZED VIEW. Before Postgres 9.4, refreshing materialized views like this was a problem, because it would lock the view while it was being refreshed. That meant that any application that wanted to query the view would have to wait until the update was completed. Since this could potentially be a long time, it meant that materialized views were mostly useless before 9.4.

As of Postgres 9.4, the refresh can be done concurrently in the background, allowing users of the table to continue querying old data until the refresh is complete. This is what we'll set up here, and it requires running the command REFRESH MATERIALIZED VIEW CONCURRENTLY.

Let's try it out.

```
sql> refresh materialized view concurrently customer_details;
sql> select * from customer_details where customer_id = 388399;
-[ RECORD 1 ]---------------+-----------------------------
customer_id                 | 388399
first_name                  | Dave
last_name                   | Copeland
email                       | dave@dave.dave
username                    | davetron5000
joined_at                   | 2015-06-25 08:28:54.327645
billing_street              | 530 Nienow Stravenue
billing_city                | West Aniyah
billing_state               | RI
billing_zipcode             | 72842-8201
shipping_address_id         | 1
shipping_street             | 530 Nienow Stravenue
shipping_city               | West Aniyah
shipping_state              | RI
shipping_zipcode            | 72842-8201
shipping_address_created_at | 2015-06-20 16:51:06.891914-04
```

Now that you know how to refresh the view, the trick is *when* to do it. This highly depends on how often the underlying data changes and how important it is for you to see the most recent data in the view. We'll look at two techniques for doing that here. The first is to create a Rake task to refresh the view on a schedule. The second is to use *database triggers* to refresh the view whenever underlying data changes.

Refreshing the View on a Schedule

The simplest way to refresh the view is to create a Rake task and then arrange for that task to be run on a regular schedule. You can do this by creating lib/tasks/refresh_materialized_views.rake and using the connection method on ActiveRecord::Base, which will allow us to execute arbitrary SQL.

```
10_materialized-views/10-data-model/shine/lib/tasks/refresh_materialized_views.rake
desc "Refreshes materialized views"
task refresh_materialized_views: :environment do
  ActiveRecord::Base.connection.execute %{
    REFRESH MATERIALIZED VIEW CONCURRENTLY customer_details
  }
end
```

You can then run it on the command line via rails:

```
$ bin/rails refresh_materialized_views
```

With this in place, you can then configure our production system to run this periodically, for example using cron. How frequently to run it depends on how recent the data should be to users, as well as how long it takes to do the refresh. If users need the data to be fairly up-to-date, you could try running it every five minutes. If users can do their jobs without the absolute latest, you could run it every hour or even every day.

If users need it to be absolutely up-to-date with the underlying tables, you can have the database itself refresh whenever the underlying data changes by using *triggers*.

Refreshing the View with Triggers

A *database trigger* is similar to an Active Record callback: it's code that runs when certain events occur. In our case, we'd want to refresh our materialized view whenever data in the tables that view is based on changes.

To do this, we'll create a database function that refreshes the materialized view, and then create several triggers that use that function when the data in the relevant tables changes. We can do this all in a Rails migration, so let's create one where we can put this code:

```
$ bin/rails g migration trigger-refresh-customer-details
invoke  active_record
create    db/migrate/20161007122606_trigger_refresh_customer_details.rb
```

First, we'll create a function to refresh the materialized view. This requires using Postgres's PL/pgSQL[6] language. It looks fairly archaic, but we don't need to use much of it.

10_materialized-views/10-data-model/shine/db/mi ... 161007122606_trigger_refresh_customer_details.rb
```
execute %{
  CREATE OR REPLACE FUNCTION
    refresh_customer_details()
    RETURNS TRIGGER LANGUAGE PLPGSQL
  AS $$
  BEGIN
    REFRESH MATERIALIZED VIEW CONCURRENTLY customer_details;
    RETURN NULL;
  EXCEPTION
    WHEN feature_not_supported THEN
      RETURN NULL;
  END $$;
}
```

The key part of this is RETURNS TRIGGER, which is what will allow you to use this function in the triggers you'll set up next. Also note the exception-handling clause that starts with EXCEPTION. This is similar to Ruby's rescue keyword and is a way to handle errors that happen at runtime. You can provide any number of WHEN clauses to indicate how to handle a particular exception. In this case, we're handling feature_not_supported, which is thrown if we run this function before the materialized view has been updated. In practice this won't happen, but in our testing environment it can, since we are resetting the database during our tests.

The form of a trigger we want will look like so:

```
CREATE TRIGGER
  refresh_customer_details
AFTER
  INSERT OR
  UPDATE OR
  DELETE
ON
  customers
FOR EACH STATEMENT
  EXECUTE PROCEDURE refresh_customer_details();
```

The code for this trigger reflects what it does: any insert, update, or delete on the customers table causes the database to run refresh_customer_details. So, we just need to set this up for each table that's relevant.

---

6.   http://www.postgresql.org/docs/9.5/static/plpgsql.html

If we assume that the list of U.S. states doesn't change, we can set up triggers for the other three tables: ADDRESSES, CUSTOMERS_SHIPPING_ADDRESSES, and CUS-TOMERS_BILLING_ADDRESSES. Since the code is almost the same for each table, we'll loop over the table names and construct the SQL dynamically.

10_materialized-views/10-data-model/shine/db/mi ... 161007122606_trigger_refresh_customer_details.rb

```ruby
class TriggerRefreshCustomerDetails < ActiveRecord::Migration[5.0]
  def up
    execute %{
      CREATE OR REPLACE FUNCTION
        refresh_customer_details()
        RETURNS TRIGGER LANGUAGE PLPGSQL
      AS $$
      BEGIN
        REFRESH MATERIALIZED VIEW CONCURRENTLY customer_details;
        RETURN NULL;
      EXCEPTION
        WHEN feature_not_supported THEN
          RETURN NULL;
      END $$;
    }
    %w(customers
       customers_shipping_addresses
       customers_billing_addresses
       addresses).each do |table|
      execute %{
        CREATE TRIGGER refresh_customer_details
        AFTER
          INSERT OR
          UPDATE OR
          DELETE
        ON #{table}
          FOR EACH STATEMENT
            EXECUTE PROCEDURE
              refresh_customer_details()
      }
    end
  end
  def down
    %w(customers
       customers_shipping_addresses
       customers_billing_addresses
       addresses).each do |table|
      execute %{DROP TRIGGER refresh_customer_details ON #{table}}
    end
    execute %{DROP FUNCTION refresh_customer_details()}
  end
end
```

After we run rails db:migrate, you can insert new customers and see the view get refreshed automatically:

```
sql> insert into customers(
    first_name,last_name,email,username,created_at,updated_at)
  values (
    'Amy','Copeland','amy@amy.dave','amytron',now(),now());
INSERT 0 1
sql> select id from customers where username = 'amytron';
  id
--------
 350002
sql> insert into customers_shipping_addresses
    (customer_id,address_id,"primary")
  values
    (350002,1,true);
INSERT 0 1
sql> insert into customers_billing_addresses
    (customer_id,address_id)
  values
    (350002,1);
INSERT 0 1
> select * from customer_details where customer_id = 350002;
-[ RECORD 1 ]-------+---------------------------
customer_id         | 350002
first_name          | Amy
last_name           | Copeland
email               | amy@amy.dave
username            | amytron
joined_at           | 2015-06-26 08:17:17.536305
billing_address_id  | 1
billing_street      | 123 any st
billing_city        | washington
billing_state       | DC
billing_zipcode     | 20001
shipping_address_id | 1
shipping_street     | 123 any st
shipping_city       | washington
shipping_state      | DC
shipping_zipcode    | 20001
```

You'll notice that the inserts took a *lot* longer to execute than before. This is the downside of this technique. The materialized view is as up-to-date as it possibly can be; however, it updates slowly. If your table will have a high volume of writes or updates, you'll be refreshing the view a lot, and this could slow down your database. You'll have to evaluate which technique will be best, based on your actual usage.

One thing you'll notice is that your tests are now failing. Let's fix those before moving on.

Altering Tests to Work with the Materialized View

The issue you should be seeing is that one of the tests in spec/features/customer_search_spec.rb is failing with a message similar to Couldn't find CustomerDetail with 'customer_id'=11. This is because we've switched the controller's show method to use CustomerDetail, which is backed by our materialized view, and that view requires that a customer have a billing address and shipping address. It's using *inner joins* (the default when you just use JOIN).

An inner join is a way to tell Postgres not to return data if there isn't data in a related table. In our case, if there is no row in customers_shipping_addresses or customers_billing_addresses for the given customer, the query backing our view won't return a row.

We could use an *outer join*, which would tell Postgres to return empty values when there isn't related data, but this should only be done if it's allowed by our business rules. In our case, it's not. Every customer must have a billing address and a primary shipping address, so instead of changing our query, we'll change our test data so it's creating valid data.

First, we need to modify the existing create_customer method you created in *Test the Typeahead Search*, on page 104 to add the requisite addresses. We'll assume the existence of a method create_address, which you'll see in a moment.

```
10_materialized-views/10-data-model/shine/spec/features/customer_search_spec.rb
def create_customer(first_name:, last_name:, email: nil)
  username = "#{Faker::Internet.user_name}#{rand(1000)}"
  email   ||= "#{username}#{rand(1000)}@" +
              "#{Faker::Internet.domain_name}"

➤ customer = Customer.create!(
    first_name: first_name,
    last_name: last_name,
    username: username,
    email: email
  )

➤ customer.create_customers_billing_address(address: create_address)
➤ customer.customers_shipping_address.create!(address: create_address,
➤                                             primary: true)
➤ customer
end
```

If you aren't familiar with some of the methods Active Record creates for you, create_customers_billing_address is provided because we've configured the relationship using a has_one.[7] Similarly, you can call create! on the customers_shipping_address relation because we used has_many.[8]

Now, let's see create_address:

```
10_materialized-views/10-data-model/shine/spec/features/customer_search_spec.rb
def create_address
  state = State.find_or_create_by!(
    code: Faker::Address.state_abbr,
    name: Faker::Address.state)

  Address.create!(
    street: Faker::Address.street_address,
    city: Faker::Address.city,
    state: state,
    zipcode: Faker::Address.zip)
end
```

With that in place, our tests should be passing again.

If you choose *not* to use triggers to maintain your materialized view, you will need to execute REFRESH MATERIALIZED VIEW customer_details in your tests. You could do this by using RSpec's hooks, which you learned about in *Using Database-Cleaner to Manage Test Data*, on page 102. Also note that the very first time you run your test, you might get an error like "ERROR: materialized view 'customer_details' has not been populated." In that case, manually refresh the materialized view in your test schema by running bin/rails dbconsole test and executing REFRESH MATERIALIZED VIEW customer_details.

The path that led us to materialized views was the promise of high performance and code simplicity. It may have felt circuitous, but it's a great demonstration of the type of power you have as a full-stack developer. By understanding the breadth of tools available to you, and how to use them, you can create solutions that are simple.

Although you had to create a materialized view and triggers to keep it updated, you were able to avoid setting up a new piece of infrastructure for caching and can get more out of the database system we already have in place. Our Rails code looks like regular Rails code (we're using Active Record to query data), and you didn't need to write a background process to keep our data updated. Eventually, you'll have complex enough query needs that

---

7. http://api.rubyonrails.org/classes/ActiveRecord/Associations/ClassMethods.html#method-i-has_one
8. http://api.rubyonrails.org/classes/ActiveRecord/Associations/ClassMethods.html#method-i-has_many

you can't use this technique, but you're getting a lot further than you would with other RDBMSs.

Next: Combining Data with a Second Source in Angular

We're about to complete our journey in creating a high-performing, usable, and clean way for our users to see a customer's details. We have our UI designed and built, and our back end is now clean, simple, and fast. We now need to bring them together in our Angular app.

With what we know about Angular, using this data in our view is pretty easy. We've seen how we can request information from the server using $http, and we've seen how to show that data in our view using Angular's templating system, along with the ng-model directive.

One thing you might have noticed is that our CustomerDetail model doesn't expose some of the billing information, such as the last four digits and expiration data of the customer's credit card. We don't store this data in our database, but we need it in our view. In the next chapter, you'll see how Angular manages that by learning more about how its asynchronous nature works.

You'll learn how to can pull data from two separate sources and have it display in the view, showing the data as it comes in for the best user experience, all without a whole lot of code.

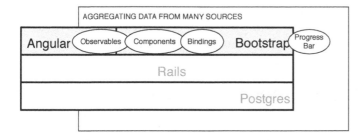

AGGREGATING DATA FROM MANY SOURCES

Angular · Observables · Components · Bindings · Bootstrap · Progress Bar

Rails

Postgres

CHAPTER 11

Asynchronously Load Data from Many Sources

At this point, our Angular app is working great, and data is coming back quickly thanks to our materialized view. We aren't fetching the credit card information, however, so our feature isn't quite complete. We'll complete it in this chapter, which will give you the opportunity to learn more about how to design a complex Angular app. You'll see how embracing a component-based design, along with the Angular's asynchronous nature, makes it easy to keep code organized and maintain a good user experience in the face of added complexity (namely, fetching the credit card information from a third party).

Up to this point, our Angular app looks like a Rails app written in JavaScript. You could think of our components as controllers and our templates as views. This is because we aren't taking full advantage of Angular's features. Angular components can be smaller, more focused, and have more intelligence than Rails views and partials. One thing we can do with this extra intelligence is fetch data from more than one source at the same time. Instead of collecting all the data and rendering a view—as we would in a classic Rails application— we can render data as it comes in. This makes our UI more responsive and provides a better user experience, especially if one of our sources of data is slow.

You'll learn about how to do that in this chapter, along with a few other tidbits of working in an Angular codebase. We'll split up our existing CustomerDetailsComponent into a hierarchy of subcomponents. We'll also fetch the credit card information from a third party and populate the UI with data as it becomes available. We'll look at how Bootstrap's progress bar UI component can be used to give the user feedback that this process is happening.

Asynchronous code can be confusing, however, especially with multiple requests in flight at once. You also might not be as familiar with observables— the underlying technology Angular uses to manage asynchronous behavior—so let's first look at how that works.

Understanding Asynchronous Requests and Observables

If you've done any JavaScript programming, you are familiar with *callbacks*. These are functions that get called after some work has completed. The simplest example is setTimeout, which takes a callback function and a number of milliseconds. After the given milliseconds have elapsed, the function is called.

In this code, the function errorMessage is executed one second later:

```
var greeting = function() {
  alert("Hello!");
};
setTimeout(greeting,1000);
```

You first saw this when using Http in Chapter 6, *Build a Dynamic UI with Angular*, on page 65, when you passed a callback to subscribe that would execute our code once we got a response from the server. I didn't really talk about *why* Http works that way. Let's do that now.

Why Asynchronous?

Contacting the server takes time. Even with all the improvements we've made in the performance of our Rails controller, fetching data over the Internet is not instantaneous. If our JavaScript were to make an Ajax call and wait for a response (called a *synchronous request*), the entire browser would be hung while it waited on the network.

To prevent this, you want to make the call in the background and let your main bits of code (and the browser in general) continue to operate while the networking request is happening. In many programming languages, this is done with threads. JavaScript does not expose the concept of threads to the user, instead requiring programmers to use callbacks managed internally by the runtime.

This means your code is often organized into three chunks: (1) the setup code to make our Ajax request, (2) the code to actually make the request, and (3) the code to run after the request has completed. Where this can get tricky is when you have more than one request. Consider this code:

```
Line 1  var base = "http://billing.example.com"
     2  self.http.get(base + "/cardholder/123").subscribe(function(response) {
     3    alert("Got card details!");
     4  });
     5  self.http.get("/customer/123.json").subscribe(function(response) {
     6    alert("Got customer!");
     7  });
     8  alert("Requests sent!");
```

Although this code looks like it runs top to bottom, it actually doesn't. Lines 1 and 2 execute first. While that Ajax call is happening, the code proceeds to line 5. After that, line 8 is called.

This means that lines 3 and 6 haven't executed yet! They'll execute when their respective Ajax calls complete, and that could happen in any order. A big part of our code—handling the responses from the server—cannot rely on any particular ordering. Following is a diagram of the overall flow.

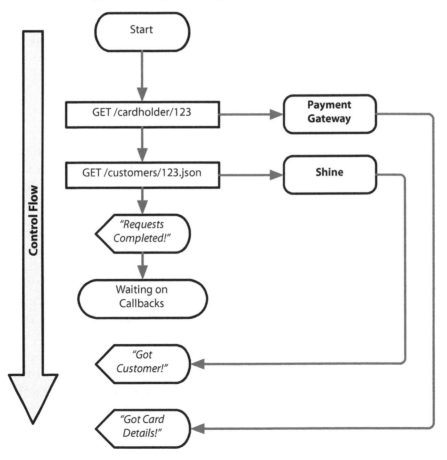

This can get confusing fast, especially if the code *does* need to run in a certain order. Consider if we needed a credit card holder ID from our customer details in order to fetch the customer's card information from our third-party billing service. We'd need to make our call to the billing service inside the callback that's called when our customer details are fetched. This creates a nested structure like so:

```
var base = "http://billing.example.com"
self.http.get("/customer/123.json").subscribe(function(response) {
  alert("Got customer!");
  self.customer = data.json().customer;
  var url = base + "/cardholder/" + self.customer.cardholder_id;
  self.http.get(url).subscribe(function(response) {
    alert("Got card details!");
  });
});
alert("Requests sent!");
```

This is called *callback hell*. It makes your client-side code hard to deal with. Partly this is just the reality of programming with an asynchronous model, but there are tools like promises and observables to help tame it. Angular uses *observables*.

Observables

We looked at observables a bit in previous chapters, and what we know about them is that instead of a passing a callback to http.get, we pass a callback to the object that http.get returns. As mentioned in *Get Data from the Back End*, on page 81, http.get returns an RxJS observable, and subscribe is a method on that observable that allows us to execute code when...well, when?

As you have come to expect by now, Angular is built on abstractions of abstractions. If you read the documentation[1] for the subscribe method of an RxJS observable, it says

> Subscribes an observer to the observable sequence.

This is not a specific explanation, and it sure doesn't sound like it has anything to do with making Ajax requests. This is because observables are a generic construct that Angular uses to implement its Ajax-handling code. If you look at the main documentation for an observable,[2] you'll see many, many methods. They might look similar to methods on Ruby's Enumerable or any other programming language's collections library.

---

1.   https://github.com/Reactive-Extensions/RxJS/blob/master/doc/api/core/operators/subscribe.md
2.   https://github.com/Reactive-Extensions/RxJS/blob/master/doc/api/core/observable.md

That's because observables are meant to allow asynchronous operations on streams of data, which is called an *observable sequence*. This may be somewhat confusing, because if you consult the documentation for Http,[3] you'll see that we're only observing a sequence of one item—the entire response:

> Calling [get] returns an Observable which will emit a single Response when a response is received.

Angular is treating a response from our Ajax request as a special case of an observable sequence. That allows it to reuse a more generic library, rather than roll its own custom mechanism (which is what both Angular 1 and jQuery do). It also means that we can make use of that generic libraries features to more cleanly structure our code.

Now that we now we are using observables, we can reexamine the previous code and structure it differently. The code needs to transform the response into the JSON object we want, and then do two things: (1) store the result in a property, and (2) kick off another Ajax request. In the language of an observable, we want to *map* the response to something else, and then *subscribe* two bits of code to that response.

You've seen the latter used for a single bit of code, and for the former, the map function allows you to encapsulate the transformation code in one place. Suppose you have the following functions (note how small and single-purpose they are):

```
var parseCustomer = function(response) {
  return response.json().customer;
};

var setCustomer = function(customer) {
  self.customer = customer;
};

var setCreditCardInfo = function(response) {
  self.credit_card_info = response.json();
}

var requestCardInfo = function(customer) {
  var url   = "http://billing.example.com" +
              "/cardholder/" +
              customer.cardholder_id;
  self.http.get(url).subscribe(function(response) {
    self.credit_card_info = response.json();
  });
}
```

---

3.   https://angular.io/docs/ts/latest/api/http/index/Http-class.html

You can use them with the observables that come back from http.get to keep the Ajax-requesting code clean and straightforward, like this:

```
var self = this;
var observable = self.http.get("/customer/123.json");

var mappedObservable = observable.map(parseCustomer);

mappedObservable.subscribe(setCustomer);
mappedObservable.subscribe(requestCardInfo);
```

To do this, start with an observable that makes the Ajax request and returns the raw JSON response when it's complete. Next, use map to create a *new* observable (mappedObservable) that notifies subscribers of the result of parseCustomer instead of the raw response. Then subscribe to that observable so that our two chunks of code can be given a nicely formatted customer instead of raw JSON. The following diagram shows what that setup looks like visually.

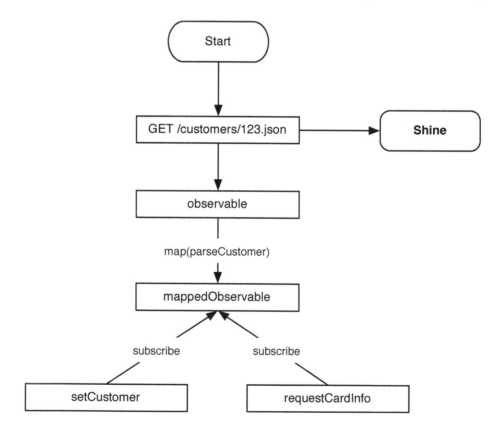

Once you get a response back from the server, observable is notified, which calls parseCustomer and then notifies the two subscribers of mappedObservable as shown in the next diagram. We'll add code like this to Shine in a moment.

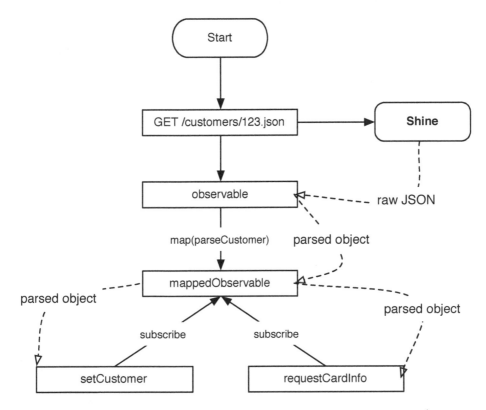

As you can see, observables are a deep topic, and we've learned most of what we need in order to do our jobs, but a detour through the documentation or *Reactive Programming with RxJS [Man15]* will reveal a powerful set of tools to manage your application as it grows in complexity.

Now that you know a bit more about the asynchronous nature of HTTP requests and how Angular manages them, let's get back to adding the credit card information to our customer detail view. The first step to doing that is to break up the existing component into several subcomponents.

Separating the App into Components

Angular intends for you to design your UI around components. Instead of one big page, you're intended to create smaller, reusable or self-contained bits of HTML and code that can be pieced together. This is a common pattern in other JavaScript libraries, such as React,[4] and it's a great way to organize complex user interfaces like our customer details page. This is different than the way Rails thinks of a UI, which is, instead, as a collection of HTML templates. You could think of partials as components, but partials are just a way to reuse HTML; there's no behavior associated with them.

Let's pick out the components from our existing UI. The following screen shows what it looked like at the end of Chapter 9, *Design Great UIs with*, on page 155:

Given the layout and design, we can quickly pick out three different components: a customer information component in the upper left, a credit card component in the upper right, and then an address component that we're using in two places for the address. The markup for both addresses is almost identical.

Let's extract all this markup into three separate components. Initially, each component will just render HTML, but you'll be able to see the shape of our code to come.

You've created a new component before, but to review, here are the basic steps:

1. Create the HTML file containing your component's markup. Since our extracted components will be nested in CustomerDetailsComponent, we'll keep them inside app/javascript/CustomerDetailsComponent and so we'll name the template the camel-cased name of the component (for example, CustomerInfoComponent.html).

---

4.   https://facebook.github.io/react

2. Create the JavaScript file to hold the component's definition using the same file name convention (so CustomerInfoComponent.ts in this example). This code will contain the selector that other components will use to refer to it. If you recall from *Set Up the Empty Component*, on page 70, we want our selectors prefixed with our app name to avoid collisions, so a good convention for your selector name would be «app_name»-«dasherized-component-name». For example, our CustomerInfoComponent's selector will be shine-customer-info.

3. Reference the component in another component's HTML using the new selector (for example, <shine-credit-card></shine-credit-card>).

4. Bring the component into your pack file (customers.js) and add it to the list of declarations in your NgModule definition.

With this information, we can now transform our complex CustomerDetailsComponent into a component that references other, simpler components. First, let's set up the customer information component. The markup is just moved from the original CustomerDetailsComponent.html:

```
11_angular-async/10-components/shine/app/javasc…tomerDetailsComponent/CustomerInfoComponent.html
<article class="panel panel-primary">
  <header class="panel-heading">
    <h1 class="h3">
      Customer
    </h1>
  </header>
  <section class="panel-body">

    <!-- markup from before -->

  </section>
  <footer class="panel-footer">
    <label for="joined">Joined</label> 12/13/2014
  </footer>
</article>
```

Note that we've moved it inside app/javascript/CustomerDetailsComponent since it's a sub-component and not generally reusable at this point. If we were to make it more general, we could create app/javascript/CustomerInfoComponent and place the files in there, but for now, we'll leave it inside the directory for CustomerDetailsComponent. The code for the component is fairly bare-bones. Note the selector name, shine-customer-info:

```
11_angular-async/10-components/shine/app/javasc…ustomerDetailsComponent/CustomerInfoComponent.ts
import { Component } from "@angular/core";
import   template   from "./CustomerInfoComponent.html";

var CustomerInfoComponent = Component({
  selector: "shine-customer-info",
```

```
  template: template
}).Class({
  constructor: [
    function() {
    }
  ]
});

export { CustomerInfoComponent };
```

We can now remove the markup from CustomerDetailsComponent.html and replace it with our new selector:

```
<section class="customer-details" *ngIf="customer">
<form>
  <div class="row">
    <div class="col-md-6">
      <shine-customer-info></shine-customer-info>
      <article class="panel panel-default">
        <header class="panel-heading">
          <h2 class="h4">
            Shipping Address
          </h2>
        </header>
        <!-- rest of the code -->
```

Finally, we'll bring it into app/javascript/packs/customers.js and add it to our NgModule:

```
11_angular-async/10-components/shine/app/javascript/packs/customers.js
import "polyfills";

import { Component, NgModule     } from "@angular/core";
import { BrowserModule           } from "@angular/platform-browser";
import { FormsModule             } from "@angular/forms";
import { platformBrowserDynamic  } from "@angular/platform-browser-dynamic";
import { HttpModule              } from "@angular/http";
import { RouterModule            } from "@angular/router";

import { CustomerSearchComponent  } from "CustomerSearchComponent";
import { CustomerDetailsComponent } from "CustomerDetailsComponent";
import { CustomerInfoComponent    } from
  "CustomerDetailsComponent/CustomerInfoComponent";

// code as before...

var CustomerAppModule = NgModule({
  imports:     [
    BrowserModule,
    FormsModule,
    HttpModule,
    routing
  ],
  declarations: [
    CustomerSearchComponent,
```

```
      CustomerDetailsComponent,
➤     CustomerInfoComponent,
      AppComponent
    ],
    bootstrap: [ AppComponent ]
})
.Class({
    constructor: function() {}
});

platformBrowserDynamic().bootstrapModule(CustomerAppModule);
```

If you reload the page, you should see the same UI as before. We've success-fully extracted a component. You should be able to repeat those steps for the credit card component and the address component. In the end, here's what CustomerDetailsComponent.html looks like:

```
11_angular-async/10-components/shine/app/javascript/CustomerDetailsComponent/template.html
<section class="customer-details" *ngIf="customer">
<form>
  <div class="row">
    <div class="col-md-6">
      <shine-customer-info></shine-customer-info>
      <shine-address></shine-address>
    </div>
    <div class="col-md-6">
      <article class="panel panel-default">
        <header class="panel-heading">
          <h2 class="h4">
            Billing Info
          </h2>
        </header>
        <section class="panel-body">
          <shine-credit-card></shine-credit-card>
          <hr>
          <shine-address></shine-address>
        </section>
      </article>
    </div>
  </div>
</form>
</section>
```

And, with the new components brought into customers.js, here's how it looks:

```
11_angular-async/10-components/shine/app/javascript/packs/customers.js
import "polyfills";

import { Component, NgModule    } from "@angular/core";
import { BrowserModule          } from "@angular/platform-browser";
import { FormsModule            } from "@angular/forms";
import { platformBrowserDynamic } from "@angular/platform-browser-dynamic";
```

```
import { HttpModule            } from "@angular/http";
import { RouterModule          } from "@angular/router";

import { CustomerSearchComponent  } from "CustomerSearchComponent";
import { CustomerDetailsComponent } from "CustomerDetailsComponent";
import { CustomerInfoComponent    } from
   "CustomerDetailsComponent/CustomerInfoComponent";
import { AddressComponent      } from
   "CustomerDetailsComponent/AddressComponent";
import { CreditCardComponent   } from
   "CustomerDetailsComponent/CreditCardComponent";

// code as before...

var CustomerAppModule = NgModule({
  imports:       [
    BrowserModule,
    FormsModule,
    HttpModule,
    routing
  ],
  declarations: [
    CustomerSearchComponent,
    CustomerDetailsComponent,
    CustomerInfoComponent,
    AddressComponent,
    CreditCardComponent,
    AppComponent
  ],
  bootstrap: [ AppComponent ]
})
.Class({
  constructor: function() {}
});

platformBrowserDynamic().bootstrapModule(CustomerAppModule);
```

I won't show the rest of the extracted code here; it's mostly boilerplate and copy/paste. You can reference the downloaded code samples, or see Appendix 3, *Customer Details Extracted Components*, on page 287 for the listing.

Although this only looks like Rails partials for the moment, Angular components are more powerful. As you'll see, there is a more clearly defined interface to passing data between them, and we also have a way to encapsulate code that's specific to the component if we need to.

There are a couple of interesting things to note. First, app/javascript/CustomerDetailsComponent/index.html now only contains markup to lay out the page and references to other components. This makes sense, because the purpose of the CustomerDetailsComponent is now just to arrange the other components it needs.

Second, you'll notice that all the components we extracted use article as their outermost HTML element. The HTML spec for the article element[5] states that the element "represents a complete, or self-contained, composition in a document, page, application, or site and that is, in principle, independently distributable or reusable." If you use this tag when it's called for, you have a good clue as to where you can extract components.

Now that we've extracted these components, how do we get data into them? We're fetching the customer details already, but we're not doing anything with it since our view is just static HTML. Let's see how that works with our new component-based design.

Sharing Data Between Components

Each component displays a different part of the customer's data. We don't want each component to hit the server for their part of the UI—that would result in multiple calls fetching the same data. Instead, we'd like the components to be in charge displaying (and later, changing) the data, but have the data handed to them from somewhere else. Because we're already fetching it in the CustomerDetailsComponent, we just need a way to pass it to the other components.

Let's start with the CustomerInfoComponent, which displays the customer's name, username, join date, and email address. We have that information in CustomerDetailsComponent, so how can we pass it along to CustomerInfoComponent?

You've seen in *Changing Our Search to Use Typeahead*, on page 86 that the bind- prefix allows us to hook into a property of a component. In that section, we bound the Angular-provided ngModel of a standard input field to the keywords property of our component that used the input fields.

This is exactly the same setup we want to achieve here. We'd like to bind the customer property of CustomerInfoComponent to the customer property of the containing component, CustomerDetailsComponent.

To do this, we'll set up the binding in the view template in CustomerDetailsComponent.html. We'll also need to configure CustomerInfoComponent to declare that customer is a property to which we can bind.

To set up the binding, use bind-customer="customer", like so:

```
11_angular-async/20-fetch-data/shine/app/javascript/CustomerDetailsComponent/template.html
<section class="customer-details" *ngIf="customer">
<form>
  <div class="row">
```

---

5. https://www.w3.org/TR/html5/sections.html#the-article-element

```
<div class="col-md-6">
  <shine-customer-info bind-customer="customer">
  </shine-customer-info>

<!-- rest of the template... -->
```

This means that the customer property of CustomerInfoComponent should be *bound* to the customer properly of the parent component, CustomerDetailsComponent. The binding means that changes made in one place are viewable in the other. This will be more useful in the next chapter.

If you tried to reload the page now (and open the JavaScript console in your browser), you'll see an error similar to "Can't bind to 'customer' since it isn't a known property of 'shine-customer-info.'" Components must opt-in to having their properties set by other components. To make this work for CustomerInfo-Component, we'll use the inputs key in the object we gave to Component:

11_angular-async/20-fetch-data/shine/app/javasc ... ustomerDetailsComponent/CustomerInfoComponent.ts
```
var CustomerInfoComponent = Component({
  selector: "shine-customer-info",
  inputs: [
    "customer"
  ],
  template: template
}).Class({
  constructor: [
    function() {
      this.customer = null;
    }
  ]
});
```

The last thing to do is to use our newly bound customer in CustomerDetailsCompo-nent.html to show the customer information. While we could do something like `<input value="{{customer.first_name}}">`, we want to bind those values to the form fields, since we ultimately want to allow the user to edit them. We'll use bindon-ngModel, which we saw before in *Respond to Click Events*, on page 74.

11_angular-async/20-fetch-data/shine/app/javasc ... tomerDetailsComponent/CustomerInfoComponent.html
```
<article class="panel panel-primary customer-info" *ngIf="customer">
  <header class="panel-heading">
    <h1 class="h3">
      Customer
    </h1>
  </header>
  <section class="panel-body">
    <div class="row">
      <div class="col-md-4">
        <div class="form-group">
```

```
              <label class="sr-only" for="first-name">
                First Name
              </label>
➤             <input type="text" class="form-control" name="first-name"
➤                    bindon-ngModel="customer.first_name">
          </div>
        </div>
        <div class="col-md-4">
          <div class="form-group">
            <label class="sr-only" for="last-name">Last Name</label>
➤           <input type="text" class="form-control" name="last-name"
➤                  bindon-ngModel="customer.last_name">
          </div>
        </div>
        <div class="col-md-4">
          <div class="form-group">
            <label class="sr-only" for="username">Username</label>
            <div class="input-group">
              <div class="input-group-addon">@</div>
➤             <input type="text" class="form-control" name="username"
➤                    bindon-ngModel="customer.username">
            </div>
          </div>
        </div>
      </div>
      <div class="form-group">
        <label class="sr-only" for="email">Email</label>
➤       <input type="text" class="form-control" name="email"
➤              bindon-ngModel="customer.email">
      </div>
    </section>
    <footer class="panel-footer">
➤     <label for="joined">Joined</label> {{customer.joined_at}}
    </footer>
</article>
```

If you reload the page, you should no longer see the static content, but should see the actual user information from the back end.

We'd like to do the same thing for AddressComponent, but we're using it in two places for two different bits of data: the billing address and the shipping address. Because our customer doesn't have a billing_address or shipping_address, but instead has fields directly on it like billing_street or shipping_state, we have a bit of dilemma.

You could use what you've just learned and pass in the customer object, and then possibly give it a flag to know which sets of keys to use (the billing_* or the shipping_* key). This feels a bit hacky. Instead, let's use the CustomerDetailsComponent for what it's for: orchestrating the use of its subcomponents.

What this means it that before we pass customer to the subcomponents, we'll make some changes to it so that we can pass only the data we'd like. While we could change the back end to pass us an object more friendly to our problem, the issue at hand is a front-end concern, so let's solve it here, in the front end.

If we could copy the billing_* fields to a subobject called billing_address (and do the same for the shipping_* fields), we could write markup like this, and pass it to the AddressComponent like so:

```
<shine-address addressType="Shipping"
               bind-address="customer.shipping_address">
</shine-address>

<!-- AND -->

<shine-address addressType="Billing"
               bind-address="customer.billing_address">
</shine-address>
```

This way, AddressComponent can just worry about addresses, and not the particulars of where the values come from.

When looking at observables earlier in this chapter, I mentioned the map function. It allows you to transform the data you get from the observable before passing it to the subscribers. Let's use that to do this transformation.

By default, map is not available, since Angular is trying to keep the size of the JavaScript needed to a minimum. We can bring it in by adding an import to it at the top of our file:

```
11_angular-async/20-fetch-data/shine/app/javascript/CustomerDetailsComponent/index.ts
import { Component }       from "@angular/core";
import { ActivatedRoute } from "@angular/router";
import { Http }            from "@angular/http";
import                     "rxjs/add/operator/map";
import    template         from "./template.html";
```

Now, let's rewrite the routeSuccess function to use map. The code is a bit more verbose than you might like, but it more clearly demonstrates what objects' functions are being called on. In particular, note that map returns a *new* observable, and only subscribers to *that* observable will get the mapped value. (Also note that we haven't yet defined parseCustomer, but we will in a moment.)

```
11_angular-async/20-fetch-data/shine/app/javascript/CustomerDetailsComponent/index.ts
var routeSuccess = function(params) {
  var observable = self.http.get(
    "/customers/" + params["id"] + ".json"
  );
```

```
    var mappedObservable = observable.map(parseCustomer)

    mappedObservable.subscribe(
      function(customer) { self.customer = customer; },
      observableFailed
    );
  }
  self.activatedRoute.params.subscribe(routeSuccess,observableFailed);
```

Note the use of map. We're transforming the original observable using the to-be-defined parseCustomer method, which means that the callback we give to subscribe will have a customer as an object, not unparsed JSON. This also means that any additional subscribers we might add later will get the parsed value.

Last, add parseCustomer so that it copies the address fields into sub-objects:

```
11_angular-async/20-fetch-data/shine/app/javascript/CustomerDetailsComponent/index.ts
var parseCustomer = function(response) {
  var customer = response.json().customer;

  customer.billing_address = {
    street:  customer.billing_street,
    city:    customer.billing_city,
    state:   customer.billing_state,
    zipcode: customer.billing_zipcode
  };

  customer.shipping_address = {
    street:  customer.shipping_street,
    city:    customer.shipping_city,
    state:   customer.shipping_state,
    zipcode: customer.shipping_zipcode
  };

  return customer;
}
var routeSuccess = function(params) {
```

With this in place, we can write our markup the way we saw it earlier:

```
<section class="customer-details" *ngIf="customer">
<form>
  <div class="row">
    <div class="col-md-6">
      <shine-customer-info bind-customer="customer">
      </shine-customer-info>
      <shine-address
        addressType="Shipping"
        bind-address="customer.shipping_address">
      </shine-address>
    </div>
```

```
    <div class="col-md-6">
      <article class="panel panel-default">
        <header class="panel-heading">
          <h2 class="h4">
            Billing Info
          </h2>
        </header>
        <section class="panel-body">

          <!-- credit card marup... -->

          <hr>
          <shine-address
            addressType="Billing"
            bind-address="customer.billing_address">
          </shine-address>
        </section>
      </article>
    </div>
  </div>
</form>
</section>
```

Next, we have to configure AddressComponent to allow setting address via binding.
We also want to allow setting addressType so that we can render the proper
heading ("Shipping" versus "Billing").

11_angular-async/20-fetch-data/shine/app/javascript/CustomerDetailsComponent/AddressComponent.ts
```
var AddressComponent = Component({
  selector: "shine-address",
  inputs: [
    "address",
    "addressType"
  ],
  template: template
}).Class({
  constructor: [
    function() {
      this.address     = null;
      this.addressType = null;
    }
  ]
});
```

Finally, we can rewrite the template to use the address object our component
will have access to (and render the proper heading using addressType):

11_angular-async/20-fetch-data/shine/app/javascript/CustomerDetailsComponent/AddressComponent.html
```
<article class="panel panel-default">
  <header class="panel-heading">
    <h2 class="h4">
      {{addressType}} Address
```

```
        </h2>
      </header>
      <section class="panel-body">
        <div class="form-group">
          <label class="sr-only" for="street-address">
            Street Address
          </label>
➤         <input type="text" class="form-control" name="street-address"
➤                bindon-ngModel="address.street">
        </div>
        <div class="row">
          <div class="col-md-6">
            <div class="form-group">
              <label class="sr-only" for="city">City</label>
➤             <input type="text" class="form-control" name="city"
➤                    bindon-ngModel="address.city">
            </div>
          </div>
          <div class="col-md-2">
            <div class="form-group">
              <label class="sr-only" for="state">State</label>
➤             <input type="text" class="form-control" name="state"
➤                    bindon-ngModel="address.state">
            </div>
          </div>
          <div class="col-md-4">
            <div class="form-group">
              <label class="sr-only" for="zip">Zip</label>
➤             <input type="text" class="form-control" name="zip"
➤                    bindon-ngModel="address.zipcode">
            </div>
          </div>
        </div>
      </section>
    </article>
```

If you reload the page, you'll see that it all works, and the address components are using the address from the back end instead of the static content.

There are two problems, however. Our acceptance test and our JavaScript unit test are both broken. Our acceptance test should be complaining that it can't find the user details on the details page. This is surprising since we know they are showing up in the form fields. If we add a puts page.html before the failing expectation (a handy technique discussed in *Debugging Browser-Based Tests*, on page 108), we can see that Angular isn't rendering HTML that uses the value attribute (this might be hard to see because Webpack has minified the HTML):

```
<input
  class="form-control
  ng-untouched
  ng-pristine
  ng-valid"
  name="username"
  type="text"
  ng-reflect-name="username"
  ng-reflect-model="earlene_abernathy350">
```

Angular sets the value of form fields after the page loads, so when we write expect(page).to have_content("earlene_abernathy350"), it fails because that string is not considered content by Capybara. Ah, the joys of full-stack web development!

We can change our expectation by using the have_selector matcher. This asserts that a given CSS selector successfully identifies an element on the page. In this case, the selector [ng-reflect-model='earlene_abernathy350'] would successfully locate this input.

Here's the change needed to our acceptance test:

11_angular-async/20-fetch-data/shine/spec/features/customer_search_spec.rb
```
    customer = Customer.find_by!(email: "pat123@somewhere.net")
    within "section.customer-details" do
➤     expect(page).to have_selector("[ng-reflect-model='#{customer.last_name}']")
➤     expect(page).to have_selector("[ng-reflect-model='#{customer.first_name}']")
➤     expect(page).to have_selector("[ng-reflect-model='#{customer.email}']")
➤     expect(page).to have_selector("[ng-reflect-model='#{customer.username}']")
    end
  end
end
```

Running bin/rails spec SPEC=spec/features/customer_search_spec.rb should show our acceptance tests are passing again. Next, we need to fix our JavaScript unit test.

Our JavaScript test now fails with "TypeError: undefined is not an object (evaluating 'self.activatedRoute.params') in CustomerDetailsComponent.spec.js," which isn't helpful in understanding the problem. If you poke around the stack trace, you'll see something about map and this will hopefuly jog your memory: you added calls to observable.map, so the test doubles need to account for that.

You'll also need to change the test so that customer is passed to the success callback instead of the unparsed response. Here's how it looks:

```
11_angular-async/20-fetch-data/shine/spec/javascript/CustomerDetailsComponent.spec.js
var createMockHttp = function(customer) {
  var response = td.object(["json"]);
  td.when(response.json()).thenReturn({ customer: customer });

➤ var observable = td.object(["subscribe", "map"]);
➤
➤ td.when(observable.map(
➤   td.callback(response)
➤ )).thenReturn(observable);

  td.when(observable.subscribe(
➤   td.callback(customer),
    td.matchers.isA(Function))).thenReturn();

  var mockHttp = td.object(["get"]);

  td.when(
    mockHttp.get("/customers/" + customer.id + ".json")
  ).thenReturn(observable);

  return mockHttp;
}
```

This should get our tests passing again. Next, let's pull in the credit card information from our payment processor.

Pulling Data from a Second Source

It's customary to keep sensitive data like credit card information stored outside our systems, so it's natural that it wouldn't be part of the customer records we maintain (and that Shine is allowing users to examine). While we could have our Rails application pull this data when we ask for the customer details, that would be a bad user experience. The user would be waiting for all data to come back before seeing anything. It would be better to show the user the information we have, and let the information from slower requests to the payment processor show up when it's available.

So, let's have our Angular app pull the data from both sources. That way, the user can see the customer details first (since it returns quickly thanks to our materialized view) and, when the payment processor with our credit card information has responded, that information will get filled in automatically.

Rather than set up a real payment processor, we'll create a controller in Shine that can stand in for the payment processor for the purposes of demonstrating the problem and learning about the solution.

First, let's add a controller for our fake payment processor. We'll create the file app/controllers/fake_payment_processor_controller.rb and add the following code to it:

11_angular-async/30-second-data-source/shine/app/controllers/fake_payment_processor_controller.rb

```ruby
class FakePaymentProcessorController < ApplicationController
  def show
    sleep 2
    render json: {
      credit_card_info: {
        cardholder_id: params[:id],
        last_four: Faker::Business.credit_card_number[-4..-1],
        expiration_month: Faker::Business.credit_card_expiry_date.month,
        expiration_year: Faker::Business.credit_card_expiry_date.year,
        type: Faker::Business.credit_card_type,
        link: Faker::Internet.url,
      }
    }
  end
end
```

I'm using the Faker gem again to provide realistic data. This is a simulation of what the payment processor might return and is enough data to render the UI. (The link entry is for the "View Details" button that would take the user to the payment processor's site.) Next, let's add a route to it in config/routes.rb:

11_angular-async/30-second-data-source/shine/config/routes.rb

```ruby
Rails.application.routes.draw do
  devise_for :users
  root to: "dashboard#index"
  # These supercede other /customers routes, so must
  # come before resource :customers
  get "customers/ng",                to: "customers#ng"
  get "customers/ng/*angular_route", to: "customers#ng"
  resources :customers, only: [ :index, :show ]
  get "credit_card_info/:id", to: "fake_payment_processor#show"
end
```

Now, if you have the cardholder's ID with the payment processor, you can request /credit_card_info/«cardholder_id» and get back a realistic payload. Here we've also added a call to sleep to simulate the slowness of the third-party payment system. This will allow you to see how we can handle the user experience when data comes in at different times. But first, we have to fetch the data.

This means you need to know the cardholder ID for the customer. Let's suppose that our company sends the customer's ID to the payment processor as the cardholder ID. Our Angular app should not have to know this bit of business logic, so let's put that in the Rails application so that our Angular app can just access cardholder_id from the given customer.

This is easy enough to do by creating the method cardholder_id on CustomerDetail to return customer_id. We also want this to be included in the JSON sent back from

CustomersController. You can do this by overriding serializable_hash on CustomerDetail. Rails uses this method to figure out what keys and values to serialize as JSON (or XML, or whatever other serialization format you might choose to use).

11_angular-async/30-second-data-source/shine/app/models/customer_detail.rb

```
class CustomerDetail < ApplicationRecord
  self.primary_key = 'customer_id'

➤  def cardholder_id
➤    self.customer_id
➤  end

➤  def serializable_hash(options = nil)
➤    super.merge({ cardholder_id: cardholder_id })
➤  end
end
```

Now that we have the cardholder ID coming from the back end, where should we use it? We could make CreditCardComponent just a dumb view of credit card information. That would keep CreditCardComponent simple, but require that CustomerDetailsComponent handle the work of fetching the credit card information. Let's instead make CreditCardComponent a richer component that's capable of fetching its own data.

We'll do this by passing the cardholder ID to CreditCardComponent and have *it* fetch the credit card details from the third-party payment processor. We'll modify CustomerDetailsComponent.html to pass it in:

11_angular-async/30-second-data-source/shine/app/javascript/CustomerDetailsComponent/template.html

```
    <article class="panel panel-default">
      <header class="panel-heading">
        <h2 class="h4">
          Billing Info
        </h2>
      </header>
      <section class="panel-body">
➤       <shine-credit-card
➤         bind-cardholder_id="customer.cardholder_id">
➤       </shine-credit-card>
        <hr>
        <shine-address
          addressType="Billing"
          bind-address="customer.billing_address">
        </shine-address>
      </section>
    </article>
  </div>
 </div>
</form>
</section>
```

Now, we'll configure CreditCardComponent to accept that as input:

```
11_angular-async/30-second-data-source/shine/ap.../CustomerDetailsComponent/CreditCardComponent.ts
var CreditCardComponent = Component({
  selector: "shine-credit-card",
  inputs: [
    "cardholder_id"
  ],
  template: template
}).Class({
```

While you know how to implement the Ajax request to fetch the credit card information, it's not clear where that code should go. In CustomerDetailsComponent, we put the Ajax request inside the callback used when routing was complete. That's because that is when we could first access the customer ID whose data should be fetched. When will we know the cardholder ID?

It's not necessarily inside ngOnInit. Instead, we need a callback when our bound properties change or, to be more specific, when CustomerDetailsComponent sets the value on customer that we've bound to cardholder_id. We can accomplish this by implementing another life-cycle hook: ngOnChanges.

ngOnChanges[6] is called after bound properties have changed. That's exactly what we want! The parameter to this function is an object whose keys are the properties with changes and the values are instances of SimpleChange,[7] which provides the attribute currentValue that contains the new value of the property.

With this knowledge, you can implement ngOnChanges to fetch the credit card information using the cardholder ID passed to us by CustomerDetailsComponent. You'll need to inject an instance of Http as well:

```
11_angular-async/30-second-data-source/shine/ap.../CustomerDetailsComponent/CreditCardComponent.ts
import { Component } from "@angular/core";
import { Http     } from "@angular/http";
import   template   from "./CreditCardComponent.html";

// code as before...

}).Class({
  constructor: [
    Http,
    function(http) {
      this.http          = http;
      this.cardholder_id = null;
    }
  ],
```

---

6. https://angular.io/docs/ts/latest/api/core/index/OnChanges-class.html
7. https://angular.io/docs/ts/latest/api/core/index/SimpleChange-class.html

```
ngOnChanges: function(changes) {
  if (changes.cardholder_id) {
    if (changes.cardholder_id.currentValue) {
      this.cardholder_id = changes.cardholder_id.currentValue;
      this.fetchCreditCardInfo();
    }
    else {
      this.cardholder_id    = null;
      this.credit_card_info = null;
    }
  }
},
```

All the if statements make sure we're getting changes about the cardholder ID. You'll notice we're deferring to the function fetchCreditCardInfo. Here's what that looks like:

11_angular-async/30-second-data-source/shine/ap.../CustomerDetailsComponent/CreditCardComponent.ts

```
},
fetchCreditCardInfo: function() {
  var self = this;
  self.http.get("/credit_card_info/" + self.cardholder_id).
    subscribe(
      function(response) {
        self.credit_card_info = response.json().credit_card_info;
      },
      function(response) {
        window.alert(response);
      }
  );
}
```

This function sets credit_card_info. You can now use this in CreditCardComponent.html to show the the credit card info we've fetched to the user. Note that we're guarding the entire thing using *ngIf="credit_card_info". If we don't do that, Angular will try to access the properties like last_four on undefined and cause an error.

11_angular-async/30-second-data-source/shine/ap... ustomerDetailsComponent/CreditCardComponent.html

```
<article class="credit-card-info" *ngIf="credit_card_info">
  <div class="row">
    <div class="col-md-7">
      <p class="h4">
        ****-****-****-{{credit_card_info.last_four}}
        <span class="label label-success">{{credit_card_info.type}}</span>
      </p>
      <p class="h5">
        <label>Expires:</label>
        {{credit_card_info.expiration_month}}/{{credit_card_info.expiration_year}}
      </p>
    </div>
```

```
    <div class="col-md-5 text-right">
➤     <a href="{{credit_card_info.link}}" class="btn btn-lg btn-default">
➤       View Details...
➤     </a>
    </div>
  </div>
</article>
```

Now when you reload the page, you'll see our customer information, shipping address, and billing address load quickly. The area for the credit card information will be blank, and a few seconds later, it will appear and the credit card data will be filled in. This demonstrates that you can create a UI where data is shown to the user as it becomes available, which is facilitated by splitting our UI up into components.

However, this does create a somewhat jarring user experience. While users wait for the slower credit card information to come back, they just see a blank spot on the screen. Let's use a handy UI component that comes with Bootstrap to let the user know the system is working.

Using Bootstrap's Progress Bar When Data Is Loading

Currently, when the slow-loading credit card information is loading, we see nothing under the "Billing Info" title. It's not clear to the user if anything is actually happening. This can be frustrating and confusing. Users are often happy to wait if something needs to take a while, so in those rare cases, feedback that we're still working can reduce this frustration and make it clear that the page is still working.

Bootstrap has a progress bar UI component that can be animated using only CSS animations. If we show this while the credit card information is loading, our UI will have some motion to it and allow us to indicate to the user that some information hasn't come in yet, but that the page is still working on it.

The basic outline of this UI component is as follows:

```
<aside class="progress">
  <div class="progress-bar"
    role="progressbar"
    style="width: 45%">
    Loading…
  </div>
</aside>
```

As with other Bootstrap UI components, you can customize this one by adding more classes on the inner div. You'll also notice that the style attribute is used to control the amount progress. In our case, the only progress we can report is that we're still loading, so we'll set the width to 100% so it simulates an indeterminate progress bar.

As mentioned earlier, we are ultimately using this to provide some animation to users to let them know the request is happening. To achieve that, we'll add progress-bar-striped and active to the inner div. We'll also use progress-bar-info so that the progress bar uses a different shade of blue than our customer information panel, making it stand out a bit more:

```
11_angular-async/30-second-data-source/shine/ap ... ustomerDetailsComponent/CreditCardComponent.html
</article>
<aside class="progress" *ngIf="!credit_card_info">
  <div class="progress-bar progress-bar-info progress-bar-striped active"
    role="progressbar" style="width: 100%">
    Loading...
  </div>
</aside>
```

Note also that we've used *ngIf="!credit_card_info" on the aside. This ensures that the animated progress bar only shows when we haven't yet received the credit card information from CustomerDetailsComponent.

Now, when you load the page, you'll see a nice, animated indicator that loading is happening, as shown in the screen that follows.

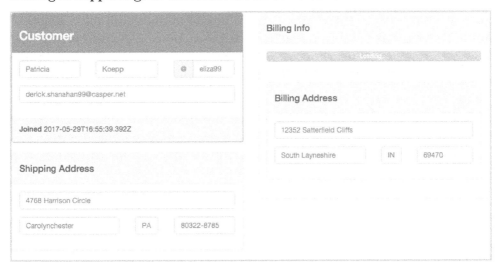

After a couple seconds, the data will be loaded, and the progress bar will be replaced with the credit card UI, as shown in the next screen.

With Angular's component-based and asynchronous design, we were able to show the user as much data as we could, as it became available. With Bootstrap's library of UI components, we easily found a way to give the user some feedback that a long-running request was happening.

Next: Sending Changes Back to the Server

In this chapter, you saw how to design your UI using components and how to pass data between them. You also saw how to initiate multiple requests to multiple locations and bring it all together asynchronously. And finally, you saw how to give the user a good experience while potentially slow-running requests were happening. But viewing data is only part of the picture.

In the next chapter, we'll add the functionality to let the user edit some of the data and have it sent back to the server and updated automatically. You'll learn more about Angular's bindings and see how to handle the disparity between our materialized view of a customer's details and the actual database model that backs it.

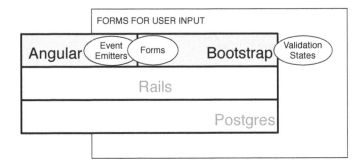

## CHAPTER 12

Wrangle Forms and Validations with Angular

So far, we've treated our application as a producer of information. It shows data quickly, easily, and in a usable way. But applications need to consume information as well, and that's what we're going to look at in this chapter. So far, you've designed a complex form that shows the user some information about a customer, and the next step is to let the user modify that information.

You could actually make this form save back to the server using what you already know. You know how to make a button, attach an event handler to execute when a user clicks it, and how to make an Ajax request. Instead of doing that, however, let's make this form more interactive. First, we'll add some basic validation to the components and use Bootstrap's form validation styles to indicate when the user has made an error. This will test your full-stack mettle, as neither Angular nor Bootstrap were designed to work together. Second, we'll arrange for the customer's data to be saved as the user makes changes—no save button required.

By adding these two features, you'll learn some more advanced Angular concepts. You'll learn how Angular manages model changes in forms, which is how you'll know which Bootstrap styles to apply where. But you'll go even deeper on components, creating a reusable text field component that notifies listeners via *event emitters* when the value it's managing changes. That's how you'll know when to save data back to the server.

At the end of the chapter, our form will be fully interactive, and the code behind it will consist of small, simple, reusable classes and components—exactly what you'd want to manage a growing application.

First, let's look at how form validation works between Angular and Bootstrap.

Marrying Angular's and Bootstrap's Form Validations

Bootstrap provides classes that, when applied to form elements, can indicate to the user that the data in that element is correct or incorrect. Angular provides features to describe the valid state of data in a form element as well as a way to check a field's validity with code. We just need to connect Bootstrap's styles with Angular's form validations.

For our form, we'll keep things simple. We'll require that every field has a value, and we'll additionally require that zip code fields look like zip codes. We may need more sophisticated validations in the future, but this will be enough to learn how they work.

 Don't make these changes to all the text fields just yet. We're going to make a generic component in the next section so that you don't have to. For now, just follow along on one or two components so you can see how everything fits together.

Angular's form validations use HTML5 validations, such as required.[1] This means that we can add the validations we need using those standard attributes. For all of the text fields, we'll add the required attribute, like so:

```
<input type="text" class="form-control" name="first_name"
       required
       bindon-ngModel="customer.first_name">
```

For the zip code fields, we'll add an additional attribute, pattern:

```
<input type="text" class="form-control" name="zip"
       required
       pattern="\d\d\d\d\d(-\d\d\d\d)?"
       bindon-ngModel="customer.zipcode">
```

If you've never used pattern before, it takes a regular expression that the field must match in order to be considered valid. Because we're dealing with U.S. zip codes, we want to allow either exactly five digits (20002) or a plus-4 format, which includes an additional four digits after a hyphen (94118-2345). This tells

---

1. http://www.w3.org/TR/2011/WD-html5-20110525/common-input-element-attributes.html#attr-input-required

Angular what our validations are. Before we see how to access a field's validity with code, let's see what Bootstrap offers us to create the user experience.

We'll use two of Bootstrap's features: form validation classes that show our form components with colored outlines, and the alert class, which we've seen before in *Style the Flash*, on page 23 and gives the user an explicit error message.

We'll use the has-warning validation class on the element we've given the form-group class to, and our text field will have a yellow outline. We'll also create an alert to give the user an error message that might look like this:

Pat	Jones	pat123
This field is required		

pattyj@somewhere.net

Joined 12/13/2014

Given these features of Bootstrap, how do you use them? First you need to know if a field's value is considered valid so that you can conditionally apply these styles.

To access the field's validity programmatically, you can declare *template reference variables*. A template reference variable is a variable you can create that only exists inside our template and is attached to something in that template. To be more specific, you can declare a variable that holds the model that powers a text field, so you can then examine that model to see if its value is valid.

You've seen before how Angular recognizes special prefixes to unlock particular features. For example, we've been using bind-, on- and bindon- in various elements to wire bits of our code together. To create a template reference variable, we use the prefix ref-, like so:

```
<div class="form-group">
  <label class="sr-only" for="first_name">First Name</label>
  <input type="text" class="form-control" name="first_name"
         required
         ref-firstName="ngModel"
         >
</div>
```

This tells Angular that, inside our template, firstName is a reference to the model of the input field we've created for the customer's first name. ngModel is the name of an attribute Angular exposes so that we can refer to the underlying model explicitly.

With this variable declared, we can use it in our template to create conditional markup. This variable exposes a few properties we can use to check the validation state. Note that this is the validation state of the *control*, which *includes* the value. This is somewhat subtle, but it allows you to differentiate between an invalid value in a control the user hasn't interacted with and a control that they have.

It might help to sort all this out by examining these properties of the template reference variable:

- pristine is true if the user hasn't interacted with the control. If the user has, dirty is true.

- touched is true if the control has been visited (meaning it's achieved and then lost focus). untouched is true if the control hasn't been visited.

- valid is true if the current value passes the existing validation checks. invalid is true if it hasn't.

Using this, we can now modify our UI so that when a value is invalid, we highlight the field using Bootstrap's form validation classes and also show the user an error message.

First, we'll arrange to have has-warning added to our form-group if the value is invalid. We can do this by binding the class attribute like so:

```
<div bind-class="( firstName.invalid && firstName.dirty ) ?
                 'form-group has-warning' :
                 'form-group'">
  <!-- field markup -->
</div>
```

This means that if firstName is both invalid and dirty (in other words, the user modified the value to be invalid), we set the class of the div to be "form-group has-warning"; otherwise we set it to "form-group" (which it has to have in both cases). Because we've bound the value to class, it will change as firstName's value changes. Note that this is actual code being executed, so we can (and will in *Customizing the Component's Behavior and Appearance*, on page 230) extract it into a help function of our component. For now, it's easier to see it all in one place, so we've inlined it.

You can now combine this technique with both *ngIf and Bootstrap's alert component to create a more explicit error message:

```
<aside *ngIf="model.invalid && model.dirty"
       class="alert alert-danger">
  <small>This is required</small>
</aside>
```

Putting it all together, here is our complete text field for the customer's first name, with full validation and necessary UI to make it clear to the user:

```
<div bind-class="( firstName.invalid && firstName.dirty ) ?
                  'form-group has-warning' :
                  'form-group'">
  <label class="sr-only" for="first_name">
    First Name
  </label>
  <input type="text" class="form-control" name="first-name"
         required
         bindon-ngModel="customer.first_name"
         ref-firstName="ngModel"
         >
  <aside *ngIf="firstName.invalid && firstName.dirty"
    class="alert alert-danger">
    <small>This is required</small>
  </aside>
</div>
```

In the context of our form, it looks like our initial mock-up:

The great thing about this is that you didn't have to write a lot of code. The downside is that it required a lot of new markup that you'd have to replicate across all of the text fields to allow them to be validated. You'll notice that there's nothing Shine-specific about this snippet of markup; it is just a generic text field managing a value for a required field. You could use almost this exact markup for every text field on the page.

So, let's do that! Angular encourages a component-based design, and a component can be anything. Let's turn what we've just learned into a self-contained, generic text field component and reuse that everywhere on the page. That will save us a lot of duplicated markup and make it easier to get our work done— exactly why we chose Angular in the first place.

Reusing Markup with a Generic Text Field Component

You've already seen how to reuse markup when we created the AddressComponent in Chapter 11, *Asynchronously Load Data*, on page 193. Our TextFieldComponent is even more generic, so we will need to have a few more properties that the user has to set. To make this generic, we need to get a few bits of information from the user:

- The name of the field being edited

- A label to use for the field

- An optional flag for the addon (you'll recall from *Form Add-Ons*, on page 166 that we added nicely styled @ in front of the username control)

Let's see how those values would be used in our markup. A completely generic version of our text field would now look like this:

```
12_angular-forms/10-text-component/shine/app/javascript/TextFieldComponent/template.html
<div bind-class="( model.invalid && model.dirty ) ?
                  'form-group has-warning' :
                  'form-group'">
  <label class="sr-only" attr.for="{{field_name}}">
    {{label}}
  </label>
  <div bind-class="addon ? 'input-group' : ''">
    <div *ngIf="addon" class="input-group-addon">{{addon}}</div>
    <input type="text" class="form-control" attr.name="{{field_name}}"
           required
           bindon-ngModel="object[field_name]"
           ref-model="ngModel"
           >
  </div>
  <aside *ngIf="model.invalid && model.dirty"
    class="alert alert-danger">
    <small>This is required</small>
  </aside>
</div>
```

Note that we've put this in app/javascript/TextFieldComponent, and not in app/java-script/CustomerDetailsComponent, because this component is intended to be totally generic. There are a few notable differences between this and the markup we saw in the previous section. First, we had to handle the addon. This means that if addon is true, our markup works properly and renders like so:

```
<div class="input-group">
  <div class="input-group-addon">@</div>

  <!-- form control markup -->

</div>
```

Without it, the class input-group on the outermost div is omitted, leaving us with an empty div (turns out, leaving it there causes odd rendering issues when we aren't using an addon):

```
<div>

  <!-- form control markup -->

</div>
```

Second, we're using code like attr.for="{{field_name}}". You might think we should be doing for="{{field_name}}", but this won't work. You'll get an error like "Can't bind to 'for' since it isn't a known property of label." This is because Angular is trying to set the property for on its internal representation of a label, and it has no for property. We really want to set the underlying label element's for attribute. It's a subtle difference.

To do that, prefix the property with attr., which tells Angular that we want to set the for attribute of the underlying HTML element.

The final odd bit is that we're using bindon-ngModel="object[field_name]". Because the other parts of the markup just use field_name directly (for example, attr.name="field_name"), this sticks out as strange.

If you just bind to the field we're managing using bindon-ngModel="field_name", the changes won't be seen on the customer object containing the value. It's not clear to me why this is, but our overall feature definitely won't work if you bind directly to the field, So, bind to object[field_name], which would be like binding to customer.first_name.

With this markup created, our component's JavaScript is fairly bare-bones:

```
12_angular-forms/10-text-component/shine/app/javascript/TextFieldComponent/index.ts
import { Component } from "@angular/core";
import    template    from "./template.html";

var TextFieldComponent = Component({
```

```
  selector: "shine-text-field",
  template: template,
  inputs: [
    "object",
    "field_name",
    "label",
    "addon"
  ]
}).Class({
  constructor: [
    function() {
      this.object     = null;
      this.field_name = null;
      this.label      = null;
      this.addon      = null;
    }
  ]
});

export { TextFieldComponent };
```

Finally, we need to tell our NgModule in app/javascript/packs/customers.js about our new component:

12_angular-forms/10-text-component/shine/app/javascript/packs/customers.js
```
import "polyfills";

import { Component, NgModule    } from "@angular/core";
import { BrowserModule          } from "@angular/platform-browser";
import { FormsModule            } from "@angular/forms";
import { platformBrowserDynamic } from "@angular/platform-browser-dynamic";
import { HttpModule             } from "@angular/http";
import { RouterModule           } from "@angular/router";

import { CustomerSearchComponent  } from "CustomerSearchComponent";
import { CustomerDetailsComponent } from "CustomerDetailsComponent";
import { CustomerInfoComponent    } from
  "CustomerDetailsComponent/CustomerInfoComponent";
import { AddressComponent         } from
  "CustomerDetailsComponent/AddressComponent";
import { CreditCardComponent      } from
  "CustomerDetailsComponent/CreditCardComponent";
import { TextFieldComponent       } from "TextFieldComponent";

// code as before...

var CustomerAppModule = NgModule({
  imports:      [
    BrowserModule,
    FormsModule,
    HttpModule,
    routing
  ],
```

```
  declarations: [
    CustomerSearchComponent,
    CustomerDetailsComponent,
    CustomerInfoComponent,
    AddressComponent,
    CreditCardComponent,
➤   TextFieldComponent,
    AppComponent
  ],
  bootstrap: [ AppComponent ]
})
.Class({
  constructor: function() {}
});

platformBrowserDynamic().bootstrapModule(CustomerAppModule);
```

This allows you to replace the markup in our components with a reference to shine-text-field, like so:

```
<shine-text-field
  bind-object="customer"
  field_name="first_name"
  label="First Name">
</shine-text-field>
```

You can now replace all references to text fields with markup like this. Although it's overall less repetition, it's still repetitive, so we'll omit the entire listing here to save space.

Once you do this replacement, you should see that all of our fields now require values. While you still need to get to actually saving the data back to the server, you'll notice a few problems with the address components. If you omit the state and set the zip code to an invalid value like "abcd," the problems become apparent:

The state field is too small for the error message, and we didn't add validation that the zip code field is a valid U.S. zip code. We really should fix this before we get to saving the data.

Customizing the Component's Behavior and Appearance

There are many ways to address the odd rendering of the error message on the state field as well as add support for pattern-based validation. We'll address this using what we already know.

Because our component can't easily tell how big it will be when rendered, it can't automatically fix the error message rendering issue. While you could use some custom CSS to make it look okay, let's create a first-class feature of our component called "compact." The user of our component will know if it's going to be rendered in a small space. When we set compact on our component, we'll omit the message entirely and instead render the text field in red when there's an error. Our browser's built-in tooltip for HTML5 validations will give the user a clue as to what the error is.

For doing pattern-based validation, we'll create a new property called pattern that users can set if they want something other than the basic check for a required value. This means our AddressComponent will look like this:

12_angular-forms/20-customize-component/shine/a ... t/CustomerDetailsComponent/AddressComponent.html

```html
<article class="panel panel-default {{addressType}}">
  <header class="panel-heading">
    <h2 class="h4">
      {{addressType}} Address
    </h2>
  </header>
  <section class="panel-body">

  <!-- rest of the markup -->

      <div class="col-md-2">
        <shine-text-field
          bind-object="address"
          field_name="state"
          compact="true"
          label="State">
        </shine-text-field>
      </div>
      <div class="col-md-4">
        <shine-text-field
          bind-object="address"
          field_name="zipcode"
          pattern="\d\d\d\d\d(-\d\d\d\d)?"
          label="Zip Code">
        </shine-text-field>
```

```
        </div>
      </div>
    </section>
  </article>
```

We'll then add these new properties to TextFieldComponent:

12_angular-forms/20-customize-component/shine/app/javascript/TextFieldComponent/index.ts

```
import { Component } from "@angular/core";
import    template    from "./template.html";

var TextFieldComponent = Component({
  selector: "shine-text-field",
  template: template,
  inputs: [
    "object",
    "field_name",
    "label",
    "pattern",
    "compact",
    "addon"
  ]
}).Class({
  constructor: [
    function() {
      this.object     = null;
      this.field_name = null;
      this.label      = null;
      this.pattern    = null;
      this.compact    = false;
      this.addon      = null;
    }
  ]
});

export { TextFieldComponent };
```

With this in place, here's what we need to do:

- Don't render the error message if compact is true.

- Render the text field in red if there is a validation problem and compact is true.

- Show a different error message if pattern is set.

You can achieve the first by adding compact to our existing *ngIf. To render the text field in red, use bind.class in a similar fashion as when you added the has-warning class to our form-group. To show a different error message, you can use span elements around the different messages and *ngIf to show them based on the value of pattern. Here's what the new component looks like:

```
12_angular-forms/20-customize-component/shine/app/javascript/TextFieldComponent/template.html
<div bind-class="( model.invalid && model.dirty ) ?
                  'form-group has-warning' :
                  'form-group'">
  <label class="sr-only" attr.for="{{field_name}}">
    {{label}}
  </label>
  <div bind-class="addon ? 'input-group' : ''">
    <div *ngIf="addon" class="input-group-addon">{{addon}}</div>
    <input type="text"
           bind-class="( compact && model.invalid && model.dirty ) ?
                        'form-control alert-danger' :
                        'form-control'"
           attr.name="{{field_name}}"
           required
           bind-pattern="pattern ? pattern : '^.*$'"
           bindon-ngModel="object[field_name]"
           ref-model="ngModel"
           >
  </div>
  <aside *ngIf="!compact && model.invalid && model.dirty"
    class="alert alert-danger">
    <small>
      <span *ngIf="pattern">This is not a {{label}}</span>
      <span *ngIf="!pattern">This is required</span>
    </small>
  </aside>
</div>
```

With this change in place, our validations look a lot better in AddressComponent:

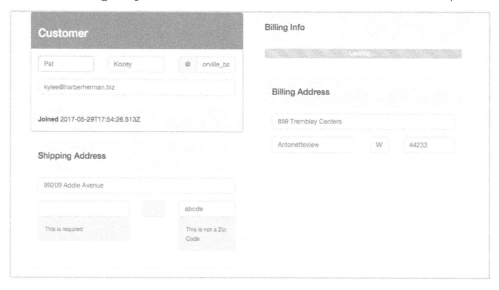

Notice where the logic ended up. We created new properties of our component —these are additional ways to customize it that users can take advantage of. Their effect on the component was purely in how it looked in different situations, and we were able to put that logic in the template, which makes sense.

That being said, the expressions we're using to adjust the behavior of our component are somewhat complex and duplicated. Let's extract them to a testable function. For our case, we'll create two: modelValid and validationPattern.

modelValid will accept the model and return true if it's both valid and pristine. Our test looks like this:

```
12_angular-forms/30-extract-functions/shine/spec/javascript/TextFieldComponent.spec.js
import "./SpecHelper";
import { TextFieldComponent } from "TextFieldComponent";

var component = null;

describe("TextFieldComponent", function() {
  beforeEach(function() {
    component = new TextFieldComponent();
  });

  describe("modelValid", function() {
    it("returns false if the model is dirty and invalid", function() {
      var model = {
        dirty: true,
        invalid: true
      }
      expect(component.modelValid(model)).toBe(false);
    });
    it("returns true if the model is dirty but valid", function() {
      var model = {
        dirty: true,
        invalid: false
      }
      expect(component.modelValid(model)).toBe(true);
    });
    it("returns true if the model is invalid but not dirty", function() {
      var model = {
        dirty: false,
        invalid: true
      }
      expect(component.modelValid(model)).toBe(true);
    });
  });
});
```

To make it pass, we'll move the logic we have in our template to a new function of our component. Note that the logic is reversed to make the function more positive. Functions that are negative (for example, modelInvalid) can be confusing.

12_angular-forms/30-extract-functions/shine/app/javascript/TextFieldComponent/index.ts
```
    ],
➤    modelValid: function(model) {
➤      return !(model.invalid && model.dirty);
➤    },
➤    validationPattern: function() {
➤      if (this.pattern) {
➤        return this.pattern;
➤      }
➤      else {
➤        return "^.*$";
➤      }
➤    }
  });

  export { TextFieldComponent };
```

Now, let's create a test for validationPattern that handles the logic of checking if pattern has been set and, if not, uses a default pattern that matches everything:

12_angular-forms/30-extract-functions/shine/spec/javascript/TextFieldComponent.spec.js
```
  describe("validationPattern", function() {
    it("returns a catch-all if pattern is null",function() {
      component.pattern = null;
      expect(component.validationPattern()).toBe("^.*$")
    });
    it("returns the pattern if it's set",function() {
      var pattern = "abcde";
      component.pattern = pattern;
      expect(component.validationPattern()).toBe(pattern);
    });
  });
});
```

Making this pass is as easy as moving the logic into another new function:

12_angular-forms/30-extract-functions/shine/app/javascript/TextFieldComponent/index.ts
```
➤    validationPattern: function() {
➤      if (this.pattern) {
➤        return this.pattern;
➤      }
➤      else {
➤        return "^.*$";
➤      }
➤    }
  });

  export { TextFieldComponent };
```

If you run our JavaScript tests with bundle exec rake karma, you should see everything pass. You can now clean up the markup with these functions:

```
12_angular-forms/30-extract-functions/shine/app/javascript/TextFieldComponent/template.html
➤ <div bind-class="modelValid(model) ?
➤                       'form-group has-warning' :
➤                       'form-group'">
    <label class="sr-only" attr.for="{{field_name}}">
      {{label}}
    </label>
    <div bind-class="addon ? 'input-group' : ''">
      <div *ngIf="addon" class="input-group-addon">{{addon}}</div>
➤     <input type="text"
➤             bind-class="( compact && !modelValid(model) ) ?
➤                           'form-control alert-danger' :
➤                           'form-control'"
➤             attr.name="{{field_name}}"
➤             required
➤             bind-pattern="validationPattern()"
➤             bindon-ngModel="object[field_name]"
➤             ref-model="ngModel"
➤             >
    </div>
➤   <aside *ngIf="!compact && !modelValid(model)"
➤     class="alert alert-danger">
      <small>
        <span *ngIf="pattern">This is not a {{label}}</span>
        <span *ngIf="!pattern">This is required</span>
      </small>
    </aside>
  </div>
```

You might think that we should have made a function like form-GroupClass(model) that encapsulates both the model validation check as well as the logic around which CSS classes to apply—we *are* repeating form-group and form-control twice, after all.

However, this would move view concerns into the component class, meaning you would have two places to check to understand how a component was styled. It's much easier to go to one place—the view template—to find out what CSS is being applied to your elements. It's a subtle distinction, but it helps keep the code understandable as it gets more complex.

Now, we have a functioning, useful component that is composed of clean, tested code. This will be invaluable in the next section when we detect changes to the customer and save them back to the server.

Listening for User Change Events

We now have everything in place to allow the user to edit data in our Angular app, including validations and user feedback using Bootstrap. Now, we need to save that data back to the server whenever it changes.

We could certainly add a button to CustomerDetailsComponent, add a click handler to it, and do an Ajax POST to the server with the customer data. But, in the interest of learning something we don't already know, let's design the app so that whenever the user tabs off of a control, that change is saved back to the server automatically. This allows us to take a look at a new way components can communicate: *event emitters*.

Communicate Between Parent and Child Components with Event Emitters

You've seen how a parent component can communicate to a child component using bindings. When you write bind-customer="customer", you're passing information from the parent to the child, and changes to customer can be seen by the parent. But those changes can't be reacted to. Put another way, the parent doesn't know when data changes; it has to check.

To notify the parent of changes happening in a child component, the child component can emit an event that the parent can listen for. This keeps the child and parent components de-coupled, but allows for structured communication. Angular provides a basic way to do this using an EventEmitter.[2]

So, what events should we emit? We need to know whenever the value of a TextFieldComponent has changed, so we'll allow anyone using a TextFieldComponent to receive events when that happens. To set this up, we'll advertise an output for others to bind to called valueChanged, and we'll initialize that as an EventEmitter:

```
12_angular-forms/40-saving-to-server/shine/app/javascript/TextFieldComponent/index.ts
import { EventEmitter,
         Component } from "@angular/core";
import   template    from "./template.html";

var TextFieldComponent = Component({
  selector: "shine-text-field",
  template: template,
  inputs: [
    "object",
    "field_name",
    "label",
```

---

2. https://angular.io/api/core/EventEmitter

```
      "pattern",
      "compact",
      "addon"
➤   ],
➤   outputs: [
➤     "valueChanged"
➤   ]
  }).Class({
    constructor: [
      function() {
        this.object       = null;
        this.field_name   = null;
        this.label        = null;
        this.pattern      = null;
        this.compact      = false;
        this.addon        = null;
➤       this.valueChanged = new EventEmitter();
      }
    ],
```

The way to use this is to call emit with whatever information you want sub-scribers to receive. In our case, we want to emit the field name and the new value, so we'll end up writing code like so:

```
this.valueChanged.emit({
  field_name: this.field_name,
  value: model.value // we'll see what 'model' is and where it comes from below
});
```

Where does that code go? Because we want to execute this code when the user changes a value, the blur event on the field seems like a logical time to do it. Alternatively, we could notify subscribers as the user types, but that would be an overwhelming amount of events, most of which would be incomplete data, as the user would still be typing.

To hook into the blur event, you can use on-blur on our input element in TextFieldComponent.html:

```
12_angular-forms/40-saving-to-server/shine/app/javascript/TextFieldComponent/template.html
<div bind-class="modelValid(model) ?
                  'form-group' :
                  'form-group has-warning'">
  <label class="sr-only" attr.for="{{field_name}}">
    {{label}}
  </label>
  <div bind-class="addon ? 'input-group' : ''">
    <div *ngIf="addon" class="input-group-addon">{{addon}}</div>
➤   <input type="text"
➤         bind-class="( compact && !modelValid(model) ) ?
➤                      'form-control alert-danger' :
```

```
                              'form-control'"
            attr.name="{{field_name}}"
            required
            bind-pattern="validationPattern()"
            bindon-ngModel="object[field_name]"
            ref-model="ngModel"
            on-blur="blur(model)"
              >
  </div>
  <aside *ngIf="!compact && !modelValid(model)"
    class="alert alert-danger">
    <small>
      <span *ngIf="pattern">This is not a {{label}}</span>
      <span *ngIf="!pattern">This is required</span>
    </small>
  </aside>
</div>
```

The blur function is where we'll emit our event. But we need to make sure we don't emit an event if the value hasn't changed, or if the value is invalid. You already know how to check if the model is valid, and you can reuse the model-Valid function you extracted in the previous section.

To check if the value has changed, you first need to store the original value. Because we're binding our input field to a field on the customer, that field is being changed as the user types, even if the user types invalid values. So, we need to save the value we were given when the component was initialized. You saw how to hook into this using ngOnInit in *Extract Details from the Route*, on page 140.

12_angular-forms/40-saving-to-server/shine/app/javascript/TextFieldComponent/index.ts
```
  },
  ngOnInit: function() {
    if (this.object && this.field_name) {
      this.originalValue = this.object[this.field_name];
    }
    else {
      this.originalValue = null;
    }
  },
  blur: function(model) {
    if (this.modelValid(model)) {
      if (this.originalValue != model.value) {
        this.valueChanged.emit({
          field_name: this.field_name,
          value: model.value
        });
        this.originalValue = model.value;
      }
```

```
      }
    }
  });
  export { TextFieldComponent };
```

Now, we can implement blur:

12_angular-forms/40-saving-to-server/shine/app/javascript/TextFieldComponent/index.ts

```
  blur: function(model) {
    if (this.modelValid(model)) {
      if (this.originalValue != model.value) {
        this.valueChanged.emit({
          field_name: this.field_name,
          value: model.value
        });
        this.originalValue = model.value;
      }
    }
  }
  });
  export { TextFieldComponent };
```

With this in place, how does the parent hook into it? What we've done is create our own custom event much like the Angular-provided click and blur events, so a parent component will specify on-valueChanged in the view template to connect their code with our event. Here's how that looks in CustomerInfoComponent:

12_angular-forms/40-saving-to-server/shine/app/ ... tomerDetailsComponent/CustomerInfoComponent.html

```
<article class="panel panel-primary customer-info" *ngIf="customer">
  <header class="panel-heading">
    <h1 class="h3">
      Customer
    </h1>
  </header>
  <section class="panel-body">
    <div class="row">
      <div class="col-md-4">
        <shine-text-field
          bind-object="customer"
          field_name="first_name"
          on-valueChanged="save($event)"
          label="First Name">
        </shine-text-field>
      </div>
```

And here's a simple version of save that just logs the contents of the event:

```
save: function(update) {
  console.log("Saving " + update.field_name + " = " +
                          update.value);
}
```

If you open up your browser's JavaScript console and change a user's first name, you can see this being logged, as shown in the following screen.

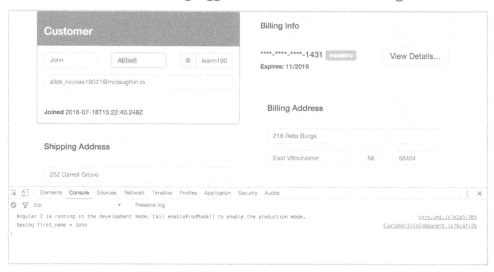

We've set all this up so that TextFieldComponent doesn't have to worry about where the updated values need to get saved—we could use this component for data that isn't about our customers. CustomerInfoComponent, however, *does* know about customers and could be the place to save this information.

But think about how we're fetching the information. Currently, CustomerDetailsComponent—the component powering the page—fetches the customer data and passes it along to the child components. It seems logical, then, that CustomerDetailsComponent should do the saving, too. So, let's have CustomerInfoComponent and AddressComponent emit their own events so that CustomerDetailsComponent can listen for them and save them.

Pass Events from Child to Grandparent Components

For CustomerInfoComponent, we'll set up the output property customerInfoChanged and have save pass along the event:

12_angular-forms/40-saving-to-server/shine/app/…ustomerDetailsComponent/CustomerInfoComponent.ts

```
import { EventEmitter,
         Component } from "@angular/core";
import    template    from "./CustomerInfoComponent.html";

var CustomerInfoComponent = Component({
  selector: "shine-customer-info",
  inputs: [
    "customer"
  ],
  outputs: [
```

```
      "customerInfoChanged"
    ],
    template: template
  }).Class({
    constructor: [
      function() {
        this.customer            = null;
        this.customerInfoChanged = new EventEmitter();
      }
    ],
    save: function(update) {
      this.customerInfoChanged.emit(update);
    }
  });

  export { CustomerInfoComponent };
```

We'll do the same thing for AddressComponent, but instead use the output property addressChanged, which reinforces the generic nature of this component:

12_angular-forms/40-saving-to-server/shine/app/ ... ipt/CustomerDetailsComponent/AddressComponent.ts

```
import { EventEmitter,
         Component } from "@angular/core";
import    template    from "./AddressComponent.html";

var AddressComponent = Component({
  selector: "shine-address",
  inputs: [
    "address",
    "addressType"
  ],
  outputs: [
    "addressChanged"
  ],
  template: template
}).Class({
  constructor: [
    function() {
      this.address        = null;
      this.addressType    = null;
      this.addressChanged = new EventEmitter();
    }
  ],
  save: function(update) {
    this.addressChanged.emit(update);
  }
});

export { AddressComponent };
```

Don't forget to add on-valueChanged to all uses of shine-text-field in both CustomerIn-foComponent.html and AddressComponent.html. (I'm omitting that code listing here for space concerns, but it's all in the downloadable code bundle on the book's companion website.)

Last, CustomerDetailsComponent needs to hear these events. There is a subtlety here, in that we're using AddressComponent twice: once for the shipping address and once for the billing address. The events we're going to receive are only that "an address changed"; we won't necessarily know *which* address.

We can deal with this by binding the event to different functions in CustomerDetailsComponent:

```
12_angular-forms/40-saving-to-server/shine/app/javascript/CustomerDetailsComponent/template.html
<section class="customer-details" *ngIf="customer">
<form>
  <div class="row">
    <div class="col-md-6">
➤     <shine-customer-info
➤       bind-customer="customer"
➤       on-customerInfoChanged="saveCustomer($event)">
➤     </shine-customer-info>
➤     <shine-address
➤       addressType="Shipping"
➤       bind-address="customer.shipping_address"
➤       on-addressChanged="saveShippingAddress($event)">
➤     </shine-address>
    </div>
    <div class="col-md-6">
      <article class="panel panel-default">
        <header class="panel-heading">
          <h2 class="h4">
            Billing Info
          </h2>
        </header>
        <section class="panel-body">
          <shine-credit-card
            bind-cardholder_id="customer.cardholder_id">
          </shine-credit-card>
          <hr>
➤         <shine-address
➤           addressType="Billing"
➤           bind-address="customer.billing_address"
➤           on-addressChanged="saveBillingAddress($event)">
➤         </shine-address>
        </section>
      </article>
    </div>
  </div>
</form>
</section>
```

Notice the levels of encapsulation and where responsibilities lie. The incredibly generic TextFieldComponent just knows how to render a text field and publish changes the user makes to the value it's managing. The higher-level, but somewhat generic, AddressComponent and CustomerInfoComponent know how to render a form for more complex bits of data, but still don't know how to do anything with changes to the data they manage. Instead, they publish a higher-level event: "The customer info I'm managing has changed."

At the highest level is a specific component—CustomerDetailsComponent—that has a single purpose: render and save the customer data for the customer details screen in Shine.

Let's make the latter happen, which will complete our Customer Details feature!

Saving Changes to the Server

Although you know how to make an Ajax request, saving the data has a few subtleties. First, our events only have the field that was changed along with its new value, not the entire customer record. That means that ideally, we just post the customer ID and the changed field to the server. The second subtlety is translating a generic address change like "the zip code was updated" to the more specific change of "the billing zip code was updated."

To do this, we'll create a function called saveCustomerField that accepts the name of the field *as sent from the server* (such as shipping_street) and the new value. With this information we'll use the patch function on Http and send a simple object mapping the field name to the value like { "first_name": "Pat" }. Note that you have to call subscribe on the observable returned by patch or the HTTP request won't be made:

```
12_angular-forms/40-saving-to-server/shine/app/javascript/CustomerDetailsComponent/index.ts
},
saveCustomerField: function(field_name, value) {
  var update = {};
  update[field_name] = value;
  this.http.patch(
    "/customers/" + this.customer.customer_id + ".json", update
  ).subscribe(
    function() {},
    function(response) {
      window.alert(response);
    }
  );
},
```

You can now implement saveCutomer, saveShippingAddress, and saveBillingAddress to use saveCustomerField:

```
12_angular-forms/40-saving-to-server/shine/app/javascript/CustomerDetailsComponent/index.ts
  saveCustomer: function(update) {
    this.saveCustomerField(update.field_name, update.value);
  },
  saveShippingAddress: function(update) {
    this.saveCustomerField("shipping_" + update.field_name, update.value);
  },
  saveBillingAddress: function(update) {
    this.saveCustomerField("billing_" + update.field_name, update.value);
  }
});
export { CustomerDetailsComponent };
```

All that's left is to implement the Rails side of this to actually save the data.

The most idiomatic way to do this in Rails is to have the CustomersController's update method find the CustomerDetail record, and call update on that:

```
12_angular-forms/40-saving-to-server/shine/app/controllers/customers_controller.rb
def update
  customer_detail = CustomerDetail.find(params[:id])
  customer_detail.update(params)
  head :ok
end
```

Note that you don't need to send anything back to the caller, so head :ok is sufficient to return an HTTP 200.

We'll also need to configure the route for this new method in config/routes.rb:

```
12_angular-forms/40-saving-to-server/shine/config/routes.rb
Rails.application.routes.draw do
  devise_for :users
  root to: "dashboard#index"
  # These supercede other /customers routes, so must
  # come before resource :customers
  get "customers/ng",                 to: "customers#ng"
  get "customers/ng/*angular_route", to: "customers#ng"
  resources :customers, only: [ :index, :show, :update ]
  #                                          ^^^^^^^
  get "credit_card_info/:id", to: "fake_payment_processor#show"
end
```

As you recall from *Using Materialized Views for Better Performance*, on page 179, CustomerDetail is an Active Record that provides access to our materialized view CUSTOMER_DETAILS. Like any other view, you can't modify it—a view is only for reading data. If we were to try customer_detail.update_attributes(billing_city: "Washington"), it wouldn't work.

This means that we have to write some code to figure out what tables need to be updated based on the parameters we get. We'll write this code in the update method of CustomerDetail so that our controller can continue to look like idiomatic Rails.

To make this work, update will have to pick apart the parameters it needs for updating the Customer or its Addresses. We can do that with require, which is provided by Rails's strong parameters.[3]

To deal with the mismatch in address parameters, we'll make a helper method called address_attributes that will convert fields like billing_street into street so that we can update Address records:

```
12_angular-forms/40-saving-to-server/shine/app/models/customer_detail.rb
class CustomerDetail < ApplicationRecord

  # rest of class...

  def update(params)
    Customer.transaction do
      Customer.find(self.customer_id).update(
        params.permit(:first_name, :last_name, :username, :email))

      Address.find(self.billing_address_id).update(
        address_attributes(params,"billing"))

      Address.find(self.shipping_address_id).update(
        address_attributes(params, "shipping"))
    end
  end

private

  def address_attributes(params, type)
    attributes = {
      street: params["#{type}_street"],
        city: params["#{type}_city"],
       state: State.find_by(code: params["#{type}_state"]),
     zipcode: params["#{type}_zipcode"],
    }
    attributes.delete_if { |_key,value| value.nil? }
  end
end
```

There are two unusual things about this code. The first is the use of a database transaction. This is done because we are updating multiple tables at once

---

3.   http://guides.rubyonrails.org/action_controller_overview.html#strong-parameters

and we want the update to be all-or-nothing. A database transaction makes that happen. Second, there's a call to delete_if in address_attributes. This removes any keys from the hash that have a nil value. Leaving them will cause Active Record to set their values to null in the database, which is not permitted by our database design.

If you try it now, you'll get an error from Rails like "Can't verify CSRF token authenticity." This is Rails Cross-Site Request Forgery protection[4] in action. When Rails is managing the view, it sets up this protection for you. Angular, being agnostic of the middleware part of the stack, doesn't do it the way Rails does it.

This is easily remedied with the *angular_rails_csrf* gem,[5] which we'll add to our Gemfile:

```
12_angular-forms/40-saving-to-server/shine/Gemfile
gem 'faker'
gem 'angular_rails_csrf'
```

After you install it with bundle install, everything should work! If you load Shine in your browser, find a customer, and start editing, the changes are saved the server. You can see them in the Rails log as well as in your database.

Updates May Seem Slow

Remember, where we left our materialized view in Chapter 10, *Cache Complex Queries*, on page 169 was that each change to an underlying table would use a database trigger to REFRESH MATERIALIZED VIEW CONCURRENTLY. Given the amount of data you've inserted, this is quite slow.

This means if you refresh the page after making an update, you won't see the updates. We discussed strategies to deal with this, but I thought I'd remind you of the consequences. In reality, a customer service agent—the user of Shine—would not refresh the page. They'd just move onto the next issue they had to deal with. By the time anyone needed the customer's updated data again, the view would be refreshed.

Our feature is now complete! Users can find customers, view their data, and change it as needed. It's worth pointing out that we haven't used Rails validators anywhere. Given the requirements of our data, and the features provided by Angular, we really don't need to. Our Angular app prevents bad data being

---

4. http://guides.rubyonrails.org/security.html#csrf-countermeasures
5. https://github.com/jsanders/angular_rails_csrf

submitted by users, and manages the user experience around that. Our database constraints make sure bad data that *does* get through can't be saved. Using Rails validations wouldn't add any value here.

That said, Rails validators are much more sophisticated and powerful than what you can do with HTML5 validations. They also can be a more centralized location for user-facing validation if your Rails application becomes large. (For example, if you made a second UI to manage some customer data, it would need to duplicate the Angular validations if you didn't use Rails's validations.) In those cases, you would need to devise a way for your Rails controller to send back validation errors and then to use them in your Angular app.

You already have all the tools to make this happen. You can handle errors from the server by passing a function to subscribe (we're currently just calling window.alert), and you can dynamically update your view based on data changes. Active Record errors serialize to JSON well. So, when you need more validation than Angular can give you, and you choose to use Rails's validators, you can easily integrate them with your Angular app.

Next: Everything Else

At this point, our work is done! You've created a highly complex page with a clean design, one that performs well and gives a great user experience. It took expertise in Bootstrap, Angular, and Postgres to make it happen. Take a moment to click around Shine and reflect on what you've done.

Although you've done a lot of setup and installed a lot of software, you've hardly written any code and every layer of our application is clean. You didn't write any CSS, and you've only written the JavaScript specific to the problems you're solving: no hacky data- attributes or code tightly coupled to the DOM. Our Rails controller code looks like a regular Rails controller, even though it's backed by a powerful, self-updating materialized view of our complex data.

There is so much more we could cover. We've only hit the tip of the iceberg with these technologies, but hopefully you are starting to see how employing Angular, Bootstrap, and Postgres together with Rails allows you to get a lot of great work done with little effort. You can keep leveling yourself up by opening the documentation and getting inspired.

But before I send you on your way, I want to take one last trip through these technologies to show some of the other possibilities and amazing things you can do with them. The next chapter is a grab bag of everything we didn't have space to get into earlier.

## CHAPTER 13

Dig Deeper

Throughout the book, we implemented a simple feature to search for, view, and edit customer details. This was a great framing example to learn a lot about full-stack development, from optimizing our database to creating a great user experience. Hopefully, this has emboldened you to dig deeper into the tools you're using, where you'll find easy solutions to the problems you face day to day.

And Angular, Postgres, and Bootstrap are *deep* tools. This chapter exposes you to more features that you'll find handy but that we don't have space to delve into deeply. Unlike the previous chapters, we won't wind these into a tale of feature development, but rather I'll provide terse examples with links for more information. Think of this chapter as inspiration for the work you'll be doing.

Unlocking More of Postgres's Power

For most of my career, I viewed SQL databases as dumb stores for simplistic data. Postgres has shattered that view. In this section we'll look at Postgres's many advanced column types, like JSON, arrays, and enumerated types. You'll then see that Postgres supports full-text search out of the box before finishing up with the most mundane yet frequently needed tasks: CSV export.

Modeling Your Data with Advanced Column Types

Most databases store numbers and strings. For storing more advanced structures, like arrays or maps, you typically have to create them using tables. Postgres provides more advanced types to avoid doing that, and they can be a huge time-saver. Let's go over a few of them and show how they might be useful.

Arrays

Suppose we want to add role-based security to Shine. That is, a user can have zero or more roles, and each action in Shine requires that the user has a certain role. You might need the view_billing role to view a customer's billing information, or the edit_customer role to edit a customer's data.

In most SQL databases, you would need to create two new tables: the table of roles and the join table that joins users to roles (USERS_ROLES), as illustrated in the following diagram.

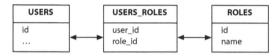

In Postgres, you can avoid all this and add an array on customers. This works pretty much like you'd expect. Active Record supports this data type by using array: true when defining the column. Here's how we'd add this to our existing USERS table:

```
> bundle exec rails g migration add_roles
```

13_dig-deeper/10-grab-bag/shine/db/migrate/20161130130034_add_roles.rb
```
class AddRoles < ActiveRecord::Migration[5.0]
  def change
    add_column :users, :roles, :string, array: true, default: []
  end
end
```

After running this migration with bundle exec rails db:migrate, we can then use this like a normal array in Ruby:

```
> bundle exec rails c
irb(main):001:0> user = User.first
=> #<User id: 1, email: "davetron5000@example.com"…
irb(main):002:0> user.roles = [ "admin", "edit_customers" ]
=> ["admin", "edit_customers"]
irb(main):003:0> user.save!
=> true
irb(main):004:0> user.reload
=> #<User id: 1, email: "davetron5000@example.com"…
irb(main):005:0> user.roles
=> ["admin", "edit_customers"]
```

You can see how Postgres stores this by going into the database directly:

```
> bundle exec rails dbconsole
shine_development=> select id,email,roles from users where id = 1;
 id | email                     | roles
----+---------------------------+-----------------------
  1 | davetron5000@example.com  | {admin,edit_customers}
```

But that's not all. An array can be searched with SQL. Suppose we want to find all the users with the role edit_customers. Postgres provides the @> operator to do just that:

```
shine_development=> update users set roles = '{admin}' where id = 2;
UPDATE 1
shine_development=> select id,email,roles from users where
                    roles @> ARRAY['admin'::varchar];
 id | email                  | roles
----+------------------------+----------------------
  1 | davetron5000@example.com | {admin,edit_customers}
  2 | foo@example.com          | {admin}
shine_development=> select id,email,roles from users where
                    roles @> ARRAY['edit_customers'::varchar];
 id | email                  | roles
----+------------------------+----------------------
  1 | davetron5000@example.com | {admin,edit_customers}
```

The ::varchar is needed to allow Postgres to compare the values in our array with the literal 'edit_customers' we used. Postgres treats string literals as the type TEXT, but Rails declared our array to be an array of VARCHAR.

This is already quite handy, but it gets better. We can *index* this array so that a query like the one shown earlier can be optimized. If we have a large USERS table, we'll see that the query is somewhat slow. If we use EXPLAIN ANALYZE on the query, we'll see the dreaded Seq Scan. As long as we're using the @> operator, however, we can improve the query by creating an index.

We can't just create a normal index, though. Postgres can only index arrays if you use a different index type. In Chapter 4, *Perform Fast Queries with*, on page 37, we created an index using a special operator class. There's an additional dimension to indexes we can control in the same way; it's called the *index type*.[1] The default, a B-Tree index, cannot index an array value. But the GIN type can. GIN[2] stands for General Inverted Index, and this index will take up more disk space and will be slower to create than a B-Tree, but it indexes arrays.

```
CREATE INDEX
  users_roles
ON
  users
USING GIN (roles)
```

---

1. http://www.postgresql.org/docs/9.1/static/indexes-types.html
2. http://www.postgresql.org/docs/9.1/static/textsearch-indexes.html

The key part of this is USING GIN. With this in place, the query is now quite fast, and our EXPLAIN ANALYZE indicates the index is being used:

```sql
sql> EXPLAIN ANALYZE
  SELECT * FROM users
  WHERE roles @> ARRAY['edit_customers'::varchar];
                            QUERY PLAN
 Bitmap Heap Scan on admin_users  (cost=9.12..268.20 rows=145 width=…
                                  (actual time=0.073..0.175 rows=145…
   Recheck Cond: (roles @> '{edit_customers}'::character varying[])
   Heap Blocks: exact=93
   -> Bitmap Index Scan on admin_users_roles
             (cost=0.00..9.09 rows=145 width=0)
             (actual time=0.056..0.056 rows=145 loops=1)
         Index Cond: (roles @> '{edit_customers}'::character varying[…
 Planning time: 0.235 ms
 Execution time: 0.219 ms
```

Generating Lots of Users

Postgres might not use this index if you don't have a lot of users —sometimes it's faster to just scan the entire table. To see the effect of this index, you can create a lot of users in the Rails console much like in db/seeds.rb.

This means that you can use an array on a large table and still get great performance out of it—performance that would certainly surpass using a join table.

HSTORE

Another common need when modeling data is storing key/value pairs. In most SQL databases, you would need to set up a generalized set of tables to do this, likely a table of possible keys, a table of possible values, and a join table to connect them to the table that needs them. An example might be user settings, as outlined in the diagram that follows.

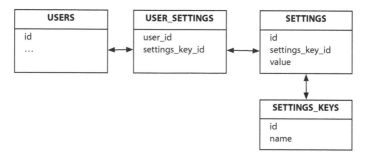

The HSTORE[3] type can solve this with a single field on USERS called settings. An HSTORE is a single-depth key/value store. Active Record supports it and treats it like a Ruby hash in your code.

This type isn't available in Postgres by default, but it can be enabled via the command enable_extension, which we can do in our Rails migration via execute. Once we've done that, we can create the column using the :hstore type:

```
> bundle exec rails g migration add_settings
```

13_dig-deeper/10-grab-bag/shine/db/migrate/20161130131705_add_settings.rb
```
class AddSettings < ActiveRecord::Migration[5.0]
  def change
    enable_extension :hstore
    add_column :users, :settings, :hstore, default: {}
  end
end
```

After we bundle exec rails db:migrate, we can treat settings just like a Ruby hash:

```
        > bundle exec rails c
irb(main):001:0> user = User.first
=> #<User id: 1, email: "davetron5000@example.com", …
irb(main):002:0> user.settings = { page_size: 20 }
=> {:page_size=>20}
irb(main):003:0> user.save!
=> true
irb(main):004:0> user.reload
=> #<User id: 1, email: "davetron5000@example.com", …
irb(main):005:0> user.settings
=> {"page_size"=>"20"}
```

Storing Deeper Hashes

 You can only store one level of depth in the hash you use with HSTORE. If you try to store a deeply nested hash, Rails will store a string representation of that hash—for example, { "page_size" => "20", "subscriptions" => "{ :offers => true }" }. Note the value of subscriptions isn't the hash { offers: true } but the *string* "{ :offers => true }". If you need to store deep structures, you should use JSON, which we'll look at in a moment.

To query this in SQL, use the -> operator, which works like Ruby's square brackets:

---

3. http://www.postgresql.org/docs/9.5/static/hstore.html

```
> bundle exec rails dbconsole
shine_development=>  select id,settings from users where
                            (settings->'page_size')::int > 0;
 id |                        settings
----+------------------------------------------------------------
  1 | "page_size"=>"20", "subscriptions"=>"{:offers=>true}"
(1 row)

shine_development=> update users set settings = '"page_size"=>"10"' where id = 2;
UPDATE 1
shine_development=>  select id,settings from users
                        where (settings->'page_size')::int > 0;
 id |                        settings
----+------------------------------------------------------------
  2 | "page_size"=>"10"
  1 | "page_size"=>"20", "subscriptions"=>"{:offers=>true}"
(2 rows)

shine_development=>  select id,settings from users
                        where (settings->'page_size')::int > 10;
 id |                        settings
----+------------------------------------------------------------
  1 | "page_size"=>"20", "subscriptions"=>"{:offers=>true}"
(1 row)
```

Note that we need to cast the result of settings->'page_size' to an int, because Postgres stores the values as strings. You can also check if an HSTORE field contains a key via the ? operator:

```
shine_development=>  select id,settings from users where (settings?'page_size');
 id |                        settings
----+------------------------------------------------------------
  2 | "page_size"=>"10"
  1 | "page_size"=>"20", "subscriptions"=>"{:offers=>true}"

shine_development=>  select id,settings from users where (settings?'foo');
 id | settings
----+----------
(0 rows)
```

Indexing options for HSTOREs are limited. You can use a GIN index to assist with the ? operator, and you can use a B-Tree index to help with testing for equality, but there isn't currently a way to index particular keys and values in an HSTORE.

Still, this is a useful data type for storing key/value data, especially if you aren't sure what keys you might need.

JSON and JSONB

Sometimes, you need to store complex, structured data that won't fit into the relational model. Either it's hierarchical or it doesn't have a small, defined set of attributes. If you were using a normal SQL database, you wouldn't be able to store this data in a useful way. You'd likely need to use a document-oriented database like CouchDB or MongoDB. Postgres, however, *can* store such data types using the JSON type.[4]

Although you can store JSON in a TEXT field (and even configure Rails to parse it for you), you can't really query a TEXT field in a useful way (for example, querying for rows that have a certain value for a JSON key). This is why many turn to document-oriented databases, because they can delve into the structure of the JSON document for querying.

Suppose we want to allow our data science team to store arbitrary insights about our customers in the database. They don't know what format they'll need, so we'll just give them a JSON column. Active Record supports this via the :json type, so we can create the column as we normally would other columns:

```
> bundle exec rails g migration add_insights_to_customers
```

13_dig-deeper/10-grab-bag/shine/db/migrate/20161130132658_add_insights_to_customers.rb
```
class AddInsightsToCustomers < ActiveRecord::Migration[5.0]
  def change
    add_column :customers, :insights, :json, default: {}
  end
end
```

After running the migration with bundle exec rails db:migrate, you can interact with this field exactly as you'd expect:

```
          > bundle exec rails c
irb(main):001:0> customer = Customer.first
=> #<Customer id: 1, first_name: "Annie", …
irb(main):002:0> customer.insights[:spendiness] = 4.5
=> 4.5
irb(main):004:0> customer.insights[:curiosity] =
{ shoes: 3, hats: 99, accessories: true }
=> {:shoes=>3, :hats=>99, :accessories=>true}
irb(main):005:0> customer.save!
irb(main):006:0> customer.reload
irb(main):007:0> customer.insights
=> {"spendiness"=>4.5, "curiosity"=>{"shoes"=>3, "hats"=>99, "accessories"=>true}}
irb(main):011:0> customer.insights["curiosity"]["shoes"]
=> 3
```

---

4. http://www.postgresql.org/docs/9.5/static/datatype-json.html

JSON columns support the -> operator (just like an HSTORE does), but this operator returns values that are also JSON types. This makes it hard to query for specific values and requires complex casting. To address this, the ->> operator is also available. ->> produces a TEXT value, which is much easier to deal with:

```
          > bundle exec rails dbconsole
shine_development=> select id,insights from customers
                    where (insights->>'spendiness')::decimal > 4;
 id |                           insights
----+-------------------------------------------------------------------
  1 | {"spendiness":4.5,"curiosity":{"shoes":3,"hats":99,"accessories":true}}
(1 row)
shine_development=> update customers set insights = '{"spendiness": 5}'
                    where id = 2;
UPDATE 1

shine_development=> select id,insights from customers
                    where (insights->>'spendiness')::decimal > 4;
 id |                           insights
----+-------------------------------------------------------------------
  2 | {"spendiness": 5}
  1 | {"spendiness":4.5,"curiosity":{"shoes":3,"hats":99,"accessories":true}}
(2 rows)

shine_development=> select id,insights from customers
                    where (insights->>'spendiness')::decimal > 4.5;
 id |      insights
----+-------------------
  2 | {"spendiness": 5}
(1 row)
shine_development=> select id,insights from customers
                    where (insights->'curiosity'->>'shoes')::decimal > 2;
 id |                           insights
----+-------------------------------------------------------------------
  1 | {"spendiness":4.5,"curiosity":{"shoes":3,"hats":99,"accessories":true}}
(1 row)
```

We can also navigate the structure more succinctly using the #>> operator. It takes an array of keys and will navigate the JSON structure, returning whatever it finds as a TEXT object. This is equivalent to the last query we ran earlier:

```
shine_development=> select id,insights from customers where
                    (insights#>>'{curiosity,shoes}')::decimal > 2;
 id |                           insights
----+-----------------------------------------------------------
  1 | {"spendiness":4.5,"curiosity":{"shoes":3,"hats":99,"acces…
```

This is obviously pretty handy. You may notice the query is a bit slow. If we EXPLAIN ANALYZE the query, we see it's doing a Seq Scan. Postgres doesn't support indexing JSON fields, but it has another data type called JSONB that works just like JSON but *can* be indexed, to a limited degree. JSONB stores a parsed representation of the JSON, so it's slower to insert but allows indexing.

In Rails, you can use :jsonb in a migration to use this type. Because we already created the column, let's convert the type in a new migration:

```
> bundle exec rails g migration switch_customer_settings_to_jsonb
```

13_dig-deeper/10-grab-bag/shine/db/migrate/20161130134926_switch_customer_settings_to_jsonb.rb
```
class SwitchCustomerSettingsToJsonb < ActiveRecord::Migration[5.0]
  def up
    change_column :customers, :insights,
      'jsonb USING CAST(insights AS jsonb)'
  end
  def down
    change_column :customers, :insights,
      'json USING CAST(insights AS json)'
  end
end
```

The bundle exec rails db:migrate might take a moment—that is a lot of rows to convert—but when it's done, we'll have some indexing options available. First, some bad news: we cannot create an index to improve our query about shoe curiosity. That query is checking if a value is greater than another value, and that cannot currently be improved with an index. But we *can* still get some value if we want to check equality.

For example, if we want everyone who's currently curious about accessories, we can improve that with an index. With what we just learned we can use a WHERE clause like (insights#>>'{curiosity,accessories}')::boolean, but this cannot be indexed. JSONB allows for a new operator, @>, which can perform the same query and it *can* be indexed. Whew!

The @> operator checks if some JSON includes some other JSON, effectively doing an equivalence check.

```
> bundle exec rails dbconsole
shine_development=> select id,insights from customers
                    where insights @>
                          '{"curiosity": { "accessories": true }}'
                    ;
 id |                           insights
----+-------------------------------------------------------------------
  1 | {"curiosity": {"hats": 99, "shoes": 3, "accessories": true}, "spend…
```

This is more cumbersome, but writing our query this way allows us to create a GIN index to improve it.

```
shine_development=> explain analyze select id,insights from customers
                    where insights@>'{"curiosity": { "accessories": true }}';
                    QUERY PLAN
-----------------------------------------------------------------------
 Seq Scan on customers  (cost=0.00..9572.03 rows=350 width=36)
                        (actual time=82.185..82.186 rows=1 loops=1)
   Filter: (insights @> '{"curiosity": {"accessories": true}}'::jsonb)
   Rows Removed by Filter: 350001
 Planning time: 0.117 ms
 Execution time: 82.206 ms

shine_development=>  create index on customers using GIN (insights);
CREATE INDEX

shine_development=> explain analyze select id,insights from customers
                    where insights @>
                            '{"curiosity": { "accessories": true }}';
                            QUERY PLAN
-------------------------------------------------------------------------------
 Bitmap Heap Scan on customers  (cost=66.71..1167.34 rows=350 width=36)
                                (actual time=0.020..0.020 rows=1 loops=1)
   Recheck Cond: (insights @> '{"curiosity": {"accessories": true}}'::jsonb)
   Heap Blocks: exact=1
   ->  Bitmap Index Scan on customers_insights_idx
         (cost=0.00..66.63 rows=350 width=0)
         (actual time=0.011..0.011 rows=1 loops=1)
         Index Cond: (insights @> '{"curiosity": {"accessories": true}}'::jsonb)
 Planning time: 0.177 ms
 Execution time: 0.045 ms
(7 rows)
```

It's hard to overstate how powerful this is. This gives you the flexibility of a document-oriented database but the performance of a relational database's queries. It also means you can write features that store both relational and free-form data that take advantage of transactional integrity, which would be impossible if you were using multiple data stores. This means that you can use Postgres for a wide variety of data-storage applications.

Active Record supports this type, but you'll still need to write SQL using these operators to do the advanced querying. For example, to perform the query we were looking at earlier, you'd need to write Ruby code like so:

```
Customer.where("insights @> ?", { curiosity: { accessories: true }}.to_json)
```

Because few databases support features like this, Active Record has no native API for this. Fortunately, where is flexible enough for us to make it work.

Enums

Rails 4 added support for enums, short for *enumerated types*,[5] which allows you to create a field that has a small number of possible values. A common use for this is for status codes. For example, we might give our customers a status of "signed_up," "verified," or "inactive."

Before Rails's support for enums, you'd need to use a string field in the database, and then something like validates_inclusion_of to be sure only the allowed types were being used. With Rails 4's enum support,[6] you can now do this more explicitly:

```ruby
class Customer < ApplicationRecord
  enum status: [ :signed_up, :verified, :inactive ]
end

c = Customer.first
c.status
# => signed_up
c.signed_up?
# => true
c.status = :foo
ArgumentError: "foo" is not a valid status
```

The problem with this is that, by default, Rails stores this in the database as a number corresponding to the index where the value falls in this array. Not only is this brittle, but also it makes the data impossible to interpret without the Ruby code.

We can tell Rails to use strings instead:

```ruby
13_dig-deeper/10-grab-bag/shine/app/models/customer.rb
class Customer < ApplicationRecord
  has_many :customers_shipping_address

  # Helper to get just the primary shipping address
  def primary_shipping_address
    self.customers_shipping_address.find_by(primary: true).address
  end
  has_one :customers_billing_address
  has_one :billing_address, through: :customers_billing_address,
                            source: :address
  enum status: {
    signed_up: "signed_up",
    verified: "verified",
    inactive: "inactive",
  }
end
```

---

5.   https://en.wikipedia.org/wiki/Enumerated_type
6.   http://api.rubyonrails.org/classes/ActiveRecord/Enum.html

It's a bit repetitive, but it makes the data easier to understand. However, it only enforces valid values from within Rails. To enforce valid values at the database, we could use a check constraint:

```
ALTER TABLE
  customers
ADD CONSTRAINT
  allowed_statuses
CHECK
  (status in ('signed_up', 'verified', 'inactive'))
```

Postgres also has support for enumerated types,[7] eliminating the need for check constraints like this. We can create a custom type named customer_status and Postgres will handle everything at the database layer, and it's all compatible with Rails.

```
> bundle exec rails g migration add_status_to_customer
```

13_dig-deeper/10-grab-bag/shine/db/migrate/20161130141129_add_status_to_customer.rb
```
class AddStatusToCustomer < ActiveRecord::Migration[5.0]
  def up
    execute %{ CREATE TYPE
               customer_status
               AS ENUM
               ('signed_up', 'verified', 'inactive' )
    }
    add_column :customers, :status, "customer_status",
               default: "signed_up", null: false
  end
  def down
    remove_column :customers, :status
    execute %{
      DROP TYPE customer_status
    }
  end
end
```

The only downside is having to repeat the values in our Active Record model, but this is a small price to pay for an explicitly modeled field in our code and database.

Postgres also has rich support for range types, various date and time types, geometric types, and even IP addresses. The documentation[8] should provide inspiration for what you can store, and how you can index it, in your database.

7.　http://www.postgresql.org/docs/9.5/static/datatype-enum.html
8.　http://www.postgresql.org/docs/9.5/static/datatype.html

Searching Free-Form Text

In addition to having advanced data types available, we can use Postgres as a full-text search engine.

In Chapter 4, *Perform Fast Queries with*, on page 37 we used LIKE to do a fuzzy search of a text field. Postgres actually supports a complete full-text search engine[9] that you can use for searching large swaths of text.

To do this, Postgres has two data types: tsvector, which represents a searchable *document*, and tsquery, which represents a query of some document. To perform a full-text search, you use the @@ operator. The left side should be a tsvector (you can turn any string type into one via the to_tsvector function) and the right side is a tsquery (similarly, you can use to_tsquery to turn a string into a tsquery).

Here's an example that searches the given string to see if it contains both "perform" and "search":

```
> bundle exec rails dbconsole
shine_development=> SELECT
                     to_tsvector(
                       'Postgres can perform a full-text search'
                     ) @@ to_tsquery('perform & search');
 ?column?
-----------
 t
(1 row)
```

You can also give to_tsquery a config name, which can help it better match the text to a query. A config is often a language, so we can use the config english and Postgres will know that if we search for performs instead of perform the string still matches, since both words are the same *normalized lexeme.*[10]

```
shine_development=> SELECT to_tsvector(
                       'english','Postgres can perform a full-text search'
                     ) @@ to_tsquery('performs & search');
 ?column?
-----------
 t
(1 row)
```

Suppose we want to allow customers to write an open-ended bio for themselves and then allow other customers to search those bios to find like-minded shoppers. We can add a new TEXT field to CUSTOMERS and create a special index on it.

---

9. http://www.postgresql.org/docs/9.5/static/textsearch-intro.html
10. https://en.wikipedia.org/wiki/Lexeme

The GIN index we looked at earlier is mostly intended for full-text search (it just happens to be useful for arrays and JSON). Let's see what it looks like.

```
> bundle exec rails g migraiton add_bio_to_customers
```

13_dig-deeper/10-grab-bag/shine/db/migrate/20161201130224_add_bio_to_customers.rb
```
class AddBioToCustomers < ActiveRecord::Migration[5.0]
  def up
    add_column :customers, :bio, :text
    execute %{
      CREATE INDEX
        customers_bio_index ON customers
      USING
        gin(to_tsvector('english', bio));
    }
  end
  def down
    remove_column :customers, :bio
  end
end
```

Note that we have to use execute because Rails doesn't provide a way to produce the string gin(to_tsvector('english', bio)) with the using: argument to create_index.

Once we bundle exec rails db:migrate, we can see that a full-text search of the bio field uses the index:

```
> bundle exec rails dbconsole
shine_development=> explain analyze select * FROM customers
                    where to_tsvector('english',bio) @@ to_tsquery('widgets');
                                QUERY PLAN
-------------------------------------------------------------------------------
 Bitmap Heap Scan on customers  (cost=209.57..4015.82 rows=1750 width=…
   Recheck Cond: (to_tsvector('english'::regconfig, bio) @@ to_tsquery…
     -> Bitmap Index Scan on customers_bio_index  (cost=0.00..209.13 ro…
         Index Cond: (to_tsvector('english'::regconfig, bio) @@ to_tsq…
 Planning time: 0.131 ms
 Execution time: 0.036 ms
```

Note that if you omit the config from the call to to_tsvector, Postgres will not be able to use the index, since that's the config we used when setting it up.

```
shine_development=> explain analyze select * from customers
                    where to_tsvector(bio) @@ to_tsquery('widgets');
                                QUERY PLAN
-------------------------------------------------------------------------------
 Seq Scan on customers  (cost=0.00..12033.00 rows=1750 width=147) (actu…
   Filter: (to_tsvector(bio) @@ to_tsquery('widgets'::text))
   Rows Removed by Filter: 350000
```

```
Planning time: 0.136 ms
Execution time: 529.359 ms
```

We can see here that it did a Seq Scan instead of using the index.

Full-text search in Postgres is extremely powerful. You can do much more than what we've just seen. You can create stop words that are not searched/indexed. You can do full-text search on concatenated fields. You can create synonyms so that, for example, a search for "database" could find strings containing "data store." You can also control how search results are ranked. All within your database!

Exporting Data to the Outside World as CSV

It's often handy to query the database and produce a comma-separated values (CSV) version of the results. This can be useful for sharing the results with nontechnical members of your team, or for pulling into a system that doesn't support SQL. Postgres makes it simple to do this via the COPY[11] command.

Suppose we want to get the names, email addresses, and IDs of all of our customers. We could do something like this:

```
> bundle exec rails dbconsole
shine_development=> COPY (
    SELECT
      id, first_name, last_name, email
    FROM
      customers
) TO '/tmp/customers.csv' WITH CSV HEADER;
```

This will run the given query, format it as CSV, and save it to /tmp/customers.csv *on the server*. This isn't always convenient, but you can use \COPY to save it to the client. If we run the same command, but using \COPY (note the backslash), it will save the CSV locally:

```
shine_development=> \COPY (
    SELECT
      id, first_name, last_name, email
    FROM
      customers
) TO '/tmp/customers.csv' WITH CSV HEADER;
```

Then /tmp/customers.csv on *our computer* will have the CSV.

---

11. http://www.postgresql.org/docs/9.5/static/sql-copy.html

Creating or Updating Records in One Statement with Upsert

Active Record provides the method find_or_create_by, which you can use to locate an existing row based on criteria, or create that row if it doesn't exist. It's a handy one-liner to avoid writing code to explicitly check the database before updating or creating a record. It's often used in conjunction with update_attributes to create or modify an existing record:

```
Customer.find_or_create_by(email: email).
        update_attributes(username: new_username)
```

Although the Ruby code is compact, this code doesn't work as it seems. First, it could run up to three SQL statements: a SELECT to try to find the customer, an INSERT to create the row if needed, and an UPDATE to change the data. There are times when executing three statements instead of one makes a difference in performance, and the previous Rails code is difficult to optimize.

The second issue with this construct is that it might not work. Suppose when we execute find_or_create_by, no customer exists with the given email address. In that case, Rails would insert a new record. Suppose further that, while that new record was being inserted, another thread or process tried to execute this code with the same email address. That thread or process would find no existing row (because the first was still executing) and try to perform an INSERT. Because there is a unique constraint on email, one of these two queries would fail.

What we really want is a way to say "insert a row, but if there is a problem, just do an update to the existing row," and do it in one statement. This is colloquially referred to as *upsert*.

Rails doesn't provide support for this. Postgres does. The syntax is clunky, but it's good to know this feature exists, if you ever need it. Here's the SQL:

```
INSERT INTO customers(
    first_name,
    last_name,
    email,
    username,
    created_at,
    updated_at
) VALUES (
    'Pat',
    'Johnson',
    'pat@thejohnsons.com',
    'pj994a',
    now(),
    now()
)
```

```
➤       ON CONFLICT (email)
➤       DO UPDATE
➤         SET first_name = excluded.first_name,
➤             last_name  = excluded.last_name,
➤             username   = excluded.username
```

The table name excluded is special. It allows you to reference the values you were attempting to insert without repeating them. This means that the above statement would insert the given row as normal if no customer existed with email of "pat@thejohnsons.com." However, if such a row *did* exist, this statement would instead *update* that row, setting the first name, last name, and username to "Pat," "Johnson," and "pj994a," respectively.

This syntax is verbose, and the only way to use this in Rails is by using the execute method on an Active Record's connection. You can derive some values from Rails and use the method quote (also on the connection) to protect against SQL injections. We might write the previous query like so:

```
Customer.connection.execute(%{
  INSERT INTO #{Customer.table_name}
  (
    first_name,
    last_name,
    username,
    created_at,
    updated_at,
    email
  ) VALUES (
    #{Customer.connection.quote(first_name)},
    #{Customer.connection.quote(last_name)},
    #{Customer.connection.quote(username)},
    now(),
    now(),
    #{Customer.connection.quote(email)}
  )
  ON CONFLICT (email)
  DO UPDATE
    SET first_name = excluded.first_name,
        last_name  = excluded.last_name,
        username   = excluded.username
})
```

This is one of those features that you hope you don't need, because the code to do it is verbose and ugly, but if you *do* need it, it's nice to know it's possible.

This completes our whirlwind tour of some of Postgres's other useful features. The documentation[12] contains more gems like these, and is quite readable, so be sure to check it out.

Leveling Up with Angular

Angular is a deep technology. What we've learned so far can take you a long way in your full-stack career and allow you to grow a large codebase that is fully unit tested and well organized. There are two other bits of Angular that you'll find useful: *pipes* and *services*. Pipes are akin to a Rails view helper—bits of code to assist in formatting text in your views. Services are a way to decompose complexity in your components or share logic between them.

Formatting View Content Using Pipes

You may have noticed that the "joined at" date in the complex view we created in Chapter 11, *Asynchronously Load Data*, on page 193, is not terribly user-friendly. It shows the entire date/time stamp in a programmery way: 2016-07-18T15:22:40.248Z. Yuck.

With what we know about JavaScript and Angular, we could add an attribute to customer that has a nicer-looking date format on it, or we could expose a function in CustomerInfoComponent to format the date. Angular provides a cleaner way called *pipes*.[13] This is best explained by an example:

13_dig-deeper/10-grab-bag/shine/app/javascript/CustomerDetailsComponent/CustomerInfoComponent.html
```
    <footer class="panel-footer">
➤     <label for="joined">Joined</label> {{customer.joined_at | date}}
    </footer>
</article>
```

Values can be piped through functions for formatting, similar to how you'd use Unix pipes on the command line. The effect of using the date pipe is to format our timestamp as a user-friendly date: "Jul 18, 2016." Pipes can be chained (again, much like the Unix command line):

```
<label for="joined">Joined</label> {{customer.joined_at | date | uppercase}}
```

This would produce "JUL 18, 2016."

Beyond the built-in pipes Angular provides, you can create your own. Suppose we want to control the way names are formatted. Because names are stored as strings, there's no enforcement of letter casing. Some customers have

---

12. http://www.postgresql.org/docs/9.5/static/index.html
13. https://angular.io/docs/ts/latest/guide/pipes.html

entered their name as "PAT," others as "pat," and even a few as "PAt"! We'd like to smooth that out by showing them in name-case. We'll make a pipe that we can use like so:

```
<h2 class="h3">
  {{customer.first_name | nameCase }} {{customer.last_name | nameCase }}
  <small>{{customer.username}}</small>
</h2>
```

To make our own pipe, we'll make a class that exposes the function transform, and that function will do the work. To keep things simple, we'll only use name case if the name is all-uppercase or all-lowercase. That'll keep us from having to special case names like "O'Farrel."

First, in app/javascript/packs/customers.js, we'll need to require our pipe class and add it to our NgModule's declarations. We'll assume it'll live in the file Name-CasePipe.js, which we'll create in a moment.

13_dig-deeper/10-grab-bag/shine/app/javascript/packs/customers.js

```
import "polyfills";

// other imports
import { TextFieldComponent } from "TextFieldComponent";
➤ import { NameCasePipe      } from "NameCasePipe";

// code as before...
var CustomerAppModule = NgModule({
  imports:       [
    BrowserModule,
    FormsModule,
    HttpModule,
    routing
  ],
  declarations: [
    CustomerSearchComponent,
    CustomerDetailsComponent,
    CustomerInfoComponent,
    AddressComponent,
    CreditCardComponent,
    TextFieldComponent,
➤    NameCasePipe,
    AppComponent
  ],
  bootstrap: [ AppComponent ]
})
.Class({
  constructor: function() {}
});

platformBrowserDynamic().bootstrapModule(CustomerAppModule);
```

Then, in app/javascript/NameCasePipe/index.ts, we'll use the Pipe function to declare our pipe, call Class on that to create our class, and implement transform:

```
13_dig-deeper/10-grab-bag/shine/app/javascript/NameCasePipe/index.ts
import { Pipe } from "@angular/core";

var NameCasePipe = Pipe({
  name: "nameCase"
}).Class({
  constructor: function() {},

  transform: function(value) {
    if (!value) { return value; }

    if ( (value.toLowerCase() === value) ||
         (value.toUpperCase() === value) ) {

      return value.charAt(0).toUpperCase() +
             value.slice(1).toLowerCase();

    }
    else {
      return value;
    }
  }
});

export { NameCasePipe };
```

To see this in action, you may need to change a user's name. Here's what I did:

```
> bundle exec rails dbconsole
shine_development=> update customers set first_name = 'PAT',
                                        last_name = 'O''Farrel' where id = 1;
shine_development=> select email from customers where id = 1;
  email
-------------------
foobar@example.com
```

I then went to the customer search and pasted in that email address (so I could be sure to find the customer I'd modified). Sure enough, the customer's name was rendered "Pat O'Farrel"!

Of course, you can't get this feature working without a bit more trouble from the JavaScript ecosystem. As of this writing, the implementation of the date pipe we first used assumes the existence of the class Intl, which is included in most modern browsers...except PhantomJS. This means, your tests will fail with an odd error such as, "Can't find variable: Intl."

Typically, there is a *shim* available, which implements the needed feature for older browsers. And typically, you can include this by referencing an online version directly in a script tag, via a service like Polyfill.io.[14] But, in our case, there's a bug in the current Intl shim that causes a *different* problem. Wonderful!

The solution is to include an older version of the shim in package.json, and set it up manually in app/javascript/packs/customers.js. We can do this with yarn add using a special syntax to indicate the version we want:

```
> yarn add intl@"1.1.0"
yarn add v0.20.3
warning No license field
[1/4] Resolving packages...
[2/4] Fetching packages...
[3/4] Linking dependencies...
[4/4] Building fresh packages...
success Saved lockfile.
success Saved 1 new dependency.
└─ intl@1.1.0
warning No license field
Done in 22.99s.
```

After that, add the following code to app/javascript/packs/customers.js:

```
13_dig-deeper/10-grab-bag/shine/app/javascript/packs/customers.js
import intl from "intl";
import "intl/locale-data/jsonp/en.js";

if (!window.Intl) {
  window.Intl = intl;
}
```

This checks if Intl exists and, if it doesn't, brings in the shim implementation that actually works. Perhaps in the future, PhantomJS will support this library or the most recent version won't be buggy and you won't have had to do all that.

Despite this setback, pipes are a great way to implement formatting across your Angular app. They can be quiet sophisticated, however, since the value being given to transform is the object, not necessarily a string. We could imagine a fullName pipe that accepts the customer object: {{ customer | fullName }}, and it could format the customer's first and last names.

Extracting Reusable Code into Services

Components are a great way to keep our front-end code organized, but sometimes, our components get complex, or we end up needing to share logic. While we can share some view logic with pipes, they don't always make sense. In an Angular app, logic can be extracted to a *service*, which is a fancy word

---

14. https://polyfill.io/v2/docs

for "a JavaScript class." This is the same concept you'd use in Ruby to create a helper class or other class to encapsulate shared logic.

The difference with Angular is that you don't create these instances yourself. You tell Angular about your service, and, in any classes that need it, tell Angular to inject that service. We've seen this with how we use Http and Router.

Let's create a simple service around observable failure. We saw in many of our classes that we wrote a function like this:

```
var observableFailed = function(result) {
  window.alert(result);
}
```

Let's create a service called AjaxFailureHandler that we can use to handle these failures the same way, without repeated code. We'd use it like so:

```
self.http.get("/credit_card_info/" + self.cardholder_id).
  subscribe(
    function(response) {
    self.credit_card_info = response.json().credit_card_info;
    },
    this.ajaxFailureHandler.handler()
  );
```

To make this work, we first define our service. It's just a plain JavaScript class, and we can use Class to create it:

```
13_dig-deeper/10-grab-bag/shine/app/javascript/AjaxFailureHandler/index.ts
import { Class } from "@angular/core";

var AjaxFailureHandler = Class({
  constructor: function() {},
  handler: function() {
    return function(response) {
      window.alert(response);
    };
  }
});

export { AjaxFailureHandler };
```

Now, wherever we want to have an instance of this class injected, we require it, add it to the providers key for the component that we want it injected into, and add it to the constructor. Here's how it would look in CreditCardComponent:

```
13_dig-deeper/10-grab-bag/shine/app/javascript/CustomerDetailsComponent/CreditCardComponent.ts
import { Component } from "@angular/core";
import { Http     } from "@angular/http";
import   template   from "./CreditCardComponent.html";

import { AjaxFailureHandler } from "AjaxFailureHandler";
```

```
var CreditCardComponent = Component({
  selector: "shine-credit-card",
  inputs: [
    "cardholder_id"
  ],
➤ providers: [
➤   AjaxFailureHandler
➤ ],
  template: template
}).Class({
  constructor: [
    Http,
➤   AjaxFailureHandler,
➤   function(http,ajaxFailureHandler) {
      this.http            = http;
      this.cardholder_id   = null;
➤     this.ajaxFailureHandler = ajaxFailureHandler;
    }
  ],

  // other methods...

  fetchCreditCardInfo: function() {
    var self = this;
    self.http.get("/credit_card_info/" + self.cardholder_id).
      subscribe(
        function(response) {
          self.credit_card_info = response.json().credit_card_info;
        },
➤       self.ajaxFailureHandler.handler()
    );
  }
// BEGIN:ngOnChanges
});

export { CreditCardComponent };
```

The providers key is how we can use Angular's dependency injection. What we wrote previously tells Angular that if anyone wants an instance of AjaxFailure-Handler injected into *their* class, create a new instance of AjaxFailureHandler and use that instance. It's a bit verbose for this simple case, but you can highly customize how instances are created, if you need to.

We can now write similar code in both CustomerSearchComponent and CustomerDetailsComponent and how our failure handling logic is centralized to one place. It might seem like a *lot* of boilerplate just to consolidate a single line of code. This example is simplified for brevity and space, but what we've done is quite powerful.

Because our service is managed by Angular, it can have code injected into it as well. For example, if we wanted to ping an external service whenever there was an Ajax failure, we could inject Http into AjaxFailureHandler and none of the *users* of AjaxFailureHandler would need to change. This is powerful, and it's not something you're used to in Rails.

Fixing Your JavaScript Tests

 You'll notice your JavaScript tests now break when you run bin/rails karma. This is because you've added a new dependency to the classes you're testing. You can satisfy that dependency by either passing in a new test double for AjaxFailureHandler, or just pass in a real instance of it via new CustomerDetailsComponent(mockRoute,mockHttp,new AjaxFailureHandler()). The code included with the book does the latter, if you'd like to see it in action.

As I've mentioned many times, Angular is a rich, deep, flexible, complex framework. Its popularity means that there are many add-ons and extensions to help you with common tasks. This popularity also means that Angular is highly *Google-able*—you can find answers to common problems easily.

Getting Everything Out of Bootstrap

Unlike Angular and Postgres, Bootstrap is smaller and more focused in its scope. Its documentation[15] is a great place to find inspiration for solving common layout and design problems. Said another way, there's not much more to learn about Bootstrap. But it's worth doing a slightly deeper dive into two handy features: icons and responsive design.

Using Glyphicons

Bootstrap includes some of the icons that are part of the Glyphicons[16] icon font. This allows you to add icons to your UI by just applying CSS classes to empty elements. Bootstrap's documentation lists the icons that are included.[17]

Our customer detail page is complex, so we used panels to create separation between the elements. But they could be made easier to navigate by adding icons to the panel titles. Let's add different icons next to each panel so that our page looks like the screen on page 273.

---

15. https://getbootstrap.com
16. http://glyphicons.com
17. http://getbootstrap.com/components/#glyphicons

We can do this by creating empty elements using the glyphicon class and an additional class named for the icon:

`13_dig-deeper/10-grab-bag/shine/app/javascript/CustomerDetailsComponent/template.html`

```html
<section class="customer-details" *ngIf="customer">
<form>

  <!-- existing markup... -->
    <article class="panel panel-default">
      <header class="panel-heading">
        <h2 class="h4">
          <i class="glyphicon glyphicon-credit-card" aria-hidden="true"></i>
          Billing Info
        </h2>
      </header>
</form>
</section>
```

This adds a credit card icon next to the title inside the panel header for the credit card information. Because the icons are purely for decoration, we use the i tag as well as aria-hidden="true" so that screen readers don't get confused and read this markup to users. The aria- tags are part of the Web Accessibility Initiative.[18]

We can write similar code to add a generic person icon next to the customer information:

`13_dig-deeper/10-grab-bag/shine/app/javascript/CustomerDetailsComponent/CustomerInfoComponent.html`

```html
<article class="panel panel-primary customer-info" *ngIf="customer">
  <header class="panel-heading">
```

---

18. https://www.w3.org/WAI

```
  <h1 class="h3">
    <i class="glyphicon glyphicon-user" aria-hidden="true"></i>
    Customer
  </h1>
</header>

<!-- rest of the markup... -->

</article>
```

For the addresses, let's add a new property to our AddressComponent called icon.
This will be the name of the Glyphicon to use. We'll default it to an envelope,
since that is a reasonable default for an address. First, we'll allow icon to be
specified as an input, and set the default value:

13_dig-deeper/10-grab-bag/shine/app/javascript/CustomerDetailsComponent/AddressComponent.ts
```
import { EventEmitter,
         Component } from "@angular/core";
import   template   from "./AddressComponent.html";

var AddressComponent = Component({
  selector: "shine-address",
  inputs: [
    "address",
    "addressType",
➤   "icon"
  ],
  outputs: [
    "addressChanged"
  ],
  template: template
}).Class({
  constructor: [
    function() {
      this.address        = null;
      this.addressType    = null;
➤     this.icon           = "envelope";
      this.addressChanged = new EventEmitter();
    }
  ],
  save: function(update) {
    this.addressChanged.emit(update);
  }
});

export { AddressComponent };
```

Now, we'll use it in our markup:

13_dig-deeper/10-grab-bag/shine/app/javascript/CustomerDetailsComponent/AddressComponent.html
```
<article class="panel panel-default {{addressType}}">
  <header class="panel-heading">
    <h2 class="h4">
```

```
      <i class="glyphicon glyphicon-{{icon}}" aria-hidden="true"></i>
      {{addressType}} Address
    </h2>
  </header>

  <!-- rest of the markup -->

</article>
```

With this new attribute in place, change app/javascript/CustomerDetailsComponent/template.html to override the value for the shipping address:

```
13_dig-deeper/10-grab-bag/shine/app/javascript/CustomerDetailsComponent/template.html
➤ <shine-address
➤   addressType="Shipping"
➤   icon="plane"
➤   bind-address="customer.shipping_address"
➤   on-addressChanged="saveShippingAddress($event)">
➤ </shine-address>
```

If you reload the page, you should see the different icons. Also note how our use of a new input property in AddressComponent worked. It reinforces that AddressComponent is a generic component that you can customize to your needs. Bootstrap's icons allow an additional bit of customization we can use.

One thing worth pointing out is that icons are a tricky subject in user experience design. Most research indicates that icons without text are extremely difficult for users to understand. We're using them here as a demonstration, but as with all design choices, be cognizant of the problem you are solving when adding icons. Purely aesthetic reasons can be valid sometimes, but they are not necessarily paramount in making a great experience for your users.

Designing for Mobile Devices with Ease

Responsive web design is a technique for designing for many different screen sizes and devices. If you've been to a website on your mobile phone that looks great but different from how it looks on your desktop computer, this is responsive design in action.

Bootstrap provides some basic tools to help with responsive design. If you recall from Chapter 9, *Design Great UIs with*, on page 155, when we looked at grid-based design, we used CSS classes that had md in them, such as col-md-6. That md means *this is the column size I want on medium-sized devices*. But there are other options, as outlined in Bootstrap's grid options documentation.[19]

---

19. http://getbootstrap.com/css/#grid-options

Suppose our complex customer detail view will be used on a mobile phone. We can quickly simulate this by resizing our browser to a narrow width. Because we used the md form of our grid, when the screen shrinks to below the medium-sized device width (992px), each grid cell takes up the full width, since this is the default (you can also see this in your browser's mobile device simulator, if it has one). Generally, this is fine, but for addresses, it's a bit extreme, as demonstrated in the following figure.

Suppose for mobile devices we're fine with the city being 100% of the width, but we want the state and zip code to be on the same line. With Bootstrap's responsive grid, making this happen is simple. In addition to the col-md classes we've used, we can add col-xs classes (xs for extra-small devices below 768px in width, that is, most smartphones).

For the city, we'll use col-xs-12, meaning we want the city's grid to be full width (this is somewhat redundant, but it's good to be explicit about our design decisions, since we'll be using other xs classes). State will be given the col-xs-4 class, meaning it should take up four grid cells at the xs size, while zip gets the remaining eight cells, which means we need the col-xs-8 class.

```
13_dig-deeper/10-grab-bag/shine/app/javascript/CustomerDetailsComponent/AddressComponent.html
    <div class="row">
      <div class="col-md-6 col-xs-12">
        <shine-text-field
          bind-object="address"
          field_name="city"
          on-valueChanged="save($event)"
          label="City">
        </shine-text-field>
      </div>
```

```
➤        <div class="col-md-2 col-xs-4">
           <shine-text-field
             bind-object="address"
             field_name="state"
             on-valueChanged="save($event)"
             compact="true"
             label="State">
           </shine-text-field>
         </div>
➤        <div class="col-md-4 col-xs-8">
           <shine-text-field
             bind-object="address"
             field_name="zipcode"
             on-valueChanged="save($event)"
             pattern="\d\d\d\d\d(-\d\d\d\d)?"
             label="Zip Code">
           </shine-text-field>
         </div>
       </div>
```

The result looks a bit better:

With just a few extra CSS classes, we've made drastically different layouts work on different screen sizes. You can even resize your browser to a larger width and watch the screen change layouts back to our original design.

In addition to a responsive grid, Bootstrap has helper classes[20] for use when doing responsive design. For example, you can use a class like hidden-xs to hide elements on small screens. This could be useful for nonessential elements that can be omitted for mobile users (like icons).

Responsive design is a deep topic, but Bootstrap gives you a few useful features to help do it more easily and without making radical changes to your markup.

---

20. http://getbootstrap.com/css/#responsive-utilities

The End

This brings us to the end of our journey. Hopefully, you've learned not just how to use Angular, Postgres, and Bootstrap, but also the value of approaching each software problem with a holistic view of the tools you are using. Some problems are best solved with a better user experience, some with improved database performance, and some require bringing all parts of the stack together.

While the book is at an end, the information provided within is just the beginning. The documentation for all of the tools we've used is excellent, and with the grounding you've got, you can now dig deeper with Angular, Postgres, and Bootstrap. And I'm willing to help if I can; just post to the book's forum.[21]

With the knowledge you've gained in this book, you now have the confidence to explore your toolset more deeply, and the curiosity to discover new and better ways to solve problems.

---

21. https://forums.pragprog.com/forums/448

Full Listing of Customer Detail Page HTML

This is the full listing of markup for the UI we designed and built in Chapter 9, *Design Great UIs with*, on page 155. It's included for completeness, but you may find it much easier to work with the source code, which you can download from the book's website.[1]

```
9-grid-based-design/10-static-ui/shine/app/javascript/CustomerDetailsComponent/template.html
<section class="customer-details" *ngIf="customer">
<form>
  <div class="row">
    <div class="col-md-6">
      <article class="panel panel-primary">
        <header class="panel-heading">
          <h1 class="h3">
            Customer
          </h1>
        </header>
        <section class="panel-body">
          <div class="row">
            <div class="col-md-4">
              <div class="form-group">
                <label class="sr-only" for="first-name">
                  First Name
                </label>
                <input type="text" class="form-control"
                       name="first-name" value="Pat">
              </div>
            </div>
            <div class="col-md-4">
              <div class="form-group">
                <label class="sr-only" for="last-name">Last Name</label>
                <input type="text" class="form-control"
                       name="last-name" value="Jones">
```

---

1. https://pragprog.com/titles/dcbang2/source_code

```html
          </div>
        </div>
        <div class="col-md-4">
          <div class="form-group">
            <label class="sr-only" for="username">Username</label>
            <div class="input-group">
              <div class="input-group-addon">@</div>
              <input type="text" class="form-control"
                     name="username" value="pat123">
            </div>
          </div>
        </div>
      </div>
      <div class="form-group">
        <label class="sr-only" for="email">Email</label>
        <input type="text" class="form-control"
               name="email" value="pattyj@somewhere.net">
      </div>
    </section>
    <footer class="panel-footer">
      <label for="joined">Joined</label> 12/13/2014
    </footer>
  </article>
  <article class="panel panel-default">
    <header class="panel-heading">
      <h2 class="h4">
        Shipping Address
      </h2>
    </header>
    <section class="panel-body">
      <div class="form-group">
        <label class="sr-only" for="street-address">
          Street Address
        </label>
        <input type="text" class="form-control"
               name="street-address" value="123 Any St">
      </div>
      <div class="row">
        <div class="col-md-6">
          <div class="form-group">
            <label class="sr-only" for="city">City</label>
            <input type="text" class="form-control"
                   name="city" value="Washington">
          </div>
        </div>
        <div class="col-md-2">
          <div class="form-group">
            <label class="sr-only" for="state">State</label>
            <input type="text" class="form-control"
                   name="state" value="DC">
```

```
        </div>
      </div>
      <div class="col-md-4">
        <div class="form-group">
          <label class="sr-only" for="zip">Zip</label>
          <input type="text" class="form-control"
                 name="zip" value="20001">
        </div>
      </div>
    </div>
  </section>
  </article>
</div>
<div class="col-md-6">
  <article class="panel panel-default">
    <header class="panel-heading">
      <h2 class="h4">
        Billing Info
      </h2>
    </header>
    <section class="panel-body">
      <article>
        <div class="row">
          <div class="col-md-7">
            <p class="h4">
              ****-****-****-1234
              <span class="label label-success">VISA</span>
            </p>
            <p class="h5">
              <label>Expires:</label> 04/19
            </p>
          </div>
          <div class="col-md-5 text-right">
            <button class="btn btn-lg btn-default">
              View Details…
            </button>
          </div>
        </div>
      </article>
      <hr>
      <article class="well well-sm">
        <header>
          <h1 class="h5">
            Billing Address
            <small>
              <input type="checkbox"> Same as shipping?
            </small>
          </h1>
        </header>
        <div class="form-group">
```

```html
                <label class="sr-only" for="street-address">
                  Street Address
                </label>
                <input type="text" class="form-control"
                       name="street-address" value="123 Any St">
              </div>
              <div class="row">
                <div class="col-md-6">
                  <div class="form-group">
                    <label class="sr-only" for="city">City</label>
                    <input type="text" class="form-control"
                           name="city" value="Washington">
                  </div>
                </div>
                <div class="col-md-2">
                  <div class="form-group">
                    <label class="sr-only" for="state">State</label>
                    <input type="text" class="form-control"
                           name="state" value="DC">
                  </div>
                </div>
                <div class="col-md-4">
                  <div class="form-group">
                    <label class="sr-only" for="zip">Zip</label>
                    <input type="text" class="form-control"
                           name="zip" value="20001">
                  </div>
                </div>
              </div>
            </article>
          </section>
        </article>
      </div>
    </div>
  </form>
</section>
```

Creating Customer Address Seed Data

This is the full listing for db/seeds.rb needed to create sample address data for all the fake customers we've been using to try out Postgres features. This is covered in Chapter 10, *Cache Complex Queries*, on page 169. It's included for completeness, but you may find it much easier to work with the source code, which you can download from the book's website.[1]

Note that for this code to work, you'll have to create the State, Address, Customers-BillingAddress, and CustomersShippingAddress models. You'll also need to create nec essary Active Record associations inside the Customer class. Although none of these are needed for Shine to function, they *are* for the seed data to work. Their code follows the seed data code.

Also note that we've added a guard around our initial code that creates customers —we don't have to create 350,000 customers again if we already have some. Also note that when you run rake db:seed, it will take a *long* time—several hours.

```ruby
10_materialized-views/10-data-model/shine/db/seeds.rb
# Guard against re-creating customers if we already have some
if Customer.all.count == 0
  350_000.times do |i|
    Customer.create!(
      first_name: Faker::Name.first_name,
       last_name: Faker::Name.last_name,
        username: "#{Faker::Internet.user_name}#{i}",
           email: Faker::Internet.user_name + i.to_s +
                  "@#{Faker::Internet.domain_name}")
    print '.' if i % 1000 == 0
  end
end

# Create all 50 states in the US
# We use find_or_create_by! so if we have to run this seed file
```

---

1.   https://pragprog.com/titles/dcbang2/source_code

```
# again, it won't blow up or create a duplicate state
State.find_or_create_by!(name: "Alabama"          , code: "AL")
State.find_or_create_by!(name: "Alaska"           , code: "AK")
State.find_or_create_by!(name: "Arizona"          , code: "AZ")
State.find_or_create_by!(name: "Arkansas"         , code: "AR")
State.find_or_create_by!(name: "California"        , code: "CA")
State.find_or_create_by!(name: "Colorado"         , code: "CO")
State.find_or_create_by!(name: "Connecticut"      , code: "CT")
State.find_or_create_by!(name: "Delaware"         , code: "DE")
State.find_or_create_by!(name: "Dist. of Columbia", code: "DC")
State.find_or_create_by!(name: "Florida"          , code: "FL")
State.find_or_create_by!(name: "Georgia"          , code: "GA")
State.find_or_create_by!(name: "Hawaii"           , code: "HI")
State.find_or_create_by!(name: "Idaho"            , code: "ID")
State.find_or_create_by!(name: "Illinois"         , code: "IL")
State.find_or_create_by!(name: "Indiana"          , code: "IN")
State.find_or_create_by!(name: "Iowa"             , code: "IA")
State.find_or_create_by!(name: "Kansas"           , code: "KS")
State.find_or_create_by!(name: "Kentucky"         , code: "KY")
State.find_or_create_by!(name: "Louisiana"        , code: "LA")
State.find_or_create_by!(name: "Maine"            , code: "ME")
State.find_or_create_by!(name: "Maryland"         , code: "MD")
State.find_or_create_by!(name: "Massachusetts"     , code: "MA")
State.find_or_create_by!(name: "Michigan"         , code: "MI")
State.find_or_create_by!(name: "Minnesota"        , code: "MN")
State.find_or_create_by!(name: "Mississippi"      , code: "MS")
State.find_or_create_by!(name: "Missouri"         , code: "MO")
State.find_or_create_by!(name: "Montana"          , code: "MT")
State.find_or_create_by!(name: "Nebraska"         , code: "NE")
State.find_or_create_by!(name: "Nevada"           , code: "NV")
State.find_or_create_by!(name: "New Hampshire"    , code: "NH")
State.find_or_create_by!(name: "New Jersey"       , code: "NJ")
State.find_or_create_by!(name: "New Mexico"       , code: "NM")
State.find_or_create_by!(name: "New York"         , code: "NY")
State.find_or_create_by!(name: "North Carolina"   , code: "NC")
State.find_or_create_by!(name: "North Dakota"     , code: "ND")
State.find_or_create_by!(name: "Ohio"             , code: "OH")
State.find_or_create_by!(name: "Oklahoma"         , code: "OK")
State.find_or_create_by!(name: "Oregon"           , code: "OR")
State.find_or_create_by!(name: "Pennsylvania"     , code: "PA")
State.find_or_create_by!(name: "Rhode Island"     , code: "RI")
State.find_or_create_by!(name: "South Carolina"   , code: "SC")
State.find_or_create_by!(name: "South Dakota"     , code: "SD")
State.find_or_create_by!(name: "Tennessee"        , code: "TN")
State.find_or_create_by!(name: "Texas"            , code: "TX")
State.find_or_create_by!(name: "Utah"             , code: "UT")
State.find_or_create_by!(name: "Vermont"          , code: "VT")
State.find_or_create_by!(name: "Virginia"         , code: "VA")
State.find_or_create_by!(name: "Washington"       , code: "WA")
State.find_or_create_by!(name: "West Virginia"    , code: "WV")
```

```ruby
State.find_or_create_by!(name: "Wisconsin"          , code: "WI")
State.find_or_create_by!(name: "Wyoming"            , code: "WY")

# Helper method to create a billing address for a customer
def create_billing_address(customer_id,state)
  billing_address = Address.create!(
    street: Faker::Address.street_address,
      city: Faker::Address.city,
     state: state,
   zipcode: Faker::Address.zip
  )

  CustomersBillingAddress.create!(customer_id: customer_id,
                                      address: billing_address)
end

# Helper method to create a shipping address for a customer
def create_shipping_address(customer_id,state,is_primary)
  shipping_address = Address.create!(
      street: Faker::Address.street_address,
        city: Faker::Address.city,
       state: state,
     zipcode: Faker::Address.zip
  )

  CustomersShippingAddress.create!(customer_id: customer_id,
                                       address: shipping_address,
                                       primary: is_primary)

end

# Cache the number of states so we don't have to query
# each time through
all_states = State.all.to_a

# For all customers
Customer.find_each do |customer|
  # Do not re-create addresses if this customer has them
  next if customer.customers_shipping_address.any?
  puts "Creating addresses for #{customer.id}..."

  # Create a billing address for them
  create_billing_address(customer.id,all_states.sample)

  # Create a random number of shipping addresses, making
  # sure we create at least 1
  num_shipping_addresses = rand(4) + 1

  num_shipping_addresses.times do |i|
    # Create the shipping address, setting the first one
    # we create as the "primary"
    create_shipping_address(customer.id,all_states.sample,i == 0)
  end
end
```

Customer Details Extracted Components

This is the full code listing for the components we extracted in *Separating the App into Components*, on page 199.

```typescript
import { Component } from "@angular/core";
import    template    from "./CustomerInfoComponent.html";

var CustomerInfoComponent = Component({
  selector: "shine-customer-info",
  template: template
}).Class({
  constructor: [
    function() {
    }
  ]
});

export { CustomerInfoComponent };
```

```html
<article class="panel panel-primary">
  <header class="panel-heading">
    <h1 class="h3">
      Customer
    </h1>
  </header>
  <section class="panel-body">

    <!-- markup from before -->

    <div class="row">
      <div class="col-md-4">
        <div class="form-group">
          <label class="sr-only" for="first-name">
            First Name
          </label>
          <input type="text" class="form-control"
          name="first-name" value="Pat">
```

```
        </div>
      </div>
      <div class="col-md-4">
        <div class="form-group">
          <label class="sr-only" for="last-name">Last Name</label>
          <input type="text" class="form-control"
          name="last-name" value="Jones">
        </div>
      </div>
      <div class="col-md-4">
        <div class="form-group">
          <label class="sr-only" for="username">Username</label>
          <div class="input-group">
            <div class="input-group-addon">@</div>
            <input type="text" class="form-control"
            name="username" value="pat123">
          </div>
        </div>
      </div>
    </div>
    <div class="form-group">
      <label class="sr-only" for="email">Email</label>
      <input type="text" class="form-control"
      name="email" value="pattyj@somewhere.net">
    </div>
  </section>
  <footer class="panel-footer">
    <label for="joined">Joined</label> 12/13/2014
  </footer>
</article>
```

11_angular-async/10-components/shine/app/javascript/CustomerDetailsComponent/AddressComponent.ts

```
import { Component } from "@angular/core";
import    template    from "./AddressComponent.html";

var AddressComponent = Component({
  selector: "shine-address",
  template: template
}).Class({
  constructor: [
    function() {
    }
  ]
});

export { AddressComponent };
```

11_angular-async/10-components/shine/app/javascript/CustomerDetailsComponent/AddressComponent.html

```
<article class="panel panel-default">
  <header class="panel-heading">
    <h2 class="h4">
      Shipping Address
```

```
      </h2>
    </header>
    <section class="panel-body">
      <div class="form-group">
        <label class="sr-only" for="street-address">
          Street Address
        </label>
        <input type="text" class="form-control"
        name="street-address" value="123 Any St">
      </div>
      <div class="row">
        <div class="col-md-6">
          <div class="form-group">
            <label class="sr-only" for="city">City</label>
            <input type="text" class="form-control"
            name="city" value="Washington">
          </div>
        </div>
        <div class="col-md-2">
          <div class="form-group">
            <label class="sr-only" for="state">State</label>
            <input type="text" class="form-control"
            name="state" value="DC">
          </div>
        </div>
        <div class="col-md-4">
          <div class="form-group">
            <label class="sr-only" for="zip">Zip</label>
            <input type="text" class="form-control"
            name="zip" value="20001">
          </div>
        </div>
      </div>
    </section>
  </article>
```

11_angular-async/10-components/shine/app/javascript/CustomerDetailsComponent/CreditCardComponent.ts

```typescript
import { Component } from "@angular/core";
import    template    from "./CreditCardComponent.html";

var CreditCardComponent = Component({
  selector: "shine-credit-card",
  template: template
}).Class({
  constructor: [
    function() {
    }
  ]
});

export { CreditCardComponent };
```

```html
<article>
  <div class="row">
    <div class="col-md-7">
      <p class="h4">
        ****-****-****-1234
        <span class="label label-success">VISA</span>
      </p>
      <p class="h5">
        <label>Expires:</label> 04/19
      </p>
    </div>
    <div class="col-md-5 text-right">
      <button class="btn btn-lg btn-default">
        View Details…
      </button>
    </div>
  </div>
</article>
```

Bibliography

[Bec10]   Kent Beck. *Test Driven Development*. The Pragmatic Bookshelf, Raleigh, NC, 2010.

[Cro08]   Douglas Crockford. *JavaScript: The Good Parts*. O'Reilly & Associates, Inc., Sebastopol, CA, 2008.

[Man15]   Sergi Mansilla. *Reactive Programming with RxJS*. The Pragmatic Bookshelf, Raleigh, NC, 2015.

[RC17]   Sam Ruby and David Bryant Copeland. *Agile Web Development with Rails 5.1*. The Pragmatic Bookshelf, Raleigh, NC, 2017.

Index

Explore Testing and Cucumber

Explore the uncharted waters of exploratory testing and delve deeper into Cucumber.

Explore It!

Uncover surprises, risks, and potentially serious bugs with exploratory testing. Rather than designing all tests in advance, explorers design and execute small, rapid experiments, using what they learned from the last little experiment to inform the next. Learn essential skills of a master explorer, including how to analyze software to discover key points of vulnerability, how to design experiments on the fly, how to hone your observation skills, and how to focus your efforts.

Elisabeth Hendrickson
(186 pages) ISBN: 9781937785024. $29
https://pragprog.com/book/ehxta

The Cucumber Book, Second Edition

Your customers want rock-solid, bug-free software that does exactly what they expect it to do. Yet they can't always articulate their ideas clearly enough for you to turn them into code. You need Cucumber: a testing, communication, and requirements tool—all rolled into one. All the code in this book is updated for Cucumber 2.4, Rails 5, and RSpec 3.5.

Matt Wynne and Aslak Hellesøy, with Steve Tooke
(334 pages) ISBN: 9781680502381. $39.95
https://pragprog.com/book/hwcuc2

Exercises and Teams

From exercises to make you a better programmer to techniques for creating better teams, we've got you covered.

Exercises for Programmers

When you write software, you need to be at the top of your game. Great programmers practice to keep their skills sharp. Get sharp and stay sharp with more than fifty practice exercises rooted in real-world scenarios. If you're a new programmer, these challenges will help you learn what you need to break into the field, and if you're a seasoned pro, you can use these exercises to learn that hot new language for your next gig.

Brian P. Hogan
(118 pages) ISBN: 9781680501223. $24
https://pragprog.com/book/bhwb

Creating Great Teams

People are happiest and most productive if they can choose what they work on and who they work with. Self-selecting teams give people that choice. Build well-designed and efficient teams to get the most out of your organization, with step-by-step instructions on how to set up teams quickly and efficiently. You'll create a process that works for you, whether you need to form teams from scratch, improve the design of existing teams, or are on the verge of a big team re-shuffle.

Sandy Mamoli and David Mole
(102 pages) ISBN: 9781680501285. $17
https://pragprog.com/book/mmteams

Secure JavaScript and Web Testing

Secure your Node applications and see how to really test on the web.

Secure Your Node.js Web Application

Cyber-criminals have your web applications in their crosshairs. They search for and exploit common security mistakes in your web application to steal user data. Learn how you can secure your Node.js applications, database and web server to avoid these security holes. Discover the primary attack vectors against web applications, and implement security best practices and effective countermeasures. Coding securely will make you a stronger web developer and analyst, and you'll protect your users.

Karl Düüna
(230 pages) ISBN: 9781680500851. $36
https://pragprog.com/book/kdnodesec

The Way of the Web Tester

This book is for everyone who needs to test the web. As a tester, you'll automate your tests. As a developer, you'll build more robust solutions. And as a team, you'll gain a vocabulary and a means to coordinate how to write and organize automated tests for the web. Follow the testing pyramid and level up your skills in user interface testing, integration testing, and unit testing. Your new skills will free you up to do other, more important things while letting the computer do the one thing it's really good at: quickly running thousands of repetitive tasks.

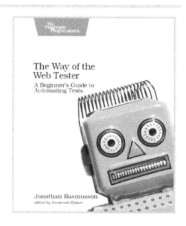

Jonathan Rasmusson
(256 pages) ISBN: 9781680501834. $29
https://pragprog.com/book/jrtest

The Modern Web

Get up to speed on the latest JavaScript techniques.

Deliver Audacious Web Apps with Ember 2

It's time for web development to be fun again, time to write engaging and attractive apps – fast – in this brisk tutorial. Build a complete user interface in a few lines of code, create reusable web components, access RESTful services and cache the results for performance, and use JavaScript modules to bring abstraction to your code. Find out how you can get your crucial app infrastructure up and running quickly, so you can spend your time on the stuff great apps are made of: features.

Matthew White
(146 pages) ISBN: 9781680500783. $24
https://pragprog.com/book/mwjsember

Reactive Programming with RxJS

Reactive programming is revolutionary. It makes asynchronous programming clean, intuitive, and robust. Use the RxJS library to write complex programs in a simple way, unifying asynchronous mechanisms such as callbacks and promises into a powerful data type: the Observable. Learn to think about your programs as streams of data that you can transform by expressing *what* should happen, instead of having to painstakingly program *how* it should happen. Manage real-world concurrency and write complex flows of events in your applications with ease.

Sergi Mansilla
(142 pages) ISBN: 9781680501292. $18
https://pragprog.com/book/smreactjs

Pragmatic Programming

We'll show you how to be more pragmatic and effective, for new code and old.

Your Code as a Crime Scene

Jack the Ripper and legacy codebases have more in common than you'd think. Inspired by forensic psychology methods, this book teaches you strategies to predict the future of your codebase, assess refactoring direction, and understand how your team influences the design. With its unique blend of forensic psychology and code analysis, this book arms you with the strategies you need, no matter what programming language you use.

Adam Tornhill
(218 pages) ISBN: 9781680500387. $36
https://pragprog.com/book/atcrime

The Nature of Software Development

You need to get value from your software project. You need it "free, now, and perfect." We can't get you there, but we can help you get to "cheaper, sooner, and better." This book leads you from the desire for value down to the specific activities that help good Agile projects deliver better software sooner, and at a lower cost. Using simple sketches and a few words, the author invites you to follow his path of learning and understanding from a half century of software development and from his engagement with Agile methods from their very beginning.

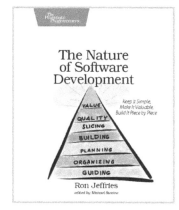

Ron Jeffries
(176 pages) ISBN: 9781941222379. $24
https://pragprog.com/book/rjnsd

The Joy of Mazes and Math

Rediscover the joy and fascinating weirdness of mazes and pure mathematics.

Mazes for Programmers

A book on mazes? Seriously?

Yes!

Not because you spend your day creating mazes, or because you particularly like solving mazes.

But because it's fun. Remember when programming used to be fun? This book takes you back to those days when you were starting to program, and you wanted to make your code do things, draw things, and solve puzzles. It's fun because it lets you explore and grow your code, and reminds you how it feels to just think.

Sometimes it feels like you live your life in a maze of twisty little passages, all alike. Now you can code your way out.

Jamis Buck
(286 pages) ISBN: 9781680500554. $38
https://pragprog.com/book/jbmaze

Good Math

Mathematics is beautiful—and it can be fun and exciting as well as practical. *Good Math* is your guide to some of the most intriguing topics from two thousand years of mathematics: from Egyptian fractions to Turing machines; from the real meaning of numbers to proof trees, group symmetry, and mechanical computation. If you've ever wondered what lay beyond the proofs you struggled to complete in high school geometry, or what limits the capabilities of the computer on your desk, this is the book for you.

Mark C. Chu-Carroll
(282 pages) ISBN: 9781937785338. $34
https://pragprog.com/book/mcmath

Past and Present

To see where we're going, remember how we got here, and learn how to take a healthier approach to programming.

Fire in the Valley

In the 1970s, while their contemporaries were protesting the computer as a tool of dehumanization and oppression, a motley collection of college dropouts, hippies, and electronics fanatics were engaged in something much more subversive. Obsessed with the idea of getting computer power into their own hands, they launched from their garages a hobbyist movement that grew into an industry, and ultimately a social and technological revolution. What they did was invent the personal computer: not just a new device, but a watershed in the relationship between man and machine. This is their story.

Michael Swaine and Paul Freiberger
(422 pages) ISBN: 9781937785765. $34
https://pragprog.com/book/fsfire

The Healthy Programmer

To keep doing what you love, you need to maintain your own systems, not just the ones you write code for. Regular exercise and proper nutrition help you learn, remember, concentrate, and be creative—skills critical to doing your job well. Learn how to change your work habits, master exercises that make working at a computer more comfortable, and develop a plan to keep fit, healthy, and sharp for years to come.

This book is intended only as an informative guide for those wishing to know more about health issues. In no way is this book intended to replace, countermand, or conflict with the advice given to you by your own healthcare provider including Physician, Nurse Practitioner, Physician Assistant, Registered Dietician, and other licensed professionals.

Joe Kutner
(254 pages) ISBN: 9781937785314. $36
https://pragprog.com/book/jkthp

Long Live the Command Line!

Use tmux and Vim for incredible mouse-free productivity.

tmux 2

Your mouse is slowing you down. The time you spend context switching between your editor and your consoles eats away at your productivity. Take control of your environment with tmux, a terminal multiplexer that you can tailor to your workflow. With this updated second edition for tmux 2.3, you'll customize, script, and leverage tmux's unique abilities to craft a productive terminal environment that lets you keep your fingers on your keyboard's home row.

Brian P. Hogan
(102 pages) ISBN: 9781680502213. $21.95
https://pragprog.com/book/bhtmux2

Practical Vim, Second Edition

Vim is a fast and efficient text editor that will make you a faster and more efficient developer. It's available on almost every OS, and if you master the techniques in this book, you'll never need another text editor. In more than 120 Vim tips, you'll quickly learn the editor's core functionality and tackle your trickiest editing and writing tasks. This beloved bestseller has been revised and updated to Vim 8 and includes three brand-new tips and five fully revised tips.

Drew Neil
(354 pages) ISBN: 9781680501278. $29
https://pragprog.com/book/dnvim2

The Pragmatic Bookshelf

The Pragmatic Bookshelf features books written by developers for developers. The titles continue the well-known Pragmatic Programmer style and continue to garner awards and rave reviews. As development gets more and more difficult, the Pragmatic Programmers will be there with more titles and products to help you stay on top of your game.

Visit Us Online

This Book's Home Page
https://pragprog.com/book/dcbang2
Source code from this book, errata, and other resources. Come give us feedback, too!

Register for Updates
https://pragprog.com/updates
Be notified when updates and new books become available.

Join the Community
https://pragprog.com/community
Read our weblogs, join our online discussions, participate in our mailing list, interact with our wiki, and benefit from the experience of other Pragmatic Programmers.

New and Noteworthy
https://pragprog.com/news
Check out the latest pragmatic developments, new titles and other offerings.

Save on the eBook

Save on the eBook versions of this title. Owning the paper version of this book entitles you to purchase the electronic versions at a terrific discount.

PDFs are great for carrying around on your laptop—they are hyperlinked, have color, and are fully searchable. Most titles are also available for the iPhone and iPod touch, Amazon Kindle, and other popular e-book readers.

Buy now at *https://pragprog.com/coupon*

Contact Us

Online Orders:	*https://pragprog.com/catalog*
Customer Service:	*support@pragprog.com*
International Rights:	*translations@pragprog.com*
Academic Use:	*academic@pragprog.com*
Write for Us:	*http://write-for-us.pragprog.com*
Or Call:	+1 800-699-7764

Lightning Source UK Ltd.
Milton Keynes UK
UKHW031101290622
405126UK00007B/1284